Kathryn Kuhn

Yale Studies
on White-Collar Crime

Wayward Capitalists

Target of the
Securities and Exchange
Commission

Susan P. Shapiro

Yale University Press
New Haven and London

Designed by Sally Harris
and set in Baskerville type by The Saybrook Press, Inc.
Printed in the United States of America by
Vail-Ballou Press, Binghamton, N.Y.

Library of Congress Cataloging in Publication Data

Shapiro, Susan P.
    Wayward capitalists.
    (Yale studies on white-collar crime)
    Includes bibliographical references and index.
    1. Securities fraud—United States. 2. White collar
crime investigation—United States. 3. United States.
Securities and Exchange commission. I. United States.
Securities and Exchange Commission. II. Title.
III. Series.
HV6697.S53   1984   364.1′68′0973   83-27337
ISBN 0-300-03116-5 (alk. paper)

The paper in this book meets the guidelines for permanence
and durability of the Committee on Production Guidelines
for Book Longevity of the Council on Library Resources.

10 9 8 7 6 5 4 3 2 1

To Ruth and Nate Shapiro

Contents

List of Figures and Tables

Foreword

No one who read the news during the decade of the 1970s could be unaware of the importance of white-collar crime in American life. Reports of corporate illegality both here and abroad and of individual cases of tax fraud, securities fraud, and bribery were coupled with the massive corruption of Watergate to draw attention to an aspect of crime less visible but arguably no less damaging to society than street crime. It is now recognized that white-collar crime takes an enormous toll not only economically, where the total value of losses far exceeds the take from street crime, but also morally. White-collar crime often entails abuse of trust by those in positions of responsibility, thus rendering shaky that world of implicit agreements and shared understandings on which all enterprise depends.

The Yale Studies on White-Collar Crime, a series initiated with this book, will shed new light on white-collar crime and its control.* Despite important individual efforts over the last several decades, there has not been an opportunity for a sustained program of research on white-collar crime since Edwin H. Sutherland first introduced the concept over forty years ago. Beginning in the mid-1970s, as a result of a substantial grant

---

*Susan Rose-Ackerman, *Corruption: A Study in Political Economy* (New York: Academic Press, 1978); Jack Katz, "Legality and equality: plea bargaining in the prosecution of white-collar crimes," *Law and Society Review* 13 (1979): 431–60; W. Michael Reisman, *Folded Lies: Bribery, Crusades and Reforms* (New York: Free Press, 1979); Jack Katz, "The social movement against white-collar crime," *Criminology Review Yearbook*, ed. Egon Bittner and Sheldon L. Messinger, 2 (1980): 161–84; Kenneth Mann, Stanton Wheeler, and Austin Sarat, "Sentencing the white-collar offender," *American Criminal Law Review* 17(1980): 479–500; Susan P. Shapiro, "Thinking About White Collar Crime: Matters of Conceptualization and Research" (Washington, D.C.: National Institute of Justice, 1980); Stanton Wheeler, David Weisburd, and Nancy Bode, "Sentencing the white-collar offender: rhetoric and reality," *American Sociological Review* 47(1982): 641–59.

from the Law Enforcement Assistance Administration, a branch of the Justice Department now known as the National Institute of Justice, a group of scholars in law and the social sciences at Yale was given such an opportunity. This series will present the principal body of new evidence and research findings to emerge from the Yale program.

The offenses studied in this series are nonviolent economic offenses that are committed by either individuals or organizations and typically employ mechanisms of fraud or collusion. Frequently they are committed by persons of above average means. However, we have focused more on the nature of the offense and how the person's occupation helped him or her to carry it out than on the social status of the offender. And although each project developed its own methods and substantive concerns, we share an important set of core commitments deriving in part from our common background as social scientists (mostly sociologists) with an interest in the legal system and in some cases with formal training in law.

First, all the studies examine an aspect of the social control of white-collar crime: what happens at the various stages of detection, investigation, prosecution, defense, adjudication, and sentencing. This means that we are necessarily focusing on persons in positions of bureaucratic or professional responsibility. In *Wayward Capitalists* it is the staff of a federal regulatory agency. In another of our inquiries it is some fifty federal judges responsible for sentencing white-collar defendants. In still another it is the U.S. attorney and his staff, and in another it is the lawyers who are hired to keep their clients from being indicted.

Second, each study presents fresh empirical data not available in published sources and gathered by a variety of social science methods. From the outset it was evident that existing published materials were simply too scanty to provide an adequate basis for understanding or analyzing white-collar crime. In addition to the special access to the staff and archives of the Securities and Exchange Commission provided Susan Shapiro for this volume, we have been granted entrée to other sources of data: the offices of a private law firm specializing in white-collar crime defense work; about 2,000 confidential presentence investigation reports prepared on convicted federal offenders; the offices of federal prosecutors, where negotiations with targets of investigation are conducted; and the chambers of federal judges, where we tape-recorded interviews about sentencing practices. Gaining access to these sources was a time-consuming process but it has paid dividends in a rich body of new findings.

Third, we make a special effort to present a portrait of the processes that is representative or typical of the actual cases being dealt with by the actors in question. It often happens in law that the "leading case" in a given area—the one that sets the legal standard—has little in common factually with the mass of cases typically handled by the legal system. Both

lawyers and journalists are likely to find their attention drawn to bizarre, exotic, or otherwise extreme cases precisely because of their special character. They would be severely misled, however, if they attempted to develop a social policy based on study of the extreme case alone.

Fourth, these studies are contributions to the field of organizational intelligence: how actors gather, process, manipulate, and control the information that leads to crucial decisions. Whether to proceed civilly or criminally, whether and for what to prosecute, how to sentence, and, for defense counsel, whether to have the client plead guilty or go to trial—these and related decisions depend heavily on information gathering and processing. The importance for decision making of the socially organized ways in which information is variously gathered, transmitted, blocked, or systematically avoided is a theme that runs throughout the books in the series.

Fifth, much of our research documents not just what actors did but how they justify their actions to themselves and to the outside world in often murky ethical or value arenas. Sentencing judges, for example, must surely decide on sentences, but they may also feel it necessary to have a principled basis for their decisions. Defense counsels often face moral dilemmas over whether inculpatory information must be given over or can be legitimately concealed, and investigators have to decide whether their evidence is strong enough to justify taking the next step, which may mean a public indictment. To some, it might seem obvious that a study of actors in the criminal justice system must give attention to the moral or ethical bases for their actions, but a long history of past research often separated inquiries about the behavior of officials from legal ideals or "the law on the books." And many scholars have been forced, because of lack of access, to study the traces of official actions in published records without being able to understand the actions from the perspectives of the actors involved. We have made a conscious effort to learn not only what actors do but how they talk and think about what they do, with a particular eye for the relevance of their talk and their actions for legal and ethical standards.

Finally, all the studies give voice to an axiom of the sociologist's craft: Individual actions are embedded in social organization. To understand an individual actor, whether it be an SEC investigator, a prosecutor, a defense attorney, a judge, or a criminal defendant, requires that we know much about the organization within which that person acts and the connections of that organization to others in a complex environment. This series documents the extraordinary degree to which actors in white-collar crime enforcement are influenced by organizational forces in their environment, though not necessarily forces beyond their influence or control.

Susan Shapiro's *Wayward Capitalists* is a striking illustration of many of these themes. She provides us with the first detailed examination of how the enforcement apparatus of the Securities and Exchange Commission works. She does so by focusing on the crucial first stage of law enforcement: the detection of illegality. As the leading watchdog agency for that most capitalist of institutions, the stock market, the SEC itself is closely watched by others for its prosecution policies. What has not been obvious, but what Shapiro makes clear, is that what the SEC prosecutes depends on the nature of the illegalities that come to its attention.

Shapiro offers an incredibly rich, detailed, and heretofore inaccessible body of data on detection mechanisms available to the SEC and the kinds of illegalities they catch. She does so by examining in detail hundreds of cases—a representative sampling of SEC investigative files over twenty-five years of agency activity—noting for each case such characteristics as what the violation was about, how it came to the agency's attention, how accurate the intelligence information was, how long the violation had been under way before detection, the type of victim, the amount of victimization, and, most importantly, the ultimate fate of the investigation: whether it was closed without action, led to civil actions or administrative proceedings, or was referred for criminal prosecution. Shapiro's conclusions are based on these findings along with a combination of other sources of information, including interviews with agency staff, participation in training seminars for new agency enforcers, and observations from within the corridors and offices of the SEC.

The central message of *Wayward Capitalists* is that where you look for illegality determines what you will find: that how the SEC's intelligence apparatus is organized will determine the kinds of violators it catches. With as many as a dozen types of illegalities and a similar number of detection devices, the results defy easy summary, but some of the suggestive policy questions may give a hint of the riches to be found within. Take the SEC's interest in policing the securities marketplace, especially in controlling insider trading. Of all the detection strategies available to the SEC, only three, which generate less than one-fifth of all its investigations, account for half of all insider trading violations: market surveillance, informants, and spin-offs from other investigations. If the SEC really wanted to concentrate on insider trading, it would allocate greater resources to these strategies, for example, by developing more sophisticated computer surveillance programs or by providing greater disclosure incentives to anonymous informants. But to do so would entail a cost, for, as Shapiro's data show, these strategies rarely catch other major offenses, particularly those involving misrepresentation, and they also tend to generate the most inaccurate intelligence. Market surveillance, for example, although it tends to find bigger cases and to find them early when it

succeeds, is the most inaccurate of all the detection devices, with more than one-third of its cases producing no real violations.

It is the merit of Shapiro's book that policy questions of this sort can be raised and systematically considered in light of her findings. The SEC, busy with its ongoing activities, has not developed a research program that routinely provides such data for its commissioners. An important policy question for the SEC raised by this book is whether it should consider developing such data on a systematic basis, so that its own policies—particularly on matters as important but as invisible as its strategies of detection—can be based on a more informed understanding of what it is accomplishing.

The authors of books in the series will acknowledge those who contributed to their individual studies, but the foreword to this first volume is an appropriate place to acknowledge, on behalf of all the authors, our gratitude to the staff of the National Institute of Justice, and especially to our project monitor, Winifred Reed, for patience as well as financial support. We also wish to acknowledge the support of the Yale community, including administrators and staff in the law school and the university, and help from many colleagues in law and the social sciences, three of whom, Abraham S. Goldstein and Dan Freed of the law school, and Albert J. Reiss, Jr., of the sociology department, have been especially close to the program throughout its several years. We owe a final, special debt of gratitude to all those persons and agencies who allowed a group of scholars to enter their worlds and their records and who put up with sometimes impertinent questions about their everyday activities.

Stanton Wheeler
Ford Foundation Professor of Law
  and the Social Sciences
Director, Yale Studies on
  White-Collar Crime
Yale University

Preface

I have never in my life purchased or directly owned a share of stock. I grew up in a home where the market was where you bought food, bulls and bears were found at the zoo, blue chips were used in tiddlywinks, a margin was something the teacher wrote comments in, security was something one always strived for, and the financial pages of the newspaper were used to line the birdcage. My invitation to the Enforcement Division of the Securities and Exchange Commission (SEC) in 1976 provided quite a rude awakening. It also provided a fantastic fifty-year journey into the worlds of Wall Street, stock fraud, and government regulation and into homes where striving after the American dream was more of a preoccupation than it was in mine. In this book, I share this journey with you by exposing systematically the interpenetrating worlds of securities investors, offenders, and enforcers, tempered, of course, by a sociological imagination. The book also provides "inside information" on SEC enforcement, derived from nonpublic enforcement records and observations of daily life inside the agency. It should, I hope, prove instructive even to those whose participation in the securities world is considerably greater than my own.

This book has had a difficult birth. Requests for access to the records that provide most of its data were repeatedly denied by SEC officials. Access was finally granted, thanks mostly to a flu epidemic in Washington and a bureaucratic bungle. Then an act of Congress mandated that most of these records be destroyed two months after my research finally got underway. Fortunately, delays in implementing the congressional order saved these records long enough for me to complete the research. But all copies of the computer tapes on which the quantitative data had been stored disappeared from the truck during a move from Connecticut to New York (ironically, they were the only things the movers managed to

lose or damage). The data were painstakingly recreated and the manuscript finally written—and then the word processor obliterated one of the chapters. The concept of "missing data" has taken on an entirely new meaning for me. Despite these misfortunes, I am fortunate to have a sizable list of persons who contributed positively to this project and to the quality of my intellectual and emotional life during its course.

Many people in Washington helped to make the research a little easier, my work pleasant, and the experience stimulating. They include Mark Richard and Winifred Reed from the Department of Justice, Lloyd Ryan from the Department of Labor, and Sam Bowens, William Carpenter, David Doherty, Ralph Ferrara, Adele Geffen, Paul Gonson, Thomas Hamill, Deborah Hechinger, Edward Herlihy, James Kennedy, Theodore Levine, Charles Moore, Ira Pearce, Irving Pollack, Gary Smith, David Tennant, and Betsy Wood from the Securities and Exchange Commission. Special thanks go to former SEC Chairman Roderick Hills, who invited me to study the agency, Stanley Sporkin, former director of its Division of Enforcement, who encouraged me to conduct the research and warmly welcomed me into the division, and Nathan Harrison, who efficiently, tirelessly, and with good humor kept me supplied with the records I needed.

Stanton Wheeler helped at virtually every stage. He first enticed me into the study of white-collar crime and then arranged my invitation to the SEC. He backed me later when agency officials had second thoughts about the research. He provided the financial and institutional support to carry off the project. He commented on the research design and on every draft and incarnation of the manuscript. And, as editor of the white-collar crime series in which this book appears, he contributed immeasurably to its final revisions and publication. Over these eight years, I have learned to count on Stan as much for his practical advice and editorial instincts as for his sociological insight and his unflagging support.

Albert J. Reiss, Jr., also provided critical feedback on the research design and on early drafts of the manuscript. His influence is reflected in many of the questions I have explored, and his creative and imaginative approach to otherwise tired sociological topics has served as a model that I have always tried to emulate. Robert Clark, Arthur Mathews, Eliot Freidson, Jennifer Savary, and Bertha Hatvary offered valuable comments on various drafts or portions of the manuscript. Richard Maisel devised a statistical solution to a problem no one else was able to solve. Marian Neal Ash of Yale University Press ably shepherded the manuscript through the publication process and with Maura D. Shaw Tantillo provided valuable editorial assistance. Finally, warm thanks go to my family and friends for their support during what was sometimes a tiresome ordeal.

Financial support for conducting the research was provided under grant number 78NI-AX-0017 from the National Institute of Justice, U.S. Department of Justice. This research was undertaken with the permission of the United States Securities and Exchange Commission. The SEC, as a matter of policy, disclaims responsibility for private publications. The views and conclusions expressed herein are those of the author and do not necessarily reflect the views of the commission, its staff, or the official position or policies of the U.S. Department of Justice.

1

False Security?

In 1980 29.8 million Americans—one of every five adults—owned stock valued at over $900 billion in American corporations (Wheeler 1983, 47; U.S. Securities and Exchange Commission 1981, 8). And countless millions of others were corporate shareholders indirectly through the securities investments of trust funds, investment companies, pension and retirement funds, and life insurance companies in which they had financial interests. These institutional investors held more than $500 billion worth of stock in 1980 (U.S. Securities and Exchange Commission 1981, 8).[1] In short, a substantial number of individuals, families, and organizations in the United States owned securities valued at about one and a half trillion dollars.

With such astronomical numbers, it would be overkill to present an argument for the enormous significance of the securities markets for the economic viability of this nation or for the economic and personal welfare, security, and quality of life of its citizens. But less obvious is the fact that this mammoth superstructure, with its enormous social and economic consequences, is precariously balanced on a very shaky foundation. That foundation is the social institution of *trust*. Trust serves as the means whereby:

- people who have too little faith in their own potential or business acumen to attempt a business venture on their own turn their money over to complete strangers to do that very thing;

1. Also included among the institutional investors are property liability insurance companies, mutual savings banks, foundations, and educational endowments, which together held about $80 billion worth of securities. Foreign investors, whose stock holdings are not reflected in any of these figures, owned American securities valued at $114.5 billion (U.S. Securities and Exchange Commission 1981, 8).

- middle-class pensioners commit their life savings to a company that purports to have developed the technology to turn sand and gravel into gold;

- Hollywood's "beautiful people" ally themselves with stodgy Wall Street bankers to shelter excess funds in an oil company promising lucrative dividends and attractive tax shelter opportunities (McClintick 1977);

- the endowment fund of Princeton University invests in a high-flying life insurance conglomerate that is earning enormous profits at a time when similar companies are losing vast amounts of money (Blundell 1974b);

- blue-collar workers, unwilling to gamble their scarce savings in the stock market, contribute to a company pension fund whose trustees do precisely that with their money;

- "when E. F. Hutton talks, people listen"—to stockbrokers, investment advisers, accountants, and lawyers—and thereupon invest their savings to build a nest egg for the future.

In the absence of trust, people would not delegate discretionary use of their funds to other entrepreneurs; Hollywood's beautiful people would become mining engineers and examine the oil wells before they invested; Princeton University officials would have personally audited the books of the insurance conglomerate; people would create their own savings plans rather than patronize pension funds and life insurance companies; and the roles of accountant, stockbroker, and investment adviser would become obsolete as investors acquired their specialized skills. In short, capitalism would break down as funds were stuffed into mattresses, savings accounts, and solo business enterprises rather than invested in the business ventures of American corporations.

Trust—the impersonal guarantee that representations of expertise or risk or financial condition can be taken at face value and that fiduciaries are not self-interested—is truly the foundation of capitalism. This taken-for-granted social technology makes it all work. It serves as the laxative that loosens money in the pockets and mattresses and bank accounts of potential investors and moves it along into the coffers of our nation's corporations. With the demise of trust, this one-and-a-half-trillion-dollar capitalist fund would surely dry up.

But how secure is this foundation, this premise of trust? Witness the experience of over 10,000 stockholders, many of them venerable institutional investors—endowments, foundations, banks, insurance companies, and pension funds holding the assets of millions of individuals—who owned stock worth about $228,000,000 in the nation's most rapidly growing financial conglomerate, the darling of Wall Street, the Equity Funding

Corporation of America (EFCA).[2] In order to increase the value of stock held by corporate insiders and to borrow money and acquire other companies, EFCA inflated its reported income by about $85,000,000 by recording nonexistent commission income on corporate financial statements. To generate needed cash, the company borrowed funds off the books through complicated bogus transactions involving foreign subsidiaries. To lend an illusion of production to one of its life insurance subsidiaries, company officials created $2 billion worth of fictitious insurance business and then sold the bogus policies to other insurance companies (a process called "reinsurance") in order to generate more cash. They obtained still more funds by killing off some of the nonexistent policyholders and filing claims for death benefits. In order to create tens of thousands of fictitious policyholder records, corporate executives and managers held "fraud parties," working through the night to fill out bogus forms. They later created a Beverly Hills office where clerks, supplied with blank credit and medical report forms and lists of common male and female names, manufactured files from scratch.

But EFCA officials were not content to mislead banks and stockholders about the financial condition and prospects of the corporation or to defraud the life insurance companies that reinsured their bogus policyholders. Officials and lower-level employees also engaged in considerable self-dealing, diverting corporate funds and resources for their personal benefit. These schemes included excessive (often outlandish) salaries, stock bonuses, and entertainment allowances; inflated expense account vouchers; free medical and psychiatric treatment under the guise of routine life insurance examinations; outright embezzlement; corporate subsidies for personal vacations, rented Rolls Royce limousines, stereo equipment, home furnishings, and legal fees for a divorce; the diversion of legitimate corporate checks and payments to personal bank accounts; unauthorized commission income; fraudulent stock option arrangements; and insider trading. In the last instance, EFCA president Stanley Goldblum, in a unique position to be aware of the impending collapse of the corporation, sold about $1,500,000 worth of personally owned, overvalued EFCA shares—much of it just days before the New York Stock Exchange halted trading in EFCA stock—to an unsuspecting public.

These malefactions—both corporate and individual—were committed over a period of almost ten years, by dozens of witting and unwitting conspirators, before the knowing eyes of perhaps seventy-five company employees, and with the complicity or, at best, the incompetence of the company's accountants and auditors. The victims of the Equity Funding

2. This account is based primarily on materials from Loeffler (1974); Dirks and Gross (1974); Soble and Dallos (1975); and Seidler, Andrews, and Epstein (1977).

fraud had not placed their trust in some risky fly-by-night business venture. They had chosen a favorite among the "cream of this country's business and financial community" (Dirks and Gross 1974, 4), a stock listed on the New York Stock Exchange, touted by *Fortune* magazine, and singled out by the *Institutional Investor* as "one of the likely star performers in 1973" (Dirks and Gross 1974, 4).

Two months after the *Institutional Investor* article had made its predictions, EFCA was in Chapter X bankruptcy and what was to become perhaps "the largest fraud-induced bankruptcy proceeding in the history of finance" (Dirks and Gross 1974, 4). EFCA's stockholders (as well as the twelve hundred holders of $22,000,000 of EFCA debentures and four banks owed $50,000,000 plus interest) paid dearly for their trust. Stockholders ultimately received twelve cents for every dollar.

The Equity Funding scandal dealt a severe blow to the social institution of trust. It causes us to inquire about the validity of this capitalist premise, about the security of its foundation. There are numerous professions employed in close observation of the capitalist beast—auditors who inspect the financial condition of corporations; securities analysts who inquire into their business prospects and operations; economists who model the stability, growth, and trends of capital markets; statisticians who quantify and analyze their functioning; and journalists, lawyers, and others who help us to monitor the behavior of business and industry. Yet, at least since the stock market crash of 1929, no one has endeavored to explore the foundation of capitalism, to audit or monitor or even offhandedly inquire about the stability, strength, viability, or vulnerability of the institution of trust.

This book does not provide a definitive, certified, independent audit of trust. The data upon which such an audit could be based do not exist and probably never will. But this book does redirect inquiry from the capitalist beast to its foundation. It examines some of the cracks in the foundation, specifically its vulnerability to "wayward capitalists," and explores the efforts—both actual and potential—to protect and refortify this foundation.

The Securities and Exchange Commission (SEC), of course, is the preeminent protector of the capital markets in this country. A New Deal agency, the SEC was born in 1934 in the aftermath of the great stock market crash and the revelation that abusive corporate financial and trading practices, which contributed to the debacle, were endemic. It is an independent regulatory agency, headed by five commissioners, with broad responsibility for the regulation of publicly held corporations, the securities markets, and the professionals who service them.

Federal securities legislation requires that companies wishing to offer securities for public sale first file with the SEC a registration statement

disclosing business and financial information and that they subsequently provide continuing and updated disclosure through annual and other periodic reports, proxy materials, and the like. The SEC processes these disclosure materials and serves as an informational conduit to investors. It does not, however, rule on or guarantee the soundness of securities offered. The agency also regulates broker-dealers, investment advisers, investment companies, public utility holding companies, stock exchanges, and national securities associations, and it plays an advisory role in the bankruptcy reorganization proceedings of publicly held companies. Agency staff have responsibility for the enforcement of the federal securities laws and the control of fraud and have authority to conduct inspections and investigations and institute civil and administrative proceedings. These responsibilities are carried out by the SEC headquarters office in Washington and regional and branch offices in fifteen cities.

The SEC is a relatively small agency as federal agencies go, with roughly two thousand employees nationwide (the Internal Revenue Service has thirty-four times as many employees) and a budget representing only about .01 percent of the annual federal budget in recent years (Office of Management and Budget 1981, Phillips and Zecher 1981, 13). Indeed, the agency is smaller than most of the corporations it regulates, and its budget is smaller than the amount of money at issue in many of the violations it investigates. Despite a long-standing reputation for diligence and effectiveness in the execution of its mandate and as the stellar enforcement agency in the federal bureaucracy (Cary 1964, 661; Ratner 1978, 2–3; Miller 1979b, D1; Subcommittee 1976, 11; Bruck 1980, 16; Karmel 1982), the SEC has actually had a cyclical history. Its half-century life course is dotted with periods of vigor and vitality (especially the New Deal period and the 1960s and 1970s), of lethargy, passivity, and ineffectiveness (particularly the 1940s and 1950s), of innovation and expansion (the post-Watergate years), and of conservative retrenchment (especially the late 1970s and 1980s).[3]

I was invited by the chairman of the SEC to visit and study the agency's Enforcement Division during a period of excitement and aggressiveness, of vigorous crusades and expansive horizons. I spent the better part of 1976 and 1977 in the Enforcement Division in Washington as an agency insider, trained with new enforcement attorneys, privy to closed commission hearings and nonpublic documents and enforcement records and able to observe day-to-day enforcement work and to talk with its practitioners. However, because my tenure coincided with such a clearly dramatic and deviant period in agency history, I also looked for data that

3. Materials on the historical development of the SEC are available in DeBedts (1964), Parrish (1970), Sobel (1977), Karmel (1982), and Seligman (1982).

would provide a historical perspective and a better picture of both typical and variable SEC enforcement practices. The agency's archives, which at the time of my research held the full investigative and enforcement records (memos, letters, testimony, documents, complaints, indictments, and the like) of every docketed SEC investigation ever conducted, perfectly met the need for comparative data to supplement my observations. These nonpublic records provided rich data on the characteristics of the offenses, offenders, and victims scrutinized by each investigation and of the nature of the investigative process, legal action taken, and eventual disposition of the case. SEC investigations are typically docketed after the earliest suspicions of illegality emerge. So the files of docketed investigations record offenses that turn out to be massive and significant, like the Equity Funding case, as well as many that do not lead to legal action of any kind because they are minor or because evidence substantiating the initial suspicions of illegality is never found. A random sample of the full enforcement record of over five hundred investigations initiated during the twenty-five years between 1948 and 1972 served as the primary source of data presented in this book.[4]

I ask in this book who the "wayward capitalists" are, what they do, whom they victimize, and how the SEC is organized to detect and control their activities. I explore the dynamic interplay between the worlds of wayward capitalism and securities regulation, examining how each affects and constrains the other. I seek to understand how enforcement strategies are adapted to the way in which offenses are organized; how offenses are differentially vulnerable to particular enforcement practices; and what difference various enforcement strategies make in the control of wayward capitalists and their abuses of trust. The intelligence or detection component of SEC enforcement work—the ways in which agency staff discover offenses—provides the setting in which these questions are posed.

Abuses of trust are not of course confined to securities markets or to wayward capitalists. They are found in the political arena (bribery and corruption, congressional self-dealing and conflicts of interest), in employer−employee relations (embezzlement, pilferage, self-dealing, expense account fraud), in the relations between business and consumers (consumer fraud; fraud by doctors, lawyers, and fiduciaries; fraud by policyholders against insurance companies and by borrowers against lending institutions), in the relations between government and its citizens (entitlement frauds concerning tax, welfare, food stamps, or medicare/medicaid; the corruption of police officers, inspectors, prosecutors, and judges; and many regulatory offenses), and in other realms of social

---

4. The appendix contains a more detailed description of the research upon which this book is based.

life as well. Therefore, an inquiry into the abuses of trust by wayward capitalists should provide insights into many other so-called white-collar crimes. And a study of the Securities and Exchange Commission and its development of enforcement strategies to respond to various forms of abuse obviously has bearing on enforcement efforts in the control of other white-collar offenses.

Therefore, this book offers even to those whose personal lives, economic fortunes, and professional or academic careers are entirely untouched by the securities markets and the threat of wayward capitalists a case study that contributes to the general understanding of white-collar crime, its control, and the regulatory process in what many consider an exemplary setting. Furthermore, it provides a rare glimpse inside a regulatory agency obtained from nonpublic records and documents, hearings and meetings, conversations and interviews, staff training seminars, and extended observation. The book supplements accounts of white-collar crimes and their enforcement which, lacking insider access, have had to rely solely upon Freedom of Information Act requests, litigated cases, published accounts of notorious crimes, interviews with incarcerated offenders or with enforcement agency personnel and reflect the biases and limited perspectives that these sources impose (Long 1980, Sutherland 1949, Clinard and Yeager 1980, Posner 1970, Geis 1967, Cressey 1953, Weaver 1977, Katzmann 1980).

I invite you—readers with direct or indirect investments in the capital markets and voluntary or involuntary dependence on them; honest, wayward, and not-so-wayward capitalists and your accomplices and legal representatives; law enforcement officials and SEC regulators; and readers with scholarly, professional, or personal interest in related abuses of trust—to join me in this insider glimpse of the worlds of wayward capitalists, their victims, and the Securities and Exchange Commission.

2
Wayward Capitalists

Americans are only too familiar with the techniques of property crime—of heists and armed robberies, muggings and purse-snatchings, shoplifting and auto theft, burglaries and break-ins. But as they valiantly attempt to protect their property by buying locks and alarms, moving to safer neighborhoods they can ill afford, altering their lifestyles, and spending tens of billions of dollars annually on property insurance, they remain vulnerable to other kinds of thieves around them. This latter group—white-collar or corporate criminals, some call them—has perfected the modus operandi of pedestrian property crime. They have learned to rob without force or violence, to steal without break-in or trespass. They need not beat their victims senseless or threaten them. Rather, they convince their victims that, if entrusted with money and property, they can protect, enhance, or increase their victims' assets. They replace force with fraud, robbery with deception. Instead of refining mechanical technology to break into a secured building, they develop social technology to become insiders in the organization. They replace trespass with trust, burglary with self-dealing.

White-collar criminals cultivate trust. They disarm the protections that have been erected around property and economic transactions and steal freely. Trust allows property thieves to steal without direct contact with victims or physical proximity to the property appropriated, hence protecting them from the risk of discovery and apprehension. Trust expands the time frame of victimization from the momentary encounter of a mugging, burglary, or shoplifting to ongoing long-term opportunities for repeated victimization. It increases the property available to thieves from often limited amounts of cash and consumer goods to entire inventories or bank accounts, business opportunities, secret information, and the like. It should therefore come as no surprise that abuses of trust are highly lu-

crative. An average robbery nets its perpetrator $338 (Sykes 1978, 94). On average, convicted federal white-collar criminals net over $300,000 (Wheeler and Rothman 1982, 1414); offenses investigated by the SEC cost their victims, on average, over $400,000.

Because trust is intrinsic to the securities world, it is a superb setting for larceny. Stockholders necessarily delegate responsibility to corporate management. Industrial secrecy and sophisticated technical procedures deprive investors of the information or expertise to fully evaluate their investments. Face-to-face transactions are replaced by brokers, middle-men, stock exchanges, and computers, in a world populated by trustees, experts, fiduciaries, advisers, brokers, and specialists. Because it is a world of "futures" transactions, in which investors pay up front for some possible future payoff, securities transactions provide wayward capitalists ample time to expropriate or exploit the front money and then disappear before their misdeeds are discovered. These inherent properties of secrecy, expertise, discretion, complex corporate hierarchies, interorganizational relationships, middlemen, and the probabilistic nature of investment outcomes provide a cover for white-collar criminals and inordinate op-portunities to keep victimized investors unwitting.

The misdeeds of wayward capitalists are variations on this theme of the manipulation of trust and the dual strategies of fraud instead of force and insider larceny instead of trespass. The offenders commit fraud through misrepresentation and stock manipulation. They abuse insider fiduciary positions through misappropriation and self-dealing. And to facilitate these misdeeds, they often violate regulations promulgated by the SEC to decrease the opportunities for abuse or protect investors: they fail to register their firms and their securities, engage in shoddy business prac-tices, fail to maintain proper books and records, and the like.

I will illustrate these misdeeds of wayward capitalists with scenarios from actual offenses investigated by the Securities and Exchange Com-mission. Because these illustrations are drawn from the random sample of SEC investigations, they portray not the Equity Fundings and other notorious acts of wayward capitalism, but rather the typical violations SEC investigators encounter day in and day out.

THE OFFENSES

MISREPRESENTATIONS

With the exception of a handful of corporate insiders who own securities of their employer, the vast majority of the investors in publicly held corporations are outside the corporation. These investors are unable to examine corporate technology, observe business operations, scrutinize

books and records, and formulate investment decisions on the basis of direct experience. They must therefore rely on information disseminated by corporations issuing securities, securities brokers, investment advisers, analysts, and the mass media in making investment decisions.

With relatively unverifiable information serving as the linchpin for securities transactions, the manipulation of information is a favorite pastime of wayward capitalists, and incomplete or fraudulent disclosures or informational imbalances between insiders and outsiders are favorite targets of SEC enforcers. Through misrepresentation or inadequate information, investors can be induced to purchase or sell securities when, given perfect information, the rational investor would do otherwise. And besides inducing "irrational" investment decisions, misrepresentations also facilitate or conceal other corporate misdeeds—acts of embezzlement or self-dealing, for example. Because of its versatile uses and facile implementation, misrepresentation is the most common element of securities violations, alleged in two-thirds of all cases in my research sample.

Most misrepresentations pertain either to characteristics of the corporation issuing securities or to details of a particular securities offering. The former include misrepresentations about (1) the status of the corporation—its business operations, financial condition, assets, and resources; (2) the future of the corporation—its prospects and risks; (3) corporate insiders—their background, compensation, financial interests, and self-dealing; and (4) corporate oversight—its registration with the SEC or self-regulatory organizations. The latter include misrepresentations about (5) the offering itself—the kind of stock; its source; the size of the offering; the market for the stock; and its current market value; (6) the role of the broker-dealers in the offering, their compensation, and the like; and (7) the return on investment—dividends, future prices, repayment of bonds, and so forth.[1]

These misrepresentations are often included in written materials disseminated to prospective investors, committed investors, or to the SEC: prospectuses, sales literature, solicitation letters, annual reports, financial statements, proxy materials, special SEC applications or filings, legal opinion letters, documents, press releases, newsletters, or general correspondence. Often they are made orally by the wayward capitalists themselves, by "bird dogs" or other stock issuer representatives or promoters, by stockbrokers or investment advisers.

---

1. Misrepresentations about (1) corporate status were found in 46 percent of all offenses; (2) corporate future in 30 percent; (3) insiders in 21 percent; (4) oversight in 10 percent; (5) the offering in 39 percent; (6) the broker-dealer's role in 7 percent; and (7) return on investment in 27 percent of all cases. The sum of these percentages exceeds 100 because many offenders made several different kinds of misrepresentations.

And on some occasions, misrepresentations are further shored up by the manipulation of physical artifacts and the creation of props. Indeed, one of the offenders in my sample referred to corporate equipment as "stage props." Several wayward capitalists in the sample planted phony ore at the entrance of mines or developed "Rube Goldberg" contraptions. Another group, representing a securities issuer that purported to have invented a plane that could fly without wings, purchased inoperable airplanes, parked them at an airport, removed their wings, and posed scantily clad women in front of them for promotional photographs. In a securities fraud not included in my sample, conspirators painted the irrigation pipes on land adjacent to their oil drilling venture bright pink (with permission from the farmer who owned the land). Atop each pipe, pieces of sheet metal bearing an *X* or *O* supposedly indicated production and steam-injected wells. "The painting and coding were intended to make the pipes look as if they were part of [the] oil facility" (McClintick 1977, 130). Less innovative wayward capitalists rented limousines, airplanes, plush offices, and prestigious mailing addresses to evidence the success of their operation. Of course, many of these ruses are necessary only where investors seek to physically inspect their investments or to deal directly with corporate officials. Fortunately for the wayward capitalists, such investors are uncommon.

The following examples drawn from my sample illustrate some of the typical contexts in which misrepresentations occur.

1. In the initial offering and sale of corporate securities:

> In the mid-1960s an evangelical preacher and his friend, a gospel singer, pilot, and oil promoter, flew around the country holding revival meetings for members of an international gospel organization. At the revival meetings, the preacher would introduce his friend to the congregation as a man devoted to the gospel movement who was blessed with success in the oil business. The promoter would then give a testimonial to God, who he claimed had given him a profitable oil lease in Wyoming as a means of helping others engaged in evangelical work. The sales presentation was imbued with the aura of religion. The two claimed that only good Christians would be allowed to purchase securities in their oil company. The promoters made misrepresentations about the presence of oil and gas in the area, the production capability of the area, and the riskiness of the venture. They misrepresented the profitability of the corporation, which was in fact consistently unprofitable and had little or no operating funds. They told investors that invested funds would be used only for drilling and property development. In fact, these funds were used to pay off the purchase price of the leases (which the corporation did not own outright, as had been represented), to pay general corporate expenses, and to support further sales promotional efforts. Investors were also deceived about the expected return on their investment and the length of time in which it should be expected. In order to lull investors into a false sense of security, early

investors were issued excessively generous checks purported to be their share of the profit. Seventy-six individuals invested about $488,000 in this scheme.

In 1959, another wayward capitalist formed a Washington corporation for the purpose of transporting fresh produce by air from Seattle to Alaska. The promoter needed to raise $300,000 for the purchase of aircraft and produce and to finance the operation. He placed newspaper ads for pilots, mechanics, and cargo handlers but made investment in the corporation a condition of employment. Indeed, personnel recruitment was simply a ruse for recruiting corporate investors. The promoter misrepresented to prospective investors that the two-month-old company had been in business for anywhere from two to four years and had established markets in Alaska. He indicated that the past operations of the company had been profitable, when clearly there were no past operations and an earlier company controlled by the promoter had been a total failure. He represented that the company owned six airplanes (it had none), and that it had complied with Federal Aviation Administration requirements and applied to register its securities (it had not). The promoter said that he had invested $180,000 of his own funds in the company (he had actually invested nothing) and that several financially prominent persons had invested funds as well. Finally, he falsely stated that the investors' money would be returned at any time. About $25,000 was obtained from eleven investors.

A loan company (which was actually an investment company) was formed in Georgia in mid-1957. An active sales campaign began, directed primarily at Georgia schoolteachers. More than thirty securities salesmen were employed by the firm and prominent ads were placed in the major Georgia education journal. Teachers were told that the company was, practically speaking, a teachers' credit union. The salesmen represented that the state superintendent of schools and other prominent persons were stock purchasers, when in fact they had invested nothing and were induced to accept stock as gifts through trickery. These men were so highly regarded that 90 percent of those who bought stock did so on the basis of this representation. Salesmen also stated that half of the company's assets would be placed in loans to teachers and secured by sound collateral; in fact only 3 percent of the funds were so used. Furthermore, they asserted that the remaining assets would be placed in short term gain and blue chip investments. Instead, these assets were invested recklessly, in the words of an SEC investigator, in "complete flops" and "cats and dogs," firms in which the company president had a proprietary interest. Because of a severe financial deficit, the company's books and records were doctored to conceal its true financial condition. And dividends were paid out, despite the lack of corporate earnings, to spur more stock sales. Additional misrepresentations concerned the safety of the investment, its expected yield, the redemption plan, assurances that investors could retrieve their money when they needed it, and corporate approval and oversight. At least 1,000 teachers invested about $750,000 in this company.

2. In subsequent attempts by broker-dealers to sell outstanding corporate securities:

A New York broker-dealer firm was created only for the purpose of distributing the securities of a Montana mining company. The firm was not

selling newly issued securities on behalf of the mining company; all shares were outstanding. Fraudulent misrepresentations were contained in several pieces of widely distributed literature. Investors were also contacted by telephone by high-pressure salesmen either before or after the mailing. Paid ads appeared in New York newspapers. Salesmen falsely stated that the company owned several mines with a proven and substantial value, validated by an assay report placing yearly net income at $1,500,000. They represented that equipment and machinery installation was near completion and that the mine would open in sixty days. Salesmen failed to disclose that the mine had been inactive since 1925 and that substantial amounts of equipment had been removed, large portions of the mine were inaccessible because of caving and flooding, the engineering reports described were made in 1920, and engineers now said that mining was not feasible. The materials failed to indicate that the stock had already been issued and falsely stated that proceeds of the stock sale would go to the mining company that had originally issued the securities. Salesmen misrepresented expected earnings, promising that the stock price would increase and that the brokerage firm would repurchase the stock, if necessary. The brokerage firm sold about 800,000 shares of the mining stock at 30–35 cents per share at a time when the over-the-counter price was 16–20 cents. It had acquired the stock at between 3 cents and 21 cents per share.

3. In attempts to purchase corporate securities:

Fraudulent purchases of the stock of the minority shareholders of a large southern insurance company were made by the company's principal officers and directors. These principals never sent financial statements to the stockholders or paid them dividends, which would have disclosed the good financial condition of the company. They concealed the fact that stock was being acquired for the principal corporate officers. Instead, they alleged that it was for persons opposed to the management, including a man who wanted to get on the board to force the payment of dividends. They misrepresented the value of the stock and the existence of a market for the stock. The purchase of these shares was facilitated by direct solicitations by the principals under assumed names, through nominees, or with the assistance of broker-dealers. As a result, the principals acquired thousands of shares of stock at grossly unfair prices and then negotiated an agreement with a securities underwriter to sell the shares at a price much higher than what they had paid. As many as 250 public shareholders lost in excess of $100,000 (based on the market value of the stock at the time of purchase).

4. In routine disclosures of a public corporation unrelated to attempts to buy or sell securities:

A corporation that financed industrial enterprises was in a hopelessly insolvent condition. However, the corporation was able to secure loans totalling more than three million dollars from thirteen different banks. This was accomplished through the preparation of false and misleading financial statements certified by a CPA firm and included in the corporation's SEC 10K annual reports for two different years. Balance sheets and financial information classified assets as current when they were not current at the time and significantly overstated current assets. They also failed to reveal

the subsidiary status of certain companies classified as customers. The CPA firm knew or should have known of the discrepancies and misstatements.

5. In the promotion of professional services in the securities industry:

Several investigations pertained to misrepresentations made by investment advisory services to potential clients about the quality of the service they offered. One firm utilized a Wall Street address as a mail drop and listed a number of well-known authors of financial books on its letterhead, falsely implying that these persons were employed members of their advisory staff. Misrepresentations in the promotional literature of the various firms concerned the size of the companies, their financial condition, their facilities for service, the background and experience of their personnel, the success of their advice to clients, and the selectivity of clientele. They assured clients of consistent profits, indicating that no other advisory services had better records. The advisory services purported to provide an in-depth independent analysis, when all they actually offered were edited reports supplied by the companies being touted. They promised that the graphs they had developed would zero in on market winners, failing to disclose the limitations of these predictions. And, finally, their representations about the limited number of subscriptions available and about the urgency for readers to subscribe were also false.

STOCK MANIPULATION

Some investment decisions are made on the basis of information concerning public corporations and the securities they issue. The misrepresentation or withholding of information renders these investments vulnerable to victimization by wayward capitalists. Often investment decisions are made after scrutinizing the trading market and price history of securities, the artificial manipulation of which provides a different version of misrepresentation and of victimization. The category of *stock manipulation* subsumes a variety of activities in which the market price or trading market of a security is artificially manipulated, usually to induce others to buy or sell these securities. A description of classic manipulation techniques of the 1920s and 1930s provides some sense of the practice in its most blatant and simple form.

The group first secures an option to purchase at a price higher than the then market quotation a large block of a stock which possesses actual or potential market appeal and an easily controllable floating supply. It is the task of the pool manager and operator to raise the market price above the option price, and, if the supply on the market remains constant, this can be accomplished only by increasing the demand. The most effective manner of inducing others to purchase is to have a favorable ticker tape record which indicates to prospective purchasers that others consider the security to be underpriced. The manager opens a number of accounts with various brokers and, fortified by a knowledge of the condition of the market obtained

from the book of a specialist, enters both buying and selling orders with a preponderance of the former so that the price is made to rise slowly upon an increasing volume of transactions. In the cruder form of operation many of these transactions will be washed sales in which the operator is both buyer and seller of the same stock; in others known as matched orders he enters orders to sell with the knowledge that some confederate is concomitantly entering orders to purchase the same amount of stock at the same price. As the price slowly rises, a complex publicity apparatus is set into motion to aid the stimulation of demand: The directors of the corporation whose stock is being manipulated, who may be members of the pool, issue favorable, but not wholly true, statements concerning the corporation's prospects; brokers, likewise interested in the operations, advise customers through market letters and customers' men to purchase the stock; subsidized tipster sheets and financial columnists in the daily papers tell glowingly of the corporation's future; "chisellers," "touts," and "wire-pluggers" are employed to disseminate false rumors of increased earnings or impending merger. As the market price passes the option price, the operator exercises his option and, increasing his sales over purchases, carefully unloads upon the public the optioned stock as well as that acquired in the process of marking up the price. But the operator does not necessarily rest with this gain. If he is able to distribute his holdings, he may sell short, and the stock, priced at an uneconomically high level and bereft of the pool's support, declines precipitately. As it approaches its normal quotation the pool covers its short position, thereby profiting both from the rise which it has engineered and the inevitable reaction. ["Market Manipulation and the Securities Exchange Act" 1937, 626–28]

Most observers believe that the widespread and flagrant abuses involving manipulative activities of this kind, which were carried on prior to and in the early years of the SEC, have since been controlled. Whether for this reason or because of investigative difficulty, manipulative activity is not a common element of most SEC investigations, nor is it quite so blatant. Only one-tenth of the investigations in the sample involved allegations of stock manipulation. A few examples of the contexts in which stock manipulation is found follow.

For two months in 1959, a man in New York purchased over 40,000 shares and sold over 18,000 shares of stock in a carpet company listed on the New York Stock Exchange. Utilizing accounts with as many as twelve different broker-dealers, he placed matched orders, engaged in wash sales, and effected numerous transactions designed to raise the price of the stock in order to induce others to buy. He placed purchase orders through brokers at a time when he did not intend to pay for the stock and allowed brokers to sell him out. This individual was only one of several persons engaged in similar

manipulative schemes, all of whom were friends and neighbors of the Chairman of the Board of the carpet company. SEC investigators suspected that the chairman had encouraged these friends to manipulate the stock, offered them jobs with the company, guaranteed them against losses, and promised them a portion of the profits so generated.

Eight New York area promoters known to be involved in organized crime cheaply acquired large blocks of stock of a dormant Florida corporation from major shareholders. Then they merged the corporation with a thinly floated public corporation. Through direct purchases, use of nominees, and placing purchase orders without any intent to pay for the stock or to honor repurchase agreements, they were able to acquire and tie up most of the floating supply of the corporate stock. For the next two months, they proceeded to manipulate the price of the stock from $2 to $12.50 per share by placing orders in nominee names and not making payment, touting the stock to prospective purchasers, and making buy-back agreements at higher prices with persons who purchased or owned stock. The promoters then attempted to sell and pledge large blocks of the stock now worth about $1,400,000. Before they were successful, the SEC suspended trading in the stock.

The president of a large corporation engaged in chemical engineering, electronics, and research, development, and the manufacture of rockets had pledged $10,000,000 worth of personally owned stock as collateral for $4,000,000 in loans. For about eight months, he instituted a manipulative scheme in order to support the price of this stock and thus protect his loan. He caused the corporation to advance money to one of several subsidiaries to purchase its own stock. Stock was only purchased at prices higher than the market price. On some days, these activities accounted for 47 to 86 percent of the total volume of trading in these corporate securities. About $1,200,000 worth of corporate stock was purchased for this purpose.

MISAPPROPRIATION

Misappropriation involves the stealing of money or property; it has been alleged in 29 percent of all cases in the sample. At least three properties of securities transactions facilitate stealing: the fact that symbolic rather than physical commodities are exchanged, the inherent "futures" context of these transactions, and the proliferation of fudiciary roles to service them.

First, investors purchase symbolic commodities, units of ownership in a business organization or economic venture evidenced in a piece of paper: a stock certificate. These investors typically are organizational outsiders, unable to scrutinize business operations. Unlike consumer frauds, in which victims have possession of physical commodities, securities frauds have almost unlimited manipulative opportunities because of their capacity to distance investors from the "goods" they have purchased. The SEC itself acknowledges this dilemma:

> Securities are by their very nature much different from almost any other type of "merchandise" for which there are established public markets. A person who wishes to purchase a new car or household

appliance—or for that matter, a peck of potatoes or a bag of beans—can pretty well determine from personal inspection the quality of the product and the reasonableness of the price in relation to other competing products. But this is not so with respect to a bond or a share of stock. An engraved certificate representing an interest in an abandoned mine or a defunct gadget manufacturer, for example, might look no less impressive than a "blue chip" security with a history of years of unbroken dividend payments. Beyond that all comparisons cease. [U.S. Securities and Exchange Commission 1978, foreword]

When an investor buys a share of a corporation, only a piece of corporate stationery, some financial statements, and a few documents need be provided. A corporation can literally be built from a ream of paper. And while investors content themselves with their symbolic ownership, their investment monies can be misappropriated and diverted. Second, investors can be kept at a distance from their corporate possessions not only physically and symbolically but temporally as well. Because securities transactions are based on the promise or expectation of some future event or return, it is possible to recruit a large group of willing investors before future events disconfirm the initial representations. The "futures" context provides a generous cushion of time in which investment funds can be stolen with impunity. Third, the securities world is by necessity staffed with fiduciaries for brokering transactions, managing publicly held corporations, and providing investment advice. Investment funds, stock certificates, and the assets and property of publicly held corporations, entrusted to fiduciaries, can be stolen, borrowed, or misused.

One occasion for misappropriation is afforded by the initial issuance and sale of corporate securities. The sample contained a substantial number of cases in which promoters created sham or bogus corporations—an investment company, a holding company, a finance company, several mining corporations, a firm that developed and marketed anti-pollution devices, one that developed and marketed life insurance and trading-stamp vending machines—generated interest in them, and subsequently sold corporate securities to the public, usually netting several hundred thousand dollars. Some of the proceeds from securities sales were used to pay promotional costs or to buy props to make the corporation look legitimate (for example, prototype machines, mining supplies), and the remainder was misappropriated by promoters, either directly or through inflated or fictitious expense claims and other ruses.

In a few cases, where offenders had ongoing relationships with potential victims, the process of creating sham organizations was considerably simplified. One stockbroker simply told his clients that he was selling some (nonexistent) bridge debentures and turnpike bonds and that he

would keep possession of these bonds until maturity. He then sent out phony receipts of their purchase and pocketed the monies provided by his clients. In another case, a life insurance salesman (and rabbi) sold $200,000 worth of bogus securities in the life insurance company to his customers.

In some cases, the issuing corporation whose stocks are offered and sold is legitimate. Nonetheless, sales of newly issued securities provide an opportunity for misappropriation by those involved in their sale. The president of a corporation that marketed his electrical inventions did not record all stock purchases (especially cash payments) on the corporate books and embezzled these monies (about $50,000). A firm serving as underwriter for three stock issuances did not report all the sales or deposit them in the escrow account. In one instance, an issuer audit discovered the practice and the issuer demanded full payment. The underwriter complied, securing these funds by misappropriating them from still another stock issuance that it had underwritten as well.

In several offenses, the source of misappropriated funds was not the proceeds from the sale of securities, but rather the operating capital of legitimate public corporations; and the recipients of these funds were those in fiduciary roles in the corporations. These practices tended to be more elaborate than classic embezzlement schemes.

> The general partner of a limited partnership in hotels and motels doubled his salary without authorization; utilized corporate funds to extend loans to himself and other businesses in which he had an interest; raised excess funds for the corporation through the issuance of securities and misappropriated the monies so generated; and simply embezzled corporate funds for his benefit and that of other business interests.

> Two officers of a corporation that made and distributed motion pictures issued a corporate check to a client, who in turn wrote a check for $10,000 to a phony bank account. This money was used to buy personal shares of corporate stock for these officers.

> Over $2,500,000 was misappropriated from a credit company by several officers and corporate counsel, who sold worthless or considerably overvalued installment contracts owned by corporations that they controlled to the credit company. Under their direction, the company made loans to businesses they controlled and then paid the interest on these loans with company funds. It transferred corporate funds to a Bahamian bank account that they controlled, recording the transaction as simply the opening of a new corporate bank account.

There is a substantial caseload involving the misappropriation of client funds by fiduciaries in the securities profession (usually stockbrokers) rather than in publicly held corporations. For example, clients order certain stock purchases and remit the necessary payment to their brokers, who then convert the funds to their own use without purchasing the securities. Brokers utilize client stock certificates that they hold in safekeeping as collateral on their own personal loans, or they simply forge

client signatures on the stock certificates, sell them, and convert the proceeds to their own use. Brokers misappropriate funds in customer credit balances or close out a customer's account without authorization, taking the check made out by the firm to the customer, forging the endorsement, and depositing the proceeds in their own personal account. Rather than abusing client assets for personal gain, brokers may generate additional personal revenue at their clients' expense. They may charge excessive and unreasonable prices for securities purchased or unreasonable mark-ups or commissions. Or they may churn a client's discretionary account, engaging in excessive and unnecessary trading to generate larger commissions.

These abuses are often supported by elaborate cover-up techniques. They include sending fictitious confirmations of stock transactions to clients, persuading clients to leave stocks and bonds with the broker for safekeeping, paying phony dividends out of the offender's pocket for (nonexistent) stocks that the client thinks are being held in safekeeping, urging clients to allow their (nonexistent) investment profits to remain with the broker for reinvestment, paying clients who demand payment with funds of other clients, falsifying books and records of the brokerage firm, and the like. One broker overpaid on his federal income tax to cover up his abuses, came to work early to intercept the mail and remove letters that might reveal his activities (and, of course, never missed work or took vacations). When a victim died, he shuffled around the accounts so that his misappropriations would not come to light when the victim's estate was probated.

It is only in the context of broker misappropriations that investigatory materials provide any insights about the motivations for participation in securities violations. (It is telling that SEC investigators apparently consider the motivations for other kinds of wayward capitalism unproblematic, obvious, or perhaps even rational.) Investigatory records contain the usual rationalism for embezzlement: expenses generated by divorce, alimony, and family illness; repaying loan sharks for gambling debts; extravagant living; liquor and cabaret bills; purchase of a new home. The sole proprietor of a broker-dealer firm misappropriated funds in an attempt to save his insolvent firm. The officers of a public corporation argued that "misappropriated" funds were needed to pay a bribe to foreign officials to get oil concessions (these allegations could not be substantiated). For some, the motivations were presumably more psychological than situational. Two embezzlers in my sample were subsequently committed to mental institutions by their families; two others committed suicide.

Some instances of misappropriation are prompted by the speculative nature of investments. Several brokers needed money to cover personal market speculations and losses. One broker lost substantial amounts of

money for clients through discretionary commodities investing and engaged in embezzlement to repay them. One salesman lost $13,000 for his firm when he pushed a particular stock and many customers cancelled their purchases. He was a mediocre salesman and feared losing his job, so he misappropriated funds to reimburse the firm.

SELF-DEALING

Self-dealing offenses are very similar to those of fiduciary misappropriation. Indeed, some of the illustrations provided in the previous section had elements of self-dealing. Self-dealing is the exploitation of insider positions for personal benefit. But the nature of personal benefit is more than simply the embezzlement or expropriation of funds. It may involve the allocation of corporate commodities or contracts to businesses in which the insider has an interest, the direction of corporate discretion in favor of insider private interests, the use of organizational resources to create new opportunities that insiders can exploit, or the use of nonmonetary corporate resources or information for personal advantage. Fourteen percent of the cases in the sample had elements of self-dealing. A few examples will show the typical situation encountered by SEC investigators.

> Several directors of a registered investment company entered into an arrangement with its custodian bank, whereby investment company funds would be used as a means of providing personal loans and credit for these persons and for other companies in which they had a financial interest. They later informed the bank that, as a condition of continued business, the bank must maintain correspondent accounts in four other banks, from which they also made substantial borrowings. To facilitate these loan transactions, the directors caused the investment companies to maintain excessive cash deposits with the banks.

> A Chicago man ran a private sole proprietorship in the business of manufacturing arc welders, torches, and cutting and filing tools. He incorporated the business, went public, and became a major shareholder and control person, influencing corporate decisions. He used the corporation for his own financial benefit, however, netting himself a great deal of money and depleting corporate coffers until its eventual bankruptcy. For example, he bought metal at 5 cents/pound but sold it to the company for 27–38 cents/pound, which then processed and sold it, though unable to make a profit. He created other personal companies that would process corporate products at great profit without performing any actual function—for example, buying saws from the corporation at $8.50 and selling them at $16, utilizing corporate resources to make the distribution.

Insider trading is another form of self-dealing. Here, people inside public corporations profit from information available to them by virtue of their corporate positions in making personal investment decisions at the expense of less well-informed investors.

A corporation was engaged in Canadian mining explorations. Several corporate insiders had seen the drilling results and were aware of some promising land on which exploration was being conducted. They decided to keep this information secret, as they wanted to purchase the land at a reasonable price. However, rumors were circulating, trading was very heavy, and the price of the stock was rising. Corporate management was concerned about the trading situation and issued a press release designed to diminish interest in and expectations about the stock. Four days later, management issued a glowing press release, announcing a major discovery of ore. The result of the first release was to lower stock prices, and of the second, to increase them. Corporate insiders had been trading on inside information since the first favorable reports seven months earlier but particularly during the interim between the press releases, and had been tipping information to their associates. No disclosures were made to the sellers with whom insiders transacted. Insiders and "tippees" made profits of $148,000 from these transactions.

A registered representative of a New York brokerage firm also served on the board of directors of a public aircraft corporation. At a board meeting he learned that the corporation was going to cut its dividend. During a break, he phoned a partner of the brokerage firm that employed him. The partner, knowing that such information had not yet been released to the public, executed orders to sell 2,000 shares for ten accounts and sell short 5,000 shares for eleven accounts, including those of clients of the director and that of his own wife. About $42,000 in profits accrued from these transactions, the greatest profit absorbed by the partner's wife.

A final example of self-dealing involves another kind of abuse of information. In insider trading offenses, parties react passively to information. In "scalping," offenders play a more active role; they tout a security after first taking a position in it and then enjoy the ensuing market reaction to the touts.

A New York investment adviser firm published material to which members of the securities industry subscribed and also provided a supplementary consultation service through which it made recommendations to broker-dealers. Two research analysts of the firm purchased stocks prior to making recommendations to clients to purchase these stocks and resold them for a profit in the market they had created. They never disclosed their holdings to clients. Together, they made profits of $39,000.

INVESTMENT SCHEMES

Investment schemes have many of the elements of misrepresentation, misappropriation, and stock manipulation. However, unlike many of these offenses, in which an attempt is made to provide a viable investment opportunity or service, investment schemes typically are designed from the beginning as con games or larceny schemes. Only 8 percent of the cases in the sample were classified as investment schemes. The following examples typify the two most common kinds of schemes, ponzi games and shell corporation swindles.

Ponzi game: A California man told investors that he could buy electronic component parts at exceptionally low prices at auctions, government surplus sales, and from bankrupt companies and later resell them at huge profits. To support his claim, he falsely stated that he held a degree in electrical engineering from an eastern university, that he held responsible positions with several large electrical companies, and that these and other connections with the electronics industry enabled him to dispose of electronic component parts at great profits. He indicated to potential investors that his need for money resulted from the exhaustion of his personal funds and the difficulty of obtaining bank loans because of the type of items being purchased. He asserted that, because of the substantial profit to be made on each transaction, money invested with him for short periods of time would yield enormous profits to the investors. He issued each investor a personal promissory note for both the principal amount invested and a profit of 40−70 percent. As the scheme progressed, he held frequent meetings with the investors, where he outlined the program, gave them the choice of being repaid, taking out part of the money, adding additional amounts of money, or letting their money ride for another investment period. Because of his readiness to pay off those desiring their money back, the majority of the investors would leave their money with him. However, proceeds from the sale of these promissory notes and investment contracts were not applied to the purchase of electronic parts; no profits were realized; and payments made to investors were derived from the paid-in capital resulting from the sale of additional securities to investors. In this particular case (he was involved in others), at least fifty to sixty people in the Salt Lake City area invested between a quarter and a half million dollars during a ten-month period. The typical ponzi game collapses because more money is being paid out as bogus dividends and misappropriated funds than is being taken in as new investment capital. This scheme ended prematurely when the promoter was indicted by the state of California for an earlier ponzi scheme.

Shell corporation swindle: Two promoters acquired control of two dormant Arizona shell corporations with no assets, issued stock to themselves for no consideration, and bought up shares from corporate shareholders for one cent apiece. They enlisted the aid of brokers in creating a market, manipulating the market price, and distributing this unregistered stock to the public. Facilitators of the scheme included promoters, broker-dealers, a transfer agent, conduits for the movement of shares, and nominees. The following month, a dinner meeting was held for brokers and investors to interest them in the issuer, describing its numerous (nonexistent) operating divisions, its assets (actually valued at only $500), and plans for future mergers and acquisitions. Within about ten months, more than 2,000,000 shares had been transferred from insiders to the public, netting somewhere between $1.5 and $7 million.

REGULATORY VIOLATIONS

Some offenses have been defined as wayward not because they defraud investors but because they violate SEC regulations. These regulations generally pertain to who is entitled to issue securities or engage in a securities business and to how that business is to be conducted. These offenses, more or less created by regulation, include registration and

technical violations, improper sales techniques, and violations of previous restrictions.

Registration Violations. Fundamental to all federal securities legislation is the requirement that before securities may be offered or sold to the public, a registration statement must be filed with the SEC and must become effective.[2] The 1933 Securities Act provides for certain exemptions from registration: private offerings to a limited number of persons or institutions (who have access to information and do not redistribute these securities); offerings restricted to the state in which the issuing company does business; offerings not in excess of specified dollar amounts and made in compliance with other regulations; and securities of governments, charitable institutions, banks, certain inter-state carriers, and small business investment companies (U.S. Securities and Exchange Commission 1978, 2). Still, a wide variety of transactions involving the offer and sale of securities are subject to SEC registration requirements. Nonetheless, some of them are not registered.

In a minority of cases in my sample, an unusual or novel interpretation of the definition of a security was involved; those offering investments were unaware that registration was required. There were a number of investigations concerning the offering of so-called unregistered invest-ment contracts—interests in citrus groves, catfish farms, Scotch whisky, warehouse receipts, rare coins, and the like—where offerers provided assorted services of farming, caretaking, storage, marketing, and distri-bution for the investors. These business opportunities were defined as investment contracts requiring registration because, in each of these cases, the investor had to rely on services provided by the offerer for the success of the investment. In another case, promoters offered cruises to Central American countries, where investor/participants would dive to recover treasures, gold, and artifacts of the Mayan civilization from sunken Spanish vessels. Since this scheme appeared to be a profit-sharing agreement, and thus a security, it was investigated for possible violation of SEC registration requirements.

Some registration violations derived from the naivete or inadvertence of those offering securities, for example, the newly emerging business enterprise whose promoter sought investment capital, unaware of the

---

2. Securities are evidence of ownership, creditorship, or debt. They are defined in the Securities Act of 1933 as "any note, stock, treasury stock, bond, debenture, evidence of indebtedness, certificate of interest or participation in any profit-sharing agreement, collateral-trust certificate, preorganization certificate, certificate of deposit for a security, fractional undivided interest in oil, gas, or other mineral rights, or, in general, any interest or instrument commonly known as a 'security,' temporary or interim certificate for, receipt for, guarantee of, or warrant or right to subscribe to or purchase, any of the forgoing" (Section 2 (1)).

need to register; the company that altered its form of capitalization and, in the process, lost its exemption from securities registration; the mistaken sale of securities in an intrastate exempted offering to someone from out of state. Other registration violations were far from inadvertent. Some involved creative and complex arrangements to cover up the violations or to present them as if exempt from registration. To qualify for the intrastate exemption, out-of-state investors were required to drive into the state of issuance to purchase their securities and to list addresses of motels, friends, or relatives as their residence in the state. In other cases, stocks were issued to a small number of nominees or trustees (qualifying for intrastate or private placement exemptions) who subsequently distributed these shares widely to the public. In one case, control stock in a corporation was channeled through Swiss and German banks and Lichtenstein trusts to launder its source and evade registration requirements.

Registration violations are found in half the investigations in the sample. Failure to register may occur during the original offering of corporate securities to the public or during the attempted resale of personally owned shares by corporate insiders, parties who purchased them pursuant to exemptive provisions, and others. Often failure to register is an intentional act associated with a more complex securities fraud. Registration or attempted registration brings securities issuers to the attention of the SEC and requires disclosure of information which, unless deceptive, would tip off SEC staff to their fraudulent schemes. Thus, only about a fifth of these cases involved registration violations exclusively; almost all the remaining cases were also coupled with elements of securities fraud. And more than half (54 percent) of the investigations of securities fraud also alleged securities nonregistration.

The Securities Exchange Act of 1934 and the Investment Company Act and Investment Advisers Act, both of 1940, require that certain securities professionals and securities organizations be registered with the commission as well. These include national securities exchanges, national securities associations, brokers and dealers engaged in an interstate over-the-counter securities business, investment companies, and investment advisers. Like the provisions for the registration of securities, these acts provide various exemptions from registration. And some securities professionals also fail to register. However, the likelihood that violations of this kind will be investigated is much lower (8 percent of the cases) for professionals than for securities themselves (52 percent). About two-thirds of the cases involving unregistered professionals also involve unregistered securities.

The nonregistration of professionals sometimes reflects naivete, inadvertence, or novel interpretations of the registration requirements.

A group of nine friends—engineers, draftsmen, and surveyors—formed an investment club. They each made a $50 deposit and a $20 monthly payment, the funds to be utilized to invest in real estate. The friends were unaware that their club had to be registered as an investment company.

An Ohio man widely advertised an investment opportunity in which investors would pay $25 with which he would buy U.S. Savings Bonds for $18.75. He would utilize the remaining $6.25 to invest in the stock market. Investors were promised a full return plus profits in nine years. The promoter had inadvertently created an investment company subject to SEC registration requirements.

An insurance company was selling variable annuity life insurance policies to residents of Arkansas. In these contracts, retirement income would be provided in units of common stock rather than in monetary units (supposedly as a hedge against inflation). The SEC argued that these were securities sales and that the insurance company was an unregistered investment company.

Sometimes securities professionals are well aware of the SEC registration requirements but are unable to register because of the terms of an injunction or conditions of probation or parole. Others anticipate that they will be denied registration because of their record of previous offenses. Some of these people simply neglect to register and continue to conduct their business. Others attempt to do business through nominees or create registered brokerage firms utilizing dummies as control persons for purposes of registration, while they actually control and conduct the business of the firm. Several investigations concerned the attempts of notorious con men or securities offenders to continue their brokerage activities through the assistance of "lady friends," neighbors, and a university professor fronting for them. Nonregistration by professionals is more likely intentional than inadvertent: 85 percent of these investigations also involved allegations of securities fraud.

Technical Violations. Many of the SEC regulations pertain specifically to the conduct of securities issuers and professionals registered with the agency or those seeking exemptions from such registration. I have labeled failures to abide by these regulations "technical violations." Although many of the regulations may have the effect of making fraudulent activity more difficult or of minimizing the likelihood of victimization, their violation is not inherently fraudulent.

About a quarter of all cases in the sample and 42 percent of those investigating the conduct of broker-dealers included allegations of technical violations by securities professionals. The most common were violations of SEC bookkeeping rules (48 percent of these cases) requiring certain books, records, ledgers, and the like to be kept and be current; delinquency or failure to file annual reports of financial condition with the SEC (44 percent); and violations of net capital rules (44 percent) that

specify the level of capitalization required for registered broker-dealers. Much less frequently, investigations pertained to violation of SEC regulations concerning the extension of credit to clients, segregation of customer accounts, use of customer securities as collateral for loans, delivery of securities, and confirmation of transactions.

Technical violations by securities issuers (8 percent of the cases) are far less common. They generally involve problems in Regulation A offerings (special securities offering where small amounts of capital are to be raised, which exempts issuers from the full and costly registration process) and general disclosure problems in the filing of annual reports, proxy materials, offering circulars and prospectuses, and similar materials.

Improper Sales Techniques and Boiler-Room Operations. Improper sales techniques were investigated in about 16 percent of the cases overall and about 27 percent of those involving broker-dealers. These offenses reflect shoddy, irresponsible, inappropriate, and often unethical sales procedures. Most common among them is the use of high-pressure sales routines and boiler rooms, a bank of telephones in a brokerage firm from which salespersons make calls across the country and pressure investors to buy speculative stocks. Other activities include improper supervision of employees, failure to consider the suitability of an investment for a particular client, failure to deliver a prospectus or confirmation of securities transactions to clients, failure to obtain the best price for securities, failure to investigate an investment opportunity sufficiently, and employing known offenders.

Previous Restrictions. Violations of previous restrictions are committed by parties whose previous offenses and sanctions prohibit them from participating in the securities industry but who continue to do so, or who fail to disclose previous sanctions upon their reemployment or renewed activity. These cases (13 percent) concern violations of injunctions, conditions of parole or probation, or SEC bars or suspensions; attempts to cover up or bypass these restrictions through the use of fronts or nominees; or failure to disclose previous sanctions in SEC registration materials. About three-quarters of these offenses are committed by broker-dealers.

THE DISTRIBUTION AND INTERRELATION OF OFFENSES

The broad categories of misrepresentation, stock manipulation, misappropriation, self-dealing, investment schemes, registration and technical violations, improper sales techniques, and violations of previous restrictions mask a great deal of variation in the modus operandi, social contexts, and strategies of violation. Indeed, these nine categories summarize 150 types of securities violations by which the research data were originally classified.

Of course, the illustrations provided earlier suggest that few securities offenses involve a single discrete act. A variety of different misrepresentations directed at different targets may be necessary to successfully consummate a transaction; fraudulent activities may create technical or other violations; different coconspirators may be enacting different offenses (for example, the stock issuer misrepresenting corporate prospects and the broker pushing these stocks in a boiler room); or the cover-up of violations may require that additional offenses be committed. For the sample of 526 cases, over 2,800 different types of illegality were investigated, 5.4 per case on average. The median number of violations per case was 4; 18 percent of the investigations considered a single type of illegal conduct, 13 percent 10 or more.[3]

Table 2.1 presents the distribution of the "abridged" offense categories for the entire sample and for stock issuers and brokers separately. Figures from the "total" column of the table were reported earlier. Since about 70 percent of the investigations in the sample involved allegations representing more than one offense category, most cases are reflected in more than one row in the table. As a result, the sum of the rows exceeds the total number of cases.

Table 2.1 reveals that misrepresentations, found in two-thirds of the investigations, and registration violations, found in a little over half, are clearly the most "popular" offenses in the sample. Misappropriations and technical violations each comprise slightly under 30 percent of the cases. Offenses such as stock manipulation, self-dealing, investment schemes, improper sales techniques, and violations of previous restrictions are each found in fewer than 17 percent of the cases.[4]

---

3. These figures are based on the 150 categories of offense. Utilizing the nine-category classification, roughly 30 percent of all investigations pertained to only one of the nine offenses, 29 percent to two offenses, 22 percent to three offenses, and 13 percent to four offenses. None of the investigations inquired about more than seven broad categories of violation.

4. The research reflects a twenty-five-year period of securities violations—from the late 1940s to the early 1970s—certainly a turbulent period of social and economic history. The distribution of offenses over this time span is remarkably stable, particularly for the most common types of violation—registration violations, misrepresentation, misappropriation, and stock manipulation. However, the proportions of some of the other offenses did increase from 1948 to 1972: from 21 percent to 32 percent for professional technical violations, from 8 percent to 18 percent for improper sales techniques, from 10 percent to 17 percent for self-dealing, and from 2 percent to 13 percent for investment schemes. And the distribution of some of the others was more cyclical. For example, boiler rooms were about three times more likely to be investigated in the 1950s than either before or after; investigations of violations of previous restrictions were almost twice as common in the late 1950s and early 1960s than either before or after. These trends reflect some mixture of the effect of changing economic conditions and illicit opportunities, growing sophistication among wayward capitalists, shifting SEC priorities, and the ubiquity of certain generic modi operandi of securities fraud and cover-up.

Table 2.1. General Categories of Securities Violations

Violations	Issuers (N)	Issuers % of cases	Both issuers and brokers (N)	% of cases	Brokers (N)	% of cases	Total (N)	% of cases
All misrepresentations	(175)	77	(59)	84	(92)	50	(350)	67
Status of corporation	(133)	58	(43)	61	(52)	28	(241)	46
Future of corporation	(91)	40	(28)	40	(27)	15	(154)	30
Corporate insiders	(49)	21	(19)	27	(30)	16	(110)	21
Corporate oversight	(31)	14	(11)	16	(11)	6	(54)	10
Stock offering	(113)	50	(37)	53	(39)	21	(201)	39
Broker-dealer's role	(6)	3	(13)	19	(18)	10	(37)	7
Return on investment	(71)	31	(30)	43	(29)	16	(139)	27
Investment advice	(4)	2	(3)	4	(2)	1	(14)	3
Stock manipulation	(22)	10	(24)	34	(6)	3	(55)	11
Misappropriations	(61)	27	(17)	24	(61)	33	(153)	29
Self-dealing	(34)	15	(17)	24	(10)	5	(71)	14
Investment schemes	(21)	9	(8)	11	(7)	4	(40)	8
Registration violations	(170)	75	(53)	76	(41)	22	(282)	54
Security	(167)	73	(53)	76	(36)	20	(269)	52
Professional	(15)	7	(8)	11	(9)	5	(40)	8
Technical violations	(22)	10	(13)	19	(102)	56	(148)	28
Issuer	(12)	5	(6)	9	(19)	10	(41)	8
Professional	(12)	5	(9)	13	(98)	54	(126)	24
Sales techniques	(9)	4	(18)	26	(51)	28	(82)	16
Improper sales techniques	(6)	3	(10)	14	(46)	25	(66)	13
Boiler room	(4)	2	(9)	13	(14)	8	(27)	5
Previous restrictions	(13)	6	(5)	7	(43)	23	(69)	13
Total cases	(228)		(70)		(183)		(522)	

Note: Total exceeds sum of columns because some investigations involve neither issuers nor brokers.

The table also reveals substantial differences in the distribution of violations between securities issuers and brokers. In almost every category of offense, the differences between cases in which securities issuers offend alone and those in which securities brokers offend alone are considerable. For example, 75 percent of the issuers alone and 22 percent of the brokers alone engage in registration violations. The illicit agendas or opportunities of these two groups clearly differ. However, when stockbrokers offend with stock issuers, their pattern of violation resembles that of stock issuers offending alone. It is the solo broker who is truly the distinctive violator. While the others are occupied with forms of securities fraud, often coupled with registration violations, solo brokers are more likely to be involved in offenses that can be contained within a brokerage firm—technical violations, improper sales techniques, and violations of previous restrictions.

But what is perhaps the most significant finding derived from these quantitative data is not the frequency of any given offense but the interconnectedness of offenses. At most, about a quarter of the technical

violations and violations of previous restrictions occurred alone with no other violations present. But this was virtually never the case for investment schemes, stock manipulation, or misappropriation. And only about a tenth of the investigations of misrepresentation, self-dealing, or improper sales techniques had no other associated violations.

The specific patterns of interconnection for those offenses are not unexpected. Investment schemes are most likely to be coupled with stock manipulation, misappropriation, misrepresentations, and registration violations. Other offenses combine misrepresentation with misappropriation, registration violations, or stock manipulation; stock manipulation with self-dealing or registration violations; and technical violations with improper sales techniques. The correlations of each of these pairs of offense are statistically significant at less than the .01 level.

There are of course a number of possible interpretations of interconnections of offenses. Some violations are said to be ancillary, serving to cover up or facilitate other offenses. Promoters selling securities in bogus oil wells would most likely intentionally fail to register their offering, lest the SEC learn of their activities. Or wayward capitalists bent on misappropriating proceeds from the sale of securities would most likely misrepresent to investors the intended use of investment monies; candor would clearly limit their recruitment of victims. Or attempts to doctor the books and records of a brokerage firm to conceal the embezzlement and self-dealing of a registered representative may create unintended technical violations concerning maintenance of books and records.

Other offenses seem to go hand in hand. For example, in order to successfully market securities in a bogus or speculative venture made respectable through blatantly fraudulent literature and other misrepresentations, brokers often rely on high-pressure sales routines and boiler rooms. On other occasions, the successful course of a single violation creates new opportunities for unrelated abuses: the opportunity to embezzle monies from off-the-books slush funds created to bribe foreign officials or, in the Equity Funding case, the death benefit scam (in which fictitious beneficiaries were "killed off" and their life insurance benefits collected) made possible by the previous creation of bogus policyholders for a different purpose. Or, finally, distinct offenses may be interconnected because corporate environments vulnerable to a single abuse are vulnerable to others as well—due to improper controls, particularly larcenous and greedy personnel, or demands by complicit co-offenders for extraordinary compensation for their added risk.

Each of these explanations of interconnectedness rings true for some of the cases in the sample. But the role of ancillary violations—especially misrepresentations and registration violations—as cover-up and facilitative strategies is clearly paramount.

THE SCOPE OF ILLEGAL ACTIVITIES

Many of the securities offenses just described do not fit the stereotypes. From our daily newspaper fare, we expect to find Fortune 500 corporations, Wall Street brokerage firms, and slick sophisticated Harvard Business School types among the ranks of the wayward capitalists. Instead, we find itinerant preachers, a part-time rabbi/insurance salesman, buddies forming an investment club, "Mom and Pop" operations, foundering brokerage firms, and so on. Data on the background characteristics of the individual and organizational offenders in my sample will be presented shortly. But data on the offenses themselves also support this observation.

One indicator of the magnitude of illegal activities is the number of their participants. Investigations in my sample scrutinized the behavior of anywhere from one to fifty individuals or organizations. If, for example, investigation of a securities fraud alleged violations by a corporation issuing securities, its president, and its chairman of the board, a brokerage firm marketing its securities, and one of its registered representatives, the number of offenders would be five. In theory, a rather limited fraud could encompass a sizeable number of offenders because of the complicity of several organizations and several roles within each of them.

Contrary to this expectation, however, the size of offender pools is typically quite small. The median number of suspects of all investigations in the sample was three, with almost a fifth of the cases pertaining to a single suspect and less than 5 percent of the cases to five or more.[5] In contrast, the Equity Funding fraud resulted in twenty-two convictions, the tip of a much larger iceberg of unindicted coconspirators and suspected participants who were not charged with criminal violations. Only 5 of the 526 offenses in the sample had more than twenty-two suspects (and most of these suspects were never formally prosecuted). One clearly cannot parlay an offense into much of anything with at most three persons and/or organizations to implement it.

Given the small number of offenders enacting securities violations, it should not be surprising that their actions touch relatively few victims. Data on numbers of victims for offenses that indeed generated specifiable victims (many violations do not) are presented in table 2.2. Numbers of securities victims range from one or two to ten thousand, although the median category is twenty-six to fifty victims. Fewer than 10 percent of the offenses generated more than five hundred victims; only 17 percent generated more than two hundred. These data characterize offenses in a somewhat different light than the common stereotype of the SEC case

---

5. Offenses involving boiler rooms and investment schemes tended to have more participants, those involving broker-dealer technical violations and violations of previous restrictions fewer participants.

Table 2.2. Numbers of Victims

Victims	(N)	% of cases
Less than 5	(23)	11
5–10	(17)	8
11–25	(30)	15
26–50	(42)	21
51–100	(29)	14
101–200	(21)	10
201–500	(17)	8
501–1,000	(6)	3
More than 1,000	(12)	6
Not specified	(6)	3
Total	(203)	

might suggest. Although a dozen cases in the sample (only 6 percent) did involve several thousand victims, it is indeed a rarity.

Another finding pertains to the geographic distribution of victims. In 12 percent of the cases, all victims came from the same city, and in 32 percent from the same state, despite the assumption that SEC jurisdiction is typically interstate.[6] In only about two-fifths of the cases were victims drawn from more than a single geographic region. Thus, the typical offense is a bit less widespread than one might expect.

What about the magnitude of offenses in economic rather than in human terms? It is very difficult, even with the finest data, to construct an indicator of the economic cost of an offense.[7] For 42 percent of the cases in the sample, it was simply impossible or inappropriate to estimate the amount of money involved. For the remaining cases, estimates were based on such data as loss to victims, profits to offenders, and amount of money involved in illegal transactions (regardless of their consequences). This variable is therefore of questionable reliability, but it does discriminate between $500 embezzled and $2,000,000 secured through a ponzi game. Its distribution is presented in table 2.3. The median cost of offenses in the sample is $100,000. Two violations cost less than $100, two others more than $35,000,000. Those offenses netting the greatest amount of

6. The SEC does have jurisdiction over intrastate fraudulent conduct. However, often these matters are deemed more appropriate for the purview of state regulatory agencies.

7. If all securities offenses involved misappropriations, the job would not be too difficult. But this is not the case. How can one attach an economic price tag to technical violations involving sloppy books and records or delinquent filings or to improper sales practices such as high-pressure sales techniques or poor employee supervision? How about cases in which economic data are available but not necessarily relevant, for example, the case of securities nonregistration, in which $100,000 worth of securities were sold but purchasers were not defrauded and indeed secured a considerable return on their investment? How about the securities swindle where "victims" actually made a profit (though perhaps not as much as if offenders had not interfered)? How about certain kinds of self-dealing, where victimization may involve fiduciary disloyalty or lost opportunities, but no economic cost to victims? Does one estimate the profits accruing to offenders?

Table 2.3. Amount of Money Involved
in the Offense

Amount	(N)	% of cases
$1,000 or less	(5)	2
$1,001–$2,500	(5)	2
$2,501–$5,000	(9)	3
$5,001–$10,000	(22)	7
$10,001–$25,000	(25)	8
$25,001–$100,000	(87)	29
$100,001–$500,000	(95)	31
$500,001–$1,000,000	(23)	8
$1,000,001–$2,500,000	(20)	7
More than $2,500,000	(14)	5
Total	(305)	
Estimate not appropriate	(221)	

money include stock manipulation, self-dealing, and boiler-room activities. Whereas 19 percent of all violations involved more than $500,000, this proportion for those offenses was, respectively, 41 percent, 36 percent, and 33 percent.

The median figure of $100,000 seems like a substantial amount of money, especially compared to the take of a single street crime. But it is actually rather insignificant; during the period covered by my study, most offerings of less than $200,000 or $300,000 were exempted from full SEC registration because of their small size. Most likely the cost distribution is biased in a downward direction because of problems of missing data. It is much easier to estimate the cost of clearcut embezzlements than of more complex schemes that tend to net much larger profits. Therefore, the less costly embezzlements are overweighting the overall cost estimates. Nonetheless, these data provide additional support for the conclusion that many SEC investigations during this period pertain to offenses that were limited in scope.

A final indicator, and the only one that deviates somewhat from the characterization of offenses as small and limited, pertains to the duration of illegal activities. Research data enumerate the number of days (or years) from the initiation of illegal activities to their cessation (whether from natural causes or SEC intervention). These data are also somewhat misleading. They do not reflect the intensity of activities, periods of inactivity, variable amounts of start-up time by offense, and so on. But data for more meaningful estimates are not available. Table 2.4 presents the distribution of offense duration.

As the table indicates, illegal activities often continue for substantial periods of time. The median offense in the sample had been ongoing for about fifteen months. At least 29 percent had been continuing for more than two years. And 79 percent of all offenses were ongoing at the time

Table 2.4. Duration of Illegal Activities

Duration	(N)	% of cases
Less than 4 months	(76)	14
4–9 months	(81)	15
9–15 months	(82)	16
15 months–2 years	(87)	17
2–4 years	(83)	16
More than 4 years	(70)	13
Not specified	(47)	9
Total	(526)	

that SEC investigation began (and presumably would have continued still longer without this "unfortunate" interruption). Of those offenses of more than four years' duration, 89 percent were still continuing, in contrast to 67 percent of those of less than four years' duration. Technical violations alone were shortest in duration (one quarter lasted more than two years) and least likely to be continuing; those involving the combination of technical and registration violations as well as securities fraud were of greatest duration (almost half lasted more than two years) and were most likely to be continuing when investigation began.

Offenses of fifteen months' duration pale, of course, in the light of the ten-year Equity Funding scandal. And perhaps it is incorrect to interpret offenses of one and two years' duration as demonstrating significant scope, especially given what are probably lengthy start-up times—to register securities, develop props and prospectuses, disseminate promotional materials, and recruit investors. These data as a whole demonstrate the difficulty in expanding the scope of offenses (to recruit additional offenders or victims or to increase the size of the take), despite an often considerable length of time. Analyses later in this book will reveal, however, that duration and other indicators of offense magnitude are positively correlated; the impact of offenses enlarges with increasing duration.

THE VICTIMS

Some of the offenses investigated by the SEC—for example, certain technical or registration violations—do not create victims. However, about two-thirds of the investigations in the sample concerned offenses in which there were victims. Unfortunately, the data pertaining to victimization are of only moderate quality. This information is not always of interest to SEC investigators and is therefore not always included in investigative records. Data were available for slightly over two hundred cases in the sample—about three-fifths of the offenses generating victims.

The underreporting of information about victims produces a serious

bias that must be considered at the outset. The most common circumstances under which data will be found in investigative records are those in which SEC investigators interview or send questionnaires to victims or utilize the fact of victimization to justify prosecution. But this is not representative of the full set of investigations undertaken by SEC staff. Where (unwitting) corporate shareholders are victimized by officers engaged in self-dealing or by others manipulating their stock, it is unlikely that they would be interviewed or included in investigative efforts, for they typically have no information to share with investigators. On the other hand, where victims are stock purchasers who were defrauded by brokers and promoters in stock sales in which they directly participated—in short, where they are witting—it is likely that their testimony would be solicited. These data may be biased, then, in overrepresenting offenses in which victims play a more dynamic role in the course of illegal activity. They may also overstate the extent of small localized victim populations, reflected earlier in table 2.2.

Offenses differ considerably in the patterns of victimization they create. Some touch only a few persons, some thousands. Victims of offenses in the sample were overwhelmingly individuals (only 8 percent of the cases included organizations among their victims) and predominantly stock purchasers at the time of their victimization. In 80 percent of the cases, they were purchasers, in 3 percent sellers, in 11 percent clients (of brokers or investment advisers), and in the remaining cases, ongoing shareholders or some combination of the above roles. (These findings are probably affected by the data biases described earlier.)

I attempted to collect data on background characteristics of victims—their wealth, sophistication, and so forth. Unfortunately, more data were missing than available. I found a few very wealthy and very sophisticated victims and a larger number of middle-class and casual or novice investors. And I saw a group of victims significant less in their number than in their considerable naivete and gullibility—investing, for example, in gold mines with phony ore planted at the entrances, dry oil wells, airplanes that were purported to fly without wings, fantastic cancer cures and diet remedies, excursions seeking sunken treasures, and machines that turned sand and gravel into gold.

Somewhat more reliable and really quite fascinating data are available on the ways in which offenders recruit their victims, their prior relationships to their victims, and prior relationships among the victims themselves. Four kinds of prior victim–offender relationships could be indentified: (1) The category of "strangers" (comprising 40 percent of the cases) includes persons who simply reply to newspaper advertisements; who own stock in a corporation, the offending officers and directors of which they never meet; who buy or sell stock through market

mechanisms and never meet the persons with whom they are transacting; who are solicited to buy stock over the telephone by high-pressure sales-men engaged in a boiler-room operation; as well as those who become the marks of con men and who may ultimately spend considerable time with the offenders before victimization is consummated. (2) A second category of victims and offenders (12 percent) had "some relationship" prior to the onset of illegal activities. They were acquaintances, business associates, members of the same church or association, fellow employees, employees and employers, teachers and students, doctors and patients. (3) A third category (10 percent), reflecting "professional/client" relationships, is more homogeneous. It includes primarily stockbrokers and their clients and occasionally lawyers and their clients. (4) The fourth category (9 percent) is composed of family and close friends of the offender. Family victims are not always "great-aunt Tillies" who have not been seen in twenty years; they include parents, siblings, and in-laws as well. For an additional 29 percent of the cases in the sample, prior relationship could not be determined or, more frequently, prior relationships reflected a mixture of the four categories. The number of victims generated by an offense tends to decrease as interpersonal intimacy increases.[8]

I found the degree of intimacy of prior victim–offender relationships surprising.[9] There are indeed more cases in the sample in which at least some of the victims and offenders were acquainted (including the mixture category) than those in which they were strangers. And even the victimiza-tion of strangers is sometimes facilitated by the fabrication of fraudulent intimacies and temporary relationships. This portrait of interpersonal intimacy conflicts with stereotypes of white-collar crime in which a chasm of interpersonal distance, disembodied transactions, cover-up techniques, middlemen, records, papers, documents, and computerization are thought to permanently separate victim and offender. Instead, the portrait has more in common with that of street crimes, a setting in which crimes among people who know each other are quite common.[10]

Some of the offenders clearly have the evil intention of victimizing their closest friends and family members, of creating and exploiting relation-ships and social networks for personal gain. Investigative records provide

8. The percentage of offenses with more than one hundred victims (28 percent of all cases) decreases from 47 percent where victim and offender are strangers to 11 percent for family and friends, to 6 percent for clients, to 4 percent for some prior relationship.

9. These unexpected findings may in part reflect the biases in the generation of victim-ization data, reported above.

10. For example, a Vera Institute study of felony arrests in New York City in the mid-1970s found that in half of all felony arrests for crimes against the person and over a third of those for property crimes, the victim had a prior relationship with the defendant (Vera 1977, xiv). Data derived from the National Crime Survey (the so-called victimization surveys) indicate that about 40 percent of the violent crimes nationwide between 1973 and 1979 were committed by nonstrangers ("Violent Crime by Strangers" 1982, 1).

hints of the humiliation and psychological trauma suffered by victims so betrayed. But there is another reality that underlies some of these data: of an unwitting securities violator who develops a new business venture; who naively evades SEC registration requirements; who in enthusiasm puffs or misrepresents the nature of his business and of investment prospects; and who, out of a need for quick capital but with few financial connections (and a desire to share these opportunities with those he cares about), turns to those around him for investment capital. Intimates and associates become the victims of ultimate securities swindles because of their accessibility and of their willingness to become involved.

Of course, recruiting victims and consummating the transactions becomes much easier as the social distance between victim and offender is lessened. And recruiting multiple victims is facilitated by tapping into ongoing social networks, as some of the sample's wayward capitalists did. A chiropractor seeking investment capital for marketing a hand cream he had invented recruited wealthy patients. A teacher in an adult education investment course recruited his students. An exterminator exploited his "professional" contacts with local residents and businessmen. A trusted member of an astrology church recruited fellow members.

One also finds contrivances by offenders to reduce the social distance between themselves and potential victims. In several cases, offenders masqueraded as traveling clergymen or missionaries, moved from town to town, attended the local church for several weeks, and soon succeeded in securing investments in some business enterprise from most of the congregation. In others, the clients or customers of an organization were approached with an offer to be let in "on the ground floor" in a business expansion. Some promoters advertised in the newspaper for employees or suppliers and only much later attempted to induce them to invest in the corporation.

The utilization of social networks for recruitment of victims is fairly common. Indeed, in only 39 percent of the offenses in the sample for which victim data are available were all victims strangers to each other. More frequently, offenses touch victim populations containing groups of associates or portions of various social networks. The sample contains cases with victim pools composed of members of particular church congregations or ethnic associations, officers at several military bases, members of political or social clubs or recreational associations, members of a professional athletic team, a textbook editor and a network of social science professors, members of investment clubs, and networks of political conservatives.

Promoters used a variety of devices to recruit victims from ongoing social networks. Some utilized "bird dogs," enthusiastic investors who innocently convince friends and associates to also invest. Some promoters

solicited investments from celebrities or community or business leaders, in the hope that their visibility or reputation for financial wisdom would induce others to invest. Some contrived special systems of social referral. One promoter created a phony beauty contest. In addition to the entrant's beauty, her "talent" in recruiting investors in a book club was a criterion of winning. Another promoter paid kickbacks to a banker who steered clients to him. Another employed a spiritualist to advise her clients during a seance to buy large quantities of stock from him. Still another solicited investments in hotel meetings where attendance was by invitation only. Subsequent lists of invitees were generated by suggestions and nominations made by attendants of previous meetings.[11]

Of course, the prior relationships so common among victims should not be attributed entirely to offender contrivance. One can find a bit of greed (even larceny) in everyone. Many victims in my sample passed along hot tips to their all too willing friends and associates. One fraud involved a social science textbook editor who tipped information concerning an investment opportunity to eminent social scientists nationwide (including members of my own profession). Another fraudulent scheme began in Canada and eventually investors included entire networks of friends and families of members of the New York Jewish community. Victims in other frauds were tipped by a family member reputed to be a big trader, by a customer to reward a restaurateur who chased him down the street to return forgotten change, by unknown persons whose steambath conversation was overheard, and by several other persons whose conversations in a boardroom and in a car dealership were also overheard.

These patterns of victimization generated by securities violations create a rather unexpected portrait of small, localized victim populations—composed of persons who are typically individual stock purchasers, who knew each other and often knew the offenders previously—and of securities offenders as scheming, manipulative con men. Clearly this portrait is influenced by biases in the data. It reflects the kind of offense for which securing victim testimony is a crucial investigatory activity, with such jury appeal that it may well result in a criminal prosecution. For cases of this kind, victim data are typically gathered to support criminal prosecution, data which would then be available in the investigatory record.

Because of these biases, the characterization cannot be generalized to the pool of all securities victims. But it cannot be dismissed either—it does reflect a substantial number of cases. The necessary corrective to these biases is a study of victimization that does not suffer from the investi-

11. David McClintick's account (1977) of how Robert Trippet and Homestake Production Company "stole from the rich" provides a particularly nice discussion of the exploitation of investor social networks in the recruitment of stock fraud victims.

gative and prosecutorial blinders that generated this data base but that obtains data on victims who know little about their victimization because of their interpersonal distance from securities violators, whose plight lacks the jury appeal of the gullible marks whose story is told in investigatory records.

THE OFFENDERS

In the 526 investigations in my sample, the conduct of over 1,900 parties—723 organizations and 1,211 individuals—was examined. As noted earlier, most violations involve few co-offenders: the median number of suspects was three. Most investigations (78 percent) pertained to both organizations and individuals, usually a single organization and associated individuals. There are few securities offenses that are inherently personal and do not create organizational complicity (though embezzlement and self-dealing are exceptions). Therefore only 5 percent of the investigations examined the conduct of individuals alone. Seventeen percent scrutinized the conduct of organizations acting alone.

Overwhelmingly, the subjects of SEC investigation are drawn from two kinds of organizations—those that issue securities and those that sell and broker them. Forty-seven percent of all individual and organizational suspects represented stock issuers; 41 percent broker-dealers. Almost half of all *cases* (as opposed to *subjects* of investigation) involved investigations of at least one broker-dealer and 57 percent of the cases investigated at least one stock issuer. About a tenth of the cases pertained to the conduct of both brokers and issuers.

Indeed, only 12 percent of the subjects of SEC investigation were affiliated with neither stock issuers nor brokers. They were drawn from investment companies, law, accounting, and public relations firms, banks, insurance companies, and private corporations; or they were investment advisers, stock promoters, shareholders, nominees, or unaffiliated individuals. Even investment companies and investment advisers, both important actors in the securities industry and the subjects of their own legislative regulations and SEC enforcement agenda, represented only 3 percent of the parties under investigation. Although there is the isolated case in which an unaffiliated individual attempts to manipulate the market of a stock or gets a tip and engages in insider trading, the opportunities for abuse and the jurisdictional issues that make an offense securities-related mean that most offenders will be drawn from the major actors in the securities industry: stock issuers and broker-dealers.

Many of the subjects of investigation were repeat offenders.[12] At least

12. There is a great deal of missing data and biased reporting on the prior record of SEC investigatory suspects in the source documents. I report these data here because, despite underreporting, the extent of prior violation is considerable.

half of the individuals and a third of the organizations had been investigated on one or more occasions by the SEC, FBI, or other law enforcement agency, usually for securities fraud. More than two-thirds of the investigations in the sample concern parties at least one of whom was a repeater. One third of the repeaters were subject to criminal proceedings, about one-quarter to civil, about one-fifth to administrative, and one-tenth to self-regulatory proceedings. Many of them experienced the most severe of the available sanctions in their earlier violations—imprisonment, permanent injunctions, and revocation of SEC registration.

Most of the wayward capitalists in the sample resided or conducted their business in the states of New York (517), California (113), Texas (111), Washington (87), and Florida (78). Thirty percent of the offenders were located in New York or New Jersey, a result of the fact that half of all stockbrokers investigated by the agency are located in that area. Overall, the New York area, the Northwest, and the Southwest contributed the greatest SEC caseload relative to their population. Of course, this does not mean that there is more illegality in these regions, only that more *investigations* are opened there. This could reflect SEC regional office policy and resources as easily as it could reflect underlying patterns of illegality.

ORGANIZATIONS

As stated above, 723 or 37 percent of the parties under investigation were organizations.[13] About 80 percent were corporations, 8 percent partnerships, and 13 percent sole proprietorships. Table 2.5 presents a general classification of these organizations on the basis of their Standard Industry Code, both overall and for stock issuers alone. This distinction is an important one, since more than half of the organizations overall are in the finance category because almost half of them were brokerage firms. Excluding finance, by far the most popular industry in which offending organizations were represented was the mining industry, comprising 35 percent of the issuers. This popularity derived from the large number of securities frauds involving oil and gas investments primarily in the Southwest and gold and silver mining investments primarily in the Northwest. The pool of stock issuers included, in smaller proportions, manufacturing firms (19 percent), finance, insurance and real estate (13 percent), and services (12 percent).

The organizations under investigation were predominantly small. Investigatory records provide little information on such corporate characteristics as total sales, profits, number of employees, and so on. And it was

13. Over half of the organizations (a third of the issuers, four-fifths of the broker-dealers) were registered with the SEC in some capacity. Seven percent of the issuers were listed on a stock exchange. Eight percent of the broker-dealers were members of a stock exchange; 35 percent where members of the National Association of Securities Dealers.

Table 2.5. Standard Industry Codes for Organizations under Investigation

Industry	Stock Issuers Only (N)	(%)	All Organizations (N)	(%)
Agriculture, forestry, and fishing	(14)	4	(15)	2
Mining	(124)	35	(127)	18
Construction	(8)	2	(11)	2
Manufacturing	(66)	19	(69)	10
Transportation, communications, electric, gas, and sanitary services	(12)	3	(12)	2
Retail trade	(9)	2	(9)	1
Finance, insurance, and real estate	(47)	13	(393)	54
Services	(43)	12	(53)	7
Shell or dummy corporations	(18)	5	(18)	2
Not specified	(13)	4	(16)	2
Total	(354)		(723)	

Note: The more specific components of the general industry categories are listed and counted below:

Agriculture, etc.—crop agriculture (4 organizations), general agriculture (7), agricultural services (2), forestry (1), fishing and hunting (1).

Mining—metals (68), oil and gas (47), minerals (12).

Construction—building construction (8), development (3).

Manufacturing—foods (14), lumber and wood (1), furniture (1), paper (2), printing (3), chemicals (4), rubber and plastics (4), primary metals (2), fabricated metals (2), machinery (4), electric machinery (16), transportation equipment (7), instruments (6), misc. manufacturing (3).

Transportation, etc.—air transportation (3), transportation service (1), communications (3), electric, gas, and sanitary services (5).

Retail trade—retail building material (7), food stores (1), furniture stores (1).

Finance, etc.—banking (3), credit agencies (15), securities (317), insurance (17), insurance agents (2), real estate (9), investment (26), finance/insurance/real estate (1), accounting (3).

Services—lodging places (2), personal services (4), business services (11), auto service (1), misc. repair (1), motion pictures (5), recreation (5), health service (5), legal service (2), educational services (4), membership organizations (8), misc. services (5).

Shell or dummy corporations reflect defunct organizations that are revitalized so that their securities can be manipulated for fraudulent purposes. Their original industrial designation is irrelevant.

impossible to obtain corporate data of this kind from other sources because all identifying information had been deleted from the data as a condition of research access. Measurement of corporate size was therefore crude, and it was possible to make even rough guesses for only 69 percent of the organizations in the sample. Bankrupt organizations (35 percent) were identified and discriminations made between small (40 percent),

medium (14 percent), large (8 percent), and extremely large (2 percent) organizations. A "Mom-and-Pop" operation, sole proprietorship, or business with fewer than fifty employees was classified as small; a Fortune 500 corporation as extremely large. Medium and large organizations filled the vast space between these boundaries. Broker-dealer firms were more likely to be bankrupt than issuers, in part because the SEC has certain technical regulations concerning maintenance of capital levels, bankruptcy, and organizational demise for broker-dealers that draw them into the enforcement stream. Broker-dealer firms were also more likely to be represented among the smaller organizations investigated.

Data on the length of time in operation were available for 72 percent of the organizations in the sample. Organizations ranged from less than a year old (about 25 percent) to more than a hundred years old. About 50 percent were less than three years old, about 10 percent were ten to twenty years old, and 8 percent were more than twenty years old. There were no substantial differences between securities issuers and brokers. It is difficult to find comparable data on the longevity of all organizations of the kind that are potential securities violators with which to compare this distribution. It appears, however, that these offending organizations are rather young. Presumably new corporations break the securities laws with their earliest attempts to raise capital, new brokerage firms in their first attempts to market securities. Whether explanations for this pattern based on inadvertence, naivete, or unsophisticated cover-up techniques are meaningful is unclear. Whatever the explanation, the organizations subject to SEC investigation are not corporate giants that have been around for a long time; they are very young and very small.

INDIVIDUALS

As noted earlier, 1,211 individuals were investigated by the SEC in cases included in my sample. Most of these individuals were in the upper tiers of organizational hierarchies. A quarter were employees and 3 percent held managerial positions, while more than half held positions of either control person (6 percent), sole proprietor (5 percent), general partner (9 percent), or officer (36 percent). Thirty-eight percent were also corporate directors; at least a third were beneficial owners of more than 10 percent of the stock of the corporation. Investigated persons affiliated with broker-dealers were slightly more likely to be employees and slightly less likely to be officers, directors, or control persons than those affiliated with issuers, but the pattern is essentially the same. It is the conduct of the leaders of securities organizations that is most likely to be investigated. Many wayward capitalists are big fish in relatively small ponds.

Crude data were available on the securities and corporate experience of about three-quarters of these offenders. Thirty-five percent (61 percent

of those affiliated with issuers and 9 percent of those with brokers) had no securities experience, and half (29 percent of those affiliated with issuers and 70 percent with brokers) had considerable securities experience. Although a substantial number of stock-issuer representatives had no securities experience, 89 percent of them did have experience in the industry in which they worked.

Suspects for whom data were available (only 15 percent) reflected a fairly wide age range: 6 percent were under 30, 30 percent were 30−39, 22 percent were 40−49, 21 percent were 50−59, 12 were 60−69, and 9 percent were over 70. Twenty-five of them died at some point between the period of their alleged involvement in illegal activity and the close of the SEC investigation. Parties affiliated with broker-dealers were somewhat younger than those affiliated with issuers. Forty-two percent of the former, in contrast to 30 percent of the latter, were under 40 years of age. Suspects in all social contexts were overwhelmingly male. The number of female suspects in the sample could be counted on two hands. They were usually spouses or girlfriends of other offenders and played secondary roles. So the majority of individual suspects are male, middle-aged, organizational leaders with considerable securities and/or industry experience—a far cry from the prototypical traditional crime suspect.

CONCLUSION

I selected the SEC investigation as the window from which to view the world of wayward capitalism. Although the view depicted considerable variability and several scenes that supported our previous stereotypes about that world, in general it revealed unfamiliar territory. The typical scenes of wayward capitalism portrayed limited, undramatic securities frauds, enacted by small numbers of co-offenders, representing small, young, often fledgling corporations, taking in relatively few, often gullible investors. Because the number of victims typically was small, the economic impact of these offenses was limited. In the typical case, offending organizations were neither prominent nor were they drawn from industries we might have expected. Nor is our view of the victim, overwhelmingly an individual purchasing securities at the time of victimization, exactly consistent with our expectation that institutional investors as well as sophisticated clients and shareholders would figure prominently in victim pools.[14]

14. Some of these unexpected findings derive from limitations and idiosyncrasies in the data retained in SEC investigative records, limitations acknowledged earlier. Other surprises perhaps come from the fact that our stereotypes depend on the notorious publicized cases and reflect the aggressive post-Watergate SEC, yet these data pertain to the previous twenty-five years of agency history and periods of greater lethargy and inaction. Indeed, the

Because this view of wayward capitalism comes courtesy of the SEC, that agency has left its mark on what we see, in the way in which it has designed and located the figurative window from which it oversees the securities world and through its selective attention to the acts and actors that parade outside this window. We behold wayward capitalism through the eyes and definitions of the SEC. It is therefore appropriate to shift attention to the process by which SEC enforcers discover wayward capitalists.

---

data provide modest evidence of a trend toward somewhat greater prominence and scope in the targets of SEC enforcement in recent years. The research data affirm that the monetary cost of victimization and the number of offenders involved in illegality have risen slightly since the Kennedy administration, the size and age of organizations subject to investigation have increased somewhat since the Johnson administration, and the proportion of national and international over localized victimizations discovered by SEC investigators modestly increased during the early Nixon years. And there have been shifts in the kinds of organizations investigated in the 1960s and early 1970s, with decreases in the relative proportions of agricultural and mining securities investigated and slight increases in those of manufacturing and services. Still, other indicators of the impact, scope, and social significance of offending considered in this chapter remained unchanged or changed in the direction of less significance. These very modest trends fly in the face of the historical evidence that posits enormous shifts in SEC enforcement vigor even within the twenty-five years before Watergate, shifts barely reflected in the data, if at all. Although these data forbid any conclusive analysis of post-Watergate change, they support the notion, developed in later chapters, that day-to-day investigative caseload is unlikely to bear the mark of agency policies as long as offenses are detected haphazardly and reactively.

3

Sources of SEC Investigation: Pathways of Intelligence

A pastor had been offered a small retainer by a gold and jade mining operation, which supposedly tithed 10 percent of its profits to a (nonexistent) evangelical organization, to scout out potential investors. The pastor became suspicious after receiving some strange mailings from the company and conferring with a mining engineer. The pastor consulted an attorney and they informed the SEC of these operations.

A corporate secretary quit her job and decided to dispose of about $4,000 of its stock that she owned. She submitted a newspaper ad to sell the securities. The newspaper, fearing either registration violations or fraud, refused to print the ad without prior SEC approval. The secretary contacted the SEC and mentioned that she didn't see what was wrong, since her boss used to sell large blocks of his personal stock all the time through ads run by the company.

A salesman for a life insurance company was fired because the premium checks he transmitted kept bouncing. The company's legal counsel contacted policyholders and learned that the salesman had been selling them nonexistent securities and certificates of deposit in the company in addition to the life insurance policies, pocketing the proceeds. The legal counsel informed the SEC, fearing that the company might be held liable for the actions of its employee.

A national brokerage firm was undergoing its annual audit. One client, contacted by the auditors, advised that the firm was holding her stock certificates in safekeeping. But the certificates could not be found. The auditors contacted the local office in which these transactions had occurred, and the errant stockbroker (who had been embezzling and misusing client funds and securities for over ten years) realized that he was finally caught. He consulted an attorney and confessed to the secretary-treasurer of the brokerage firm, who conducted an investigation and then contacted the SEC. Apparently everyone in town, from the barber to the bartender, had known that there was trouble at the brokerage office for weeks, but no one had bothered to tell the authorities.

Several persons had invested in a Scotch whisky scheme. They bought in at the time of initial production and were told that after the whisky had aged,

their investment would increase in value by at least 100 percent. After the aging process was complete, the investors found that they were having trouble selling the whisky and complained to SEC officials.

A potential investor contacted the SEC and inquired about an investment opportunity in a firm that sold and promoted personal development and success programs. The promoter's representations that investors could expect a 60 percent profit per year seemed too high.

A stockbroker notified the SEC that a man had opened a brokerage account for his sister under unusual circumstances. It turned out that actually the man had burglarized an elderly woman's home and stolen $875,000 worth of securities, which he was trying to sell.

A Florida realtor complained to SEC officials that his tenant, a boat production company, had left the state, taking furniture that belonged to him and failing to pay four months' back rent.

Editors of two financial publications reported to the SEC a luncheon conversation they had with a broker affiliated with a Canadian investment firm. He requested that they publish favorable reports concerning a particular mining stock. He felt that their reports would push up the price of the stock and offered to share any profits (perhaps as much as $1,000,000) that resulted from his purchase and sale of 100,000 shares of the stock.

A federal probation officer reported to the SEC Fort Worth regional office that one of his parolees was acting suspiciously. He had purchased an expensive Lincoln coupe in which he had already driven 16,000 miles, despite restrictions on leaving the state. His employment address was a vacant lot. The officer had heard rumors that the parolee was selling mining stock in southern Missouri and requested an investigation.

A postal inspector was investigating a subject alleged to be using the mails to defraud men's clothing and specialty shops. He placed a mail cover on the subject and thereby learned of his securities transactions with various brokerage firms. The inspector referred this information to SEC officials.

The Internal Revenue Service in auditing the tax return of a securities salesman uncovered suspicious transactions. The IRS shared this information with SEC officials, who later discovered that he had defrauded 20 investors of $90,000.

An elderly widow wrote a letter (filled with spelling and grammatical errors) to the president of the United States, stating that she had recently been offered 75 cents per share for a security that she had purchased twenty years earlier for $10 per share. She felt she had been robbed. The president's office referred her letter to the SEC.

A local Better Business Bureau received an inquiry from the manager of a professional football team, one of whose players had been solicited to buy into a limited partnership for producing and marketing catfish. The Better Business Bureau notified the SEC.

A stockbroker, suffering from a tubercular condition and mental stress, hallucinated that a customer ordered an unlimited quantity of a particular security and immediately placed an order. The next morning he learned of his purchase, for which he had insufficient funds. He informed the National Association of Securities Dealers (NASD), which informed the SEC.

In April 1965, an SEC employee noticed advertising promoting investments in Scotch whisky. In September 1967, an investor, solicited to buy these securities, inquired about them at the Denver SEC regional office. In October 1968, a London whisky competitor contacted the SEC, alleging that racketeers were in the whisky industry, one of whom was under investigation in Canada and engaged in fraudulent activities. Two months later, the SEC received a letter alleging fraud, forwarded from the U.S. State Department, that had traveled from a Minnesota whisky investor to the Minnesota Attorney General to a postal inspector to the State Department. In April 1969, the Intelligence Division of the U.S. Department of Commerce referred advertising concerning whisky investments to the SEC. In the next two months, letters from interested investors in California and Utah inquiring about these investments and from the San Francisco District Attorney alleging fraud arrived at SEC offices.

In March 1956, the Dallas Better Business Bureau requested information from the SEC after receiving reports from several investors that they had been solicited to buy stock in a mining company. In July, at least four investors requested information directly from the SEC. In September, the New Mexico Securities Commissioner alleged that the mining company had sold unregistered securities through unregistered salesmen, misrepresented corporate prospects, falsely represented that the company had been cleared by the SEC, and charged that insiders were misappropriating proceeds from the securities sale. In October, several purchasers sent letters to the SEC, and the former director and secretary-treasurer (who had resigned) notified the agency that commingling and personal use of corporate funds were common. In the next few months, the SEC received an inquiry from the Texas Securities Commission, allegations of fraud and misappropriation from the Oklahoma Securities Commissioner, additional investor complaints, and a complaint from a geologist who had consulted for the firm and feared that misrepresentations would be attributed to him.

These scenarios, uncovered during my research, represent only a small sample of the diverse sources of SEC investigations and the circumstances under which illicit activities are discovered. They demonstrate the broad diffusion of information about securities offenses, the number of potential sources of information about any given offense, and the occasions and incentives for reporting or sharing intelligence. A few of the vignettes also portray the convoluted pathways along which intelligence often travels before reaching the SEC—through individuals, employers, brokers, accountants, attorneys, and regulatory, self-regulatory, intelligence, and prosecutorial agencies—and the precariousness of this journey.

In addition to colorful anecdotes, the SEC investigative records also yield systematic data on the detection of wayward capitalism, the sources of SEC intelligence. For all but sixty-four cases (12 percent of the sample),[1] it was possible to gather from enforcement records all the suspicion

1. It was impossible to determine the investigative source of these sixty-four cases either because of missing or incomplete records or because of ambiguous or inconsistent information contained therein. I have scrutinized differences between cases with and without missing

or allegations of illegality directed to SEC enforcers prior to initiation of investigation and to reconstruct the pathways of intelligence.[2] These data provide the basis for this chapter.

REACTIVE SOURCES

From the scenarios of wayward capitalism presented in the previous chapter, it should be obvious that a wide assortment of individuals and organizations—stock issuers, brokers, investment companies, investment advisers, lawyers, accountants, bankers, investors, journalists, business associates, employers, and employees—are privy to some of the details of securities offenses. Indeed, at least forty separate categories of actors in the securities world, the financial and law enforcement communities, and their associates make unsolicited disclosures or inquiries to the SEC that generate the majority (64 percent) of agency investigations. These investigations are mobilized "reactively"; SEC investigators react to information provided by agency outsiders. Some of these outsiders are culpable themselves, some their unknowing accomplices, others their victims.

For purposes of this analysis, I have differentiated this diverse complement of actors into four somewhat heterogeneous categories on the basis of their role in securities violations or the securities world and their access to information concerning illegality. In order of decreasing centrality and access, the categories are insiders, investors, members of the securities community, and other social control agencies.

INSIDERS

As the examples given at the beginning of this chapter illustrate, a diverse group of persons and organizations share knowledge of illegality by virtue of their complicity or proximity. They are "insiders," persons or organizations participating in securities offenses, organizations that house securities offenders, or employees of these organizations.[3] Insiders

---

data on investigative source, and there is little reason to believe that the former cases are substantively different from the latter or that their exclusion from most analyses introduces any serious bias in the data.

2. The policy of recording only those allegations which preceded investigation was adopted for two reasons: (1) to isolate the sources of intelligence that *account* for the decision to undertake investigation, and (2) to eliminate the allegations that *result from* investigation (for example, investors who complain about their victimization only after they read about the investigation in the *Wall Street Journal* or offenders who offer to tell all in exchange for immunity after enforcers begin to close in).

3. One potential member is excluded from the insider category: the anonymous informant, of which there were 22 in the sample. Although some informants may be insiders— perhaps culpable, participating insiders—it is just as likely that they are not and derive their information from some other association with the offense or offenders. They are instead assigned to the "securities community" category, a general heterogenous mixture of social roles. This reflects a conservative decision, one that seeks to weight the informant role with as few specific assumptions as possible.

vary in their complicity in illegal activities. Because of the delegation of responsibility and the use of fronts, nominees, or cover-up techniques, it is often difficult to differentiate culpable from nonculpable members of organizations (Katz 1977, 1979a), even for purposes of coding research data. They share one common characteristic, though. They are positioned at the center of illegal activity, and therefore their vision is the clearest, their ability to read detail the sharpest, and the amount of behavior and information discernible to them the greatest. Insiders are potentially the richest source of intelligence.

Of course, this capacity for intelligence is undercut by the infrequent opportunities for and disincentives to their disclosure of often incriminating information to law enforcement agencies. Not surprisingly, only 9 percent of all cases in my sample were generated by insider disclosures, the smallest category of all investigative sources. Even if the contribution of anonymous informants (classified in the "securities community" category), some of whom might be insiders, were added, this category would still comprise only 14 percent of all cases. Ironically, where the quality of intelligence is highest, the quantity transmitted is lowest.

The occasions for the disclosure of information by insiders are obviously rather limited. On rare occasions, insiders openly confess lawbreaking or disclose information suggestive of illegality, or, like the former secretary, unknowingly "spill the beans." Occasionally, they direct inquiries to the SEC, raising questions that provoke agency interest, suspicion, or surveillance. But more frequently, insiders play a less direct role in the information they disclose. They report on the misdeeds of others. They grow suspicious and fear complicity, liability, or attribution of criminal responsibility for marginal acts they perhaps unknowingly committed. They feel victimized by offenders who fired them or embezzled from them and they exploit disclosure for revenge or restitution. Or they are embroiled in a conflict or power struggle with offenders and use disclosure to get the upper hand. For many, their insider status is tenuous at best. In fact, it is their limited involvement in illegality or their transition from insider to outsider through firing or resignation that affords them the incentive for disclosure.

Although the investigations generated by insider disclosures are few in number, it seems crucial to differentiate the disclosures by their attribution of blame. They fall into three categories:

1. Disclosures by *participating insiders* who shared some complicity at some point in illegal acts (38 percent of all insiders)

> An accountant solicited to invest in a mining company was later hired to do some accounting work and to help organize materials for an approaching SEC registration. In the process he discovered several irregularities in the use of company funds, which he ignored. Some time later, the accountant

had a disagreement with company officials about his compensation and either was fired or resigned. He became so angry that he made threats on the lives of some of these officials and also reported his earlier discoveries to the SEC.

2. Disclosures by *corporate representatives*, typically corporate directors, counsel, or accountants, reporting on organization-wide problems or inquiring about appropriate procedures (54 percent of all insiders)

The independent auditors of a publicly held corporation uncovered irregularities in corporate accounts and financial statements. They furnished this information to the board of directors, which reported it to the SEC and the New York Stock Exchange.

The counsel for an oil company called SEC officials. Its stock price had been rising for several months. During this period, another oil company had been negotiating to purchase some of its stock. The attorney feared that leaks were responsible for the price increase and inquired whether it would be appropriate to issue a press release so that all stockholders would be aware of the negotiations.

3. Disclosures by *employers*, reporting on the misdeeds of their employees (10 percent of all insiders)

After a customer complained that a dividend check bounced, the principal of a brokerage firm realized that one of the firm's registered representatives was misappropriating client funds. He was fired and the SEC notified.

Two employees of a brokerage firm were fired. While emptying out their desks after their departure, their employer found some documents that suggested they might be the undisclosed principals of another brokerage firm. He called the SEC.

Participating insiders contact the SEC to level basic charges of lawbreaking: fraud and misrepresentation, particularly, although embezzlement, self-dealing, registration violations, improper sales techniques, and assorted other offenses are reported as well. While 87 percent of the participating insiders allege fraud, embezzlement, or nonregistration, only 42 percent of the corporate representatives do so. Their disclosures instead pertain to a different agenda, especially reports of technical violations or the transmission of or request for information (representing 75 percent of their contacts with the SEC). Virtually all allegations made by employers pertain to either fraud or embezzlement by organizational employees.

INVESTORS

Parties who invested money in a particular security, who sold these investments, who did business with a broker-dealer or investment adviser, or who were solicited to do any of these things are among the most common

sources of SEC investigation. Investors are often the most numerous participants in illegality (thousands of them may be stockholders in a wayward corporation or clients of an illicit brokerage firm or advisory service). And investors stand the most to gain from SEC investigation of their alleged victimization. For investors and/or victims, the SEC promises both informational resources on potential investments and enforcement resources that can be invoked in attempts to secure restitution or revenge, or to assure the success of a private civil suit.

There are obstacles to the transmission of intelligence by investors, however. They include lack of knowledge of illegality, on the one hand, and absence of direct victimization, on the other. Securities violations are especially well suited for generating unwitting victims. The victims may lose a great deal of money, but they do so in a context in which a great many people lose money on perfectly legal investments in a risky market and fluctuating economy. They put their trust in persons whose activities they cannot possibly monitor or properly evaluate. And they make investments based on expectations about the future, so they must patiently await the result. Many offenders further exploit investors with elaborate cover-up schemes, "cooling out" strategies, phony dividends, physical props, and the like to insure that investors will never learn of the violations they have perpetrated and therefore have no reason to contact the SEC. And investors are also unlikely to communicate with the agency regarding offenses that do not generate victims or in which victimization is widely diffused.[4]

Despite these obstacles, investors still contribute a significant proportion (29 percent) of SEC investigations. Two distinctive groups of investors make these disclosures: "actual" investors, who have already committed funds to one or more investments or brokers about which they have lodged a complaint, and "solicited" investors, who have been offered a particular investment opportunity about which they inquire, but for which they have not yet committed funds. Actual investors usually are also victims; solicited investors usually are not. Seventy-seven percent of all cases in the investor category were generated by actual investors, 18 percent by solicited investors, and 5 percent by both.

Most securities violations touch more than one investor and therefore provide the opportunity for multiple disclosures. For 63 percent of the

---

4. The significant effect of both knowledge and victimization on investor disclosure is affirmed by the data. The proportion of investigations generated by investors is three times greater for offenses creating witting investors (36 percent) than for those creating unwitting investors (12 percent). And although only 9 percent of those investigations in which investors were not victimized by securities violations were generated by investor disclosures, that proportion is more than quadrupled (37 percent) for offenses with clearly identified victims. Witting victims are more than eight times more likely to provide intelligence to the SEC than unwitting and unvictimized investors.

investigations generated by investors, more than one investor had communicated with the SEC prior to the onset of investigation. On average, 3.7 investors complained about an offense, and the figure was even higher for investigations generated by solicited rather than actual investors. Occasionally, complaints were made by a group of investors who had banded together, but usually disclosures were made by single investors by letter, in person, or through their attorneys.

The substance of investor disclosures is by no means restricted to direct allegations of illegality. Solicited investors may inquire about a security that seems too good to be true—for example, the earlier vignette of the personal development program that promised a 60 percent yearly return on investment—or already committed investors may inquire about their stocks, brokers, or investment advisers. Investors may only suspect illegality or may simply be disgruntled by the conduct of parties with whom they have transacted business. Others may allege victimization where none, in fact, exists, as in the case of the widow whose securities had depreciated from $10 to 75 cents over a twenty-year period. After all, investments usually involve some degree of risk. Many are destined to fail regardless of the licit or illicit actions of their principals. Some investors attribute their losses to illegality when bad fortune and the market were the true culprits.

Some investors complain to the SEC after they begin to lose money on their investments—for example, the investors in Scotch whisky who had trouble disposing of the whisky after it had aged. Others communicate with the SEC after experiencing difficulties with securities professionals, after receiving bad checks from their brokers, after brokers fail to deliver stock certificates, or when they suspect embezzlement or churning. Some notify the SEC after receiving phone calls from high-pressure securities salesmen or extravagant literature touting a particular investment opportunity. Many of these solicited investors simply request information or ask about the registration status of particular securities or professionals. Unlike actual investors, they are unlikely to allege fraud, misappropriation, or mismanagement.

THE SURROUNDING "SECURITIES COMMUNITY"

A number of observers, both organizational and individual, surround illegal activities. They are neither direct participants like insiders or investors nor official observers like the SEC or other social control agencies. Rather, by virtue of their business relationships, their placement in business networks, and their proximity, they have varied opportunities to observe illegal activities. They often have access to the settings of illegality, and in some circumstances their access may be substantial and significantly greater than that of the investors.

The securities community category includes securities professionals, other surrounding business organizations, and anonymous complainants and informants. This latter assignment may be inappropriate since anonymous informants may, in fact, be either investors or insiders in illegality. The securities community category makes the fewest assumptions about their access to illegal activities. Given the suspicion that some informants and anonymous complainants are actually participants in illegality, it is appropriate to view this intelligence source as a transition between inside and outside, between the surrounding community and the actual (perhaps offending) participants.

Disclosures by members of the securities community account for 11 percent of all cases in the sample. In addition to informants (who make 44 percent of these disclosures), members of the securities community include broker-dealers and investment advisers (28 percent of them), other professionals, such as outside attorneys, outside accountants, and bankers (16 percent of them), and miscellaneous individuals and organizations, such as competitors and journalists (14 percent).

Relatively little can be said about informants and anonymous complainants as intelligence sources since, by definition, few data are available about their identities or the circumstances under which they transmit information. The major insight is derived from an examination of the allegations they make to SEC investigators. Most often, informants disclose fraud or registration violations. For example, one investigation followed allegations by an anonymous informant that a bowling center development company was insolvent and had been taken over by a gang of hoods who were manipulating the price of its stock. Other investigations were opened following informant allegations of stock manipulation, price rigging and arrangements by insiders to sell securities to a union pension fund, and charges that a brokerage firm was in financial difficulty and its sole proprietor had disappeared under suspicious circumstances.

Though less prolific an intelligence source than informants, broker-dealers have enormous potential. Brokers are middlemen; they intervene in the transactions of buyers and sellers. They are the vortex of independent information systems and must sort out and manage conflicting data. In addition, stockbrokers play an intelligence role. They are expected to know the market, to have accumulated and evaluated "hot tips," to be aware of potential opportunities as well as potential disasters.

Stockbrokers obtain the intelligence they ultimately share with SEC enforcers in various ways. Some receive information of questionable validity from stock-issuer representatives who routinely solicit them in the marketing of their securities. A Fort Worth broker received a letter from one of the principals in a previous SEC investigation that indicated that it

had changed its name and was back in business. Suspicious that the fraud was being reactivated, the broker notified the SEC. In another case, one of the representatives of a brokerage firm was approached by the president of a company whose stock was traded over-the-counter and offered one share for every four he sold. The president indicated that he had similar arrangements with broker-dealers in other cities. The brokerage firm passed along this information to the SEC. Broker insights may derive instead from the behavior or requests of their clients—to buy large quantities of relatively unknown securities or securities for which the broker could not find a market—or from the solicitation of their clients by other broker-dealers to buy certain securities at an unusually low price.

Other members of the business community transmit intelligence to the SEC as well. Accountants and attorneys are often recipients of information by virtue of the services they perform as well as by their potential as investors themselves.[5] Bankruptcy receivers sometimes discover illicit dealings in the aftermath of corporate failure. Bankers also have some access to securities transactions because of the role of securities as collateral for loans or because of the deposit or withdrawal of substantial sums of money from investor bank accounts in connection with securities investments. One investigation in the sample began after SEC officials were notified by a Wyoming bank director that two depositors had made substantial investments by check for securities that were not registered and appeared to be rather speculative.

Trade associations or competitors of stock issuers may have particularly strong incentives to report the misbehavior that they discover. One investigation followed disclosures by the attorney of a morticians' association alleging that a competitor in the memorial gardens and funeral business was selling unregistered securities. A different perspective is illustrated by disclosures from the telephone company, which originated several cases in the sample. Telephone company officials submitted information concerning extensive orders for new telephones by certain brokerage firms or substantial monthly increases in long-distance charges for certain broker-dealer accounts. This information suggested the creation of a boiler-room operation. Other investigations were generated by disclosures from landlords, journalists, and business associates. Recall earlier vignettes in which a realtor contacted the SEC after his tenant, a publicly held corporation, failed to pay the rent and absconded with some furniture, and in which two journalists notified the SEC after they were offered a substantial bribe to tout a stock.

5. This category pertains to the activities of attorneys (and accountants) independent of any involvement with any of the participants in illegality. Where they represent deviant organizations, they are classified as insiders. Where attorneys represent investors, they are classified in the investor category.

Although each of these professional and business roles is quite different, for purposes of analysis they have been aggregated into a single sub-category, "professionals." This was necessary because of their small number. Even fully aggregated, the sample contains only 28 investigations generated by professional disclosures, a mere 6 percent of all cases.

Members of the securities community, then, are often brokers of information, equipment, customers, or clientele and, by virtue of this position, are privy to substantial intelligence. Yet despite these opportunities, they rarely generate SEC investigations. Perhaps this is because community members constitute the only intelligence source without some direct involvement either in illegality (as participant or victim) or in enforcement and therefore have less to gain by contributing to investigation. Yet because of their independence from the offenders whose behavior they observe, members of the securities community could be a most significant intelligence source. Except for the aggrieved competitor, however, there appear to be few incentives for nonculpable members of the securities community to share their intelligence with the SEC.

OTHER SOCIAL CONTROL AGENCIES

Many of the investigations cited at the beginning of this chapter were opened after other law enforcement or self-regulatory agencies referred information to the SEC: for example, the probation officer whose parolee was living too well, presumably on the profits of illicit securities sales, the postal inspector who discovered incriminating mail in the course of another investigation, and all the state attorneys general and securities commissioners who referred information relating to the whisky and mining frauds. The sample contained other examples of disclosures by law enforcement or government agencies as well: a bankruptcy judge who found a disturbing pattern of illicit dealings in the cases he was hearing and spoke with his friend, the SEC General Counsel; the Federal Deposit Insurance Corporation, which discovered that securities used for collateral contributed to a bank failure; and countless investor complaints funnelled through state securities commissions, Better Business Bureaus, stock exchanges, postal inspectors, the Federal Bureau of Investigation, the Veteran's Administration, and so on.

It is not unusual that other agencies were so wise in the ways of wayward capitalists. Some of them also have enforcement responsibility for securities violations. And the paths of many of the other agencies cross those of wayward capitalists as well. Offenders also violate the tax laws and use the mails, the facilities of banking or international trade, and engage in other illicit activities that overstep SEC jurisdictional boundaries.

Therefore, a significant number of SEC investigations (30 percent of all cases in my sample) are generated by disclosures from other social control

agencies: federal regulatory agencies, the Justice Department, state securities commissions and other state regulatory agencies, private social control or self-regulatory agencies (stock exchanges, Better Business Bureaus, the National Association of Securities Dealers), and foreign agencies. Their contribution to SEC caseload is presented in table 3.1.[6] As the table indicates, most of these disclosures come from state agencies (45 percent), particularly state securities commissions (which account for over a third of all disclosures by other social control agencies). Self-regulatory agencies are also significant sources of intelligence, contributing two-fifths of the cases referred by other social control agencies.

Table 3.1 presents two unexpected findings: the small proportion of referrals from federal agencies and the high proportion of referrals from Better Business Bureaus, exceeding all categories except state securities commissions and the National Association of Securities Dealers. The former is particularly startling, given the vast intelligence sources available to federal agencies. The federal category includes referrals from the FBI and the Postal Service (for which mail fraud cases often have securities implications), requests from U.S. attorneys or the IRS to investigate the securities implications of other white-collar crimes, congressional referrals of problems of their constituents, as well as disclosures from the many other federal agencies that also regulate aspects of the business operations of publicly held corporations. Their contribution to the SEC investigative caseload remains small.

Table 3.1.   Referrals from Other Social Control Agencies

Social Control Agency	(N)	% of referrals
Federal	(25)	19
Justice Department	(12)	9
Other agencies	(14)	11
State	(59)	45
Securities commissions	(45)	35
Other agencies	(16)	12
Self-regulatory	(52)	40
Stock exchanges	(8)	6
National Association		
of Securities Dealers	(25)	19
Better Business Bureaus	(17)	13
Other	(5)	4
Total	(130)	

6. The sum of percentages in table 3.1 may exceed 100 because more than one agency may generate a particular case. For the same reason, the sum of the proportions of the components of a more general category may exceed the proportion of the general category as a whole.

The most common practice in social control agency disclosures is to pass along victim or investor complaint letters they have received; almost half of the disclosures for which data are available originate this way. In another 20 percent of the cases, agencies pass along information obtained from members of the securities community, from insiders, and from other agencies. Presumably these social control agencies seek to empty their dockets and to delegate social control initiative elsewhere. Another third of the agency referrals derive from their own ongoing enforcement activities and seek to secure information or assistance, to report on sanctions imposed, or to pass along offenses "spun-off" from these agency investigations. Non-state agencies tend to transmit intelligence to the SEC in order to dispose of potential enforcement problems; state agencies tend to do so in order to involve the SEC in ongoing enforcement activity.

Large proportions of the disclosures of state agencies allege registration violations. Federal agencies are especially likely to charge fraud and misrepresentation. Self-regulatory agencies are much less likely than other agencies to allege fraud or registration violations and much more likely to complain of technical violations and improper broker-dealer sales techniques.

THE REACTIVE STRATEGIES

As we have seen, the reactive sources of SEC intelligence are rich and extensive. But reactive intelligence suffers from several problems, particularly its dependence on disclosure incentives available to parties outside the agency. Earlier discussion noted the paradox that those with access to the richest intelligence—fearing incrimination, embarrassment, impairment of business relations, cessation of a lucrative ongoing scheme, or inconvenience—have few, if any, incentives to share information, while those with the greatest incentives are often ignorant and therefore have little to disclose. As a result, a good many misdeeds never come to light and those for which intelligence does reach the SEC are often idiosyncratic and unrepresentative. Securities offenses that are subtle, complex, or sophisticated, those without direct victimization, those best able to prolong violation, insure secrecy, minimize leaks of information, maintain insider loyalty, or minimize the collaboration of other members of the securities community and pay for their silence—in short, many of the more serious and insidious instances of wayward capitalism—are less vulnerable to disclosure than more blatant amateurish acts that generate direct loss to victims. Perhaps that is why many of the offenses investigated by the SEC appear so trivial. Furthermore, even if disclosures did not expose a biased sample of offenses, reactive sources of investigation often deliver untimely information. Since disclosures frequently must await the disaffection of a loyal conspirator, the realization of investors

that long-term dividends are not forthcoming, or the collapse of an illicit scheme, SEC enforcers are often not alerted to violation for months or even years.

The SEC, passively dependent on reactive intelligence, therefore has little control over its enforcement program. The agency must endure biased enforcement and unnecessary victimization and must forgo the strategic value of intelligence as a deterrent as well. It is not surprising that, like other law enforcement agencies, the SEC has also developed proactive strategies to detect wayward capitalists.

PROACTIVE SOURCES

Almost half of all SEC investigations are mobilized "proactively"; they are initiated by SEC staff themselves.[7] Like the reactive sources, proactive strategies can be differentiated by their amount of access to the securities world and to its illicit activities. One group of proactive detection strategies is organized on the assumption that the SEC has no special access to these settings for wayward capitalism. Investigators therefore monitor public events and communications, events accessible to journalists, attorneys, self-regulatory agencies, you, or me—to anyone with interest and persistence in analyzing the output of corporate life. I have labeled these strategies "surveillance."

A second set of proactive detection strategies is organized to exploit the very few opportunities in which agency investigators are permitted incursions into the securities world. This access is afforded by the SEC's regulatory relationships with agency registrants through routine inspections, filings, and disclosures as well as by opportunities provided by ongoing investigations. I have labeled these detection strategies "incursions."

SURVEILLANCE

The first of the proactive strategies finds the SEC an outsider to the illegal activities that it seeks to detect. Lacking any form of access to the settings of securities violations, SEC investigators attempt to observe the public behavior of their varied participants and audiences and monitor the public byproducts of illicit promotions and transactions in the hope that they might suggest illegal activity. Such surveillance is responsible for 12 percent of the investigations in the sample.

There are a number of public aspects of activities in the securities

---

7. The sum of the proportions of reactive and proactive mobilizations exceeds 100 percent because some investigations (12 percent) are mobilized by *both* proactive and reactive means.

world. Unlike many other illicit transactions, securities transactions are public, documented, advertised events and therefore susceptible to monitoring. Any visitor to the observation gallery of the New York Stock Exchange can watch as data on the latest stock transactions dance across dozens of monitors—electronic versions of the oldfashioned ticker tape. Because of the informational requirements of the securities markets and of securities trading, an enormous amount of data pertaining to the details of securities transactions—prices bid and asked, the volume of shares traded, the time of the trade, and so on—is recorded, published, and publicly disseminated. This intelligence resource provides an incredible transactional history freely available without need to penetrate institutions of privacy through infiltration or subpoena.

Then, of course, the recruitment of investors and the dissemination of information that secures their participation in illegality often requires public forums. The small-scale securities fraud may successfully avoid public performances and locate potential victims through the solicitation of acquaintances or members of investor social networks, door-to-door promotional strategies, or the use of "bird-dogs." But a large number of swindles must rely on advertising placed in newspapers, business periodicals, trade journals or other specialized publications, radio, and television, or else they forgo considerable coverage. And regardless of the need to employ these media to recruit investors, offenders often require them to promote their investment schemes. Articles placed in the mass media that tout the investment or bear favorably upon or confirm oral representations about the quality of the investment are often crucial in securing the commitment of investors. The role of the press was highlighted in an earlier vignette in which two journalists were offered perhaps as much as $1,000,000 to tout a mining stock. The public nature of these promotional devices and the assumption by naive investors that they are independent, objective, and trustworthy insure investors' commitment. Were promotional statements private, their ability to secure investment would be greatly diminished because of the presumption that they were intentionally manipulated for this purpose. Public promotional efforts provide additional grist for SEC surveillance.

Finally, other information occasionally surfaces about publicly held corporations or their members, which may bear indirectly on corporate illegality and trigger an SEC investigation. Corporations make discoveries, develop new products, earn unanticipated profits, or merge with other corporations—good fortune that may be prematurely exploited by corporate insiders through insider trading. One investigation in the sample was generated by reports in the press of a major oil strike; another was opened after Walter Winchell mentioned during a broadcast that a corporation had just discovered uranium in Texas.

And news of corporate misfortune, danger, difficulty, or deviance—unanticipated losses, bankruptcy, failed experiments or manufacturing processes, proxy battles, shareholder suits, violations by the corporation or its members—may also trigger investigation. For example, the suicide of the chairman and chief executive officer of United Brands figured prominently in the SEC investigation of corporate bribes to Honduran officials (Clinard and Yeager 1980, 169). The SEC investigations of domestic and foreign bribes and payments in the mid-1970s reportedly were generated by the Watergate investigations. One SEC enforcer watching the televised proceedings probing illicit corporate campaign contributions began to wonder about the source of these funds, the mechanisms for creating slush funds, and the disclosure of these activities to corporate stockholders.

Where surveillance uncovers successful corporations, then, SEC investigators inquire about insider self-dealing, misrepresentation, or the manipulation of successful façades for future illegality. Where it uncovers organizational difficulty or failure, they again suspect insider trading as well as the possibility of misappropriation or self-dealing as a source of failure, or the possibility that stockholders or the SEC itself were not properly apprised of the difficulties that led to failure. Organizational conflict prompts investigators to determine whether the source of conflict or the management of conflict constitutes a violation of the securities laws. Where surveillance uncovers corporations in violation of the rules or regulations of other agencies, jurisdictions, or governments, SEC enforcers determine whether correlative federal securities offenses are involved or whether the cover-up of these violations constitutes a securities violation.

Market surveillance. The monitoring of the public record of securities transactions is referred to as "market surveillance" in SEC parlance. Two-fifths of all surveillance cases (5 percent of the total sample) were generated specifically by market surveillance efforts. Market surveillance monitors data pertaining to securities prices, bids and offers, price movements, trading volume, block transactions, broker-dealer behavior, reports of insider transactions, and financial news. Where patterns exceed or vary from some specified set of parameters, the "deviant case" is isolated and further investigation is pursued. Although often the deviation is subsequently explained by market factors or other licit contingencies, these efforts often isolate instances of securities fraud, especially stock manipulation and insider trading. One investigation in the sample was instituted after SEC market surveillance discovered that the price of securities in an ice cream manufacturing and franchising company dropped from 16 5/8 to 11 7/8 in a week. Subsequent investigation

uncovered both insider trading and misrepresentation of the company's financial condition. Another investigation generated by market surveillance when the bid price for stock in a sulfur mining company rose from 5 7/8 to 9 1/2 over a one-month period was less fruitful. Investigation disclosed that market forces—the high demand for sulfur—not illegality, contributed to the rise.

Market surveillance has been likened by an SEC enforcement official to an electrocardiogram, with little "beeps" indicating the transgressions. This output is perhaps not so clear, nor do the beeps always indicate transgressions, and all transgressions may not generate beeps. Nonetheless, market surveillance reflects a fascinating attempt by agency investigators to monitor the byproducts of activities to which they have no access, to study the faint observable outlines and inferentially reconstruct their underlying texture.

At the time of this research, about thirty employees, including attorneys, analysts, accountants, and clerks, were assigned to a permanent market surveillance unit in the Enforcement Division of the Headquarters Office. In addition to SEC efforts, some surveillance responsibility has been delegated to stock exchanges and other self-regulatory organizations (see Noble 1981).

Market surveillance activities date to the inception of the SEC (*SEC Annual Report* 1935, 14–15), though with more recent developments in computer technology the capacity, sophistication, and speed of surveillance have undoubtedly increased. Still, the commission's surveillance capacity is limited. Making a pitch for congressional appropriations to fund the Market Oversight Surveillance System (MOSS), a more comprehensive computer surveillance system, former SEC Chairman Harold Williams characterized the agency's then current market surveillance capacity as technology backward: "his staff must still monitor the markets by watching the tape that reports stock trading on the major exchanges" ("A Computer Watchdog" 1980, 42).[8] Furthermore, the staff and budget allocated to market surveillance have not grown over the years, despite increased market activity, more complex transactions, and new financial instruments such as stock options and money market funds subject to oversight ("A Computer Watchdog" 1980, 42).

Non-market surveillance. I have labeled the surveillance of other public information from the securities world—newspaper articles, advertisements, promotional materials, and corporate news—"non-market surveillance." Earlier examples such as the suicide of the United Brands chairman and

---

8. Williams's successor, John Shad, has apparently decided to postpone or abandon proposals for MOSS because of the cost and the opposition from self-regulatory agencies ("SEC May Abandon Proposals" 1981, 31).

the Watergate disclosures illustrate non-market surveillance, as does a case in the sample in which an SEC staff member noticed an ad in the *Wall Street Journal* for the sale of citrus land and investment contracts in citrus groves. He sent for literature on this investment and subsequently opened an investigation of registration violations and misrepresentation. Other investigations were generated by a *Life* article on organized crime that implied linkages to a publicly held corporation and a *Fortune* article concerning opportunities for investment in the production and distribution of Scotch whisky. Slightly more than three-fifths of all investigations generated by surveillance (8 percent of all investigations) were detected specifically by non-market surveillance.

Unlike market surveillance, these activities tend to be unsystematic, fortuitous, and haphazard. There is no special unit within the SEC charged with this surveillance or any explicit set of procedures. Non-market surveillance depends primarily upon the curiosity and imagination of SEC staff. One offense in the sample was discovered through advertising found in a magazine by an SEC staff member who was waiting in a barber shop for a haircut, another through promotional material an SEC commissioner noticed in a drugstore. An advertisement on a church calendar received by another staff member prompted an investigation.

These examples highlight many of the more bizarre and irregular occasions for intelligence. A large number of agency staff members regularly scrutinize the major financial publications, local newspapers, and trade publications. In addition, the SEC has access to databanks that contain current financial news, proxy contests, routine disclosures, industry news, government affairs news, and the like. But these resources are not systematically explored.

INCURSIONS INTO THE SECURITIES WORLD

Unlike the surveillance strategies, in which public events and records are monitored by SEC investigators situated outside the securities world, incursive strategies rely on the creation of intelligence structures that reach inside that world. Intelligence strategies based on incursions exploit two types of access afforded to SEC investigators: (1) ongoing relationships with agency registrants and the intelligence opportunities provided by routine filings and SEC inspections; and (2) ongoing investigations that uncover unrelated misdeeds and "spin off" new investigations.

These incursions into the securities world are a substantial source of SEC intelligence, indeed the largest category, accounting for almost two-fifths of the investigations in the sample. The frequency is not surprising, given the considerable oversight exercised by the SEC over its registrants. Over half (57 percent) of all investigations generated by incursions followed registrant filings; 22 percent derived from inspections; and one-

quarter were spun off from previous investigations.[9] They represent 22 percent, 8 percent, and 9 percent of all cases in the sample, respectively.

Inspections and filings. The SEC has few opportunities to move from its distant surveillance outposts into the securities world, to learn the identities, financial condition, business operations, and other activities of corporations issuing securities and those offering professional services. Indeed, surveillants don't always know who or what to monitor. When issuers and professionals register with the commission, they announce the existence of an often unknown securities organization, and they activate significant incursive opportunities for SEC intelligence as well. The requirements of SEC registration include not only substantial disclosures at the time of registration, but considerable periodic reporting of financial matters and material events (with both positive and negative implications), and subsequent reports of certified independent audits.[10] Registration therefore inaugurates an ongoing intelligence stream from securities organizations to the SEC. And for securities professionals, the requirements do not stop with the periodic disclosure of information. Registered professionals, such as broker-dealers and investment advisers, must also open their business offices, files, accounts, books, and records to SEC inspection. These routine on-site inspections are conducted by SEC regional offices at most once a year, usually once every few years. Investigators can make additional "cause" inspections of a registered professional at any time.

The manifest function of both filing and inspection systems is the accumulation of data upon which sound investment decisions can be based and the insurance of sound business practices. But the discovery of illegality certainly represents their latent function. Systems that increase the SEC's access to securities activities physically (in on-site inspections) or informationally (through routine filings) are employed for intelligence purposes as well. And because they provide greater access to illegality, they generate less ambiguous data than that available through surveillance.

9. Because seven cases, or 4 percent, were generated by more than one of these sources, the sum of these percentages exceeds 100. The measure of the incidence of spin-off sources of investigation, though accurate for a case-based unit of analysis, is actually conservative where illegality is the analytic unit. Within a particular docketed case, many separate, unrelated illegal activities are often investigated and prosecuted. It is a matter of circumstance or expediency that a new case pertaining to the separate offenses is docketed, but it is by no means standard operating procedure. If one were able to count separate forms of offenses or separate offenders rather than enumerated cases, the number and proportion of offenses derived from spin-off strategies would undoubtedly increase, probably substantially.

10. Excluded from this category are unsolicitied disclosures of illegality by offenders themselves, classified for purposes of this analysis as reactive disclosures by insiders.

Since few wayward capitalists explicitly confess their misdeeds in routine disclosures and filings, one might be skeptical about the potential for intelligence. But SEC investigators are attentive not only to the substance of the disclosures, but to their underlying message as well—how they are stated, how they are supported, what facts or explanations are omitted, what can be read between the lines. Filings inadvertently tip off investigators to the possibility of illegality. In several cases in the sample, estimates of business assets or prospects —for example, oil reserves or anticipated drilling output—disclosed in filings seemed excessive to agency staff and fraud investigations were initiated. Other filings provided financial data which, when recomputed by investigators, indicated violations of SEC net capital requirements or other undisclosed financial difficulty. And some disclosures fail to implicate their source but do provide incriminating information about the registrant's business associates. Some broker-dealers, required to disclose their sources of capital and intended employees in initial registration materials, revealed the reinvolvement of persons previously barred from the securities industry. A few issuers disclosed information in their prospectuses and registration materials about intended underwriters or business associates who were not themselves registered with the SEC or whose involvement in these transactions violated the provisions of an injunction.

The intelligence opportunities afforded by SEC inspections are considerable. Much less can be hidden from a surprise physical inspection than can be concealed in written documents and filings. It is easy to lie about business operations; it is much more difficult to conceal a telephone boiler room. On-site inspections can often readily uncover violations of SEC technical regulations concerning record-keeping, reporting, and the safekeeping and segregation of customer funds and securities, as well as violations involving supervision of employees, boiler rooms, churning or inappropriate pricing practices, sales of unregistered securities, or embezzlement of customer funds.

But inspections often uncover intelligence about violations by others as well. Securities professionals do not operate in a vacuum. They work closely with customers (who may be engaged in stock manipulation or insider trading, for example), with stock issuers (who may be distributing unregistered stocks or employing fraudulent representations in their sale), and with other professionals (who may be pushing fraudulent or unregistered securities or manipulating their prices). Inspections of the files, accounts, records of transactions, solicitations, or promotional literature held by securities professionals often uncover information bearing on the illegal activities of these clients or actual or solicited business associates.

In one case in the sample, advertising found in the files of an inspected

brokerage firm disclosed the sale of notes of a Louisiana investment and loan company controlled by a notorious swindler who was engaged in fraud and self-dealing. Examination of securities transactions of a California brokerage firm during an inspection revealed that the firm had sold the president of a life insurance company 4,900 shares of its stock seven-eighths of a point below market value. Subsequent investigation revealed that the president was accumulating stock in anticipation of a future proxy fight; he had done so by defrauding the sellers of the shares and by violating SEC registration requirements.

Finally, sometimes investigators become suspicious that something illegal is underway because of disturbances in the registrant's relationship with the SEC. Several investigations in the sample followed overdue filings and other reports, the return of undelivered mail sent by the SEC to registrants, the unavailability of registrants for inspection, and a broker-dealer's claim that all his books and records had been stolen and therefore were unavailable for examination. These problems raised suspicions of financial difficulties, the involvement of registrants in other legal proceedings, or the need for cover-up or for other evasive activity.

Spin-offs. The spin-off represents a third intelligence strategy in which SEC investigators detect illegality by making incursions into the securities world. In this case, however, access is gained, not by some ongoing relationship between the SEC and parties the agency wants to scrutinize, but by independent investigation. SEC enforcers inspect offices and business operations, interview suspects, business associates, and victims, and scrutinize documents, books, and records. While on this investigative journey, they can see the other "sights," some of which may suggest unrelated offenses.

Ongoing investigations provide access to inside locations in the securities world and spin-offs explore the possibility that offenses, offenders, and victims are related, that wayward capitalists are repeat offenders, that their social networks are filled with co-offenders and other securities violators, or that a violation often generates a chain of subsequent violations as new illicit opportunities are exploited and their fallout concealed. These investigations provide richer, more detailed materials than are available in public surveillance. Many offenders have no ongoing relationship with the SEC and thus there is no opportunity comparable to filings or inspections for careful monitoring or scrutiny of their private behavior. But once they are implicated in an SEC investigation, the possibility of penetrating this privacy is available in the "Formal Order of Investigation," a decree authorized by the commission providing subpoena-like powers. Formal orders can compel testimony and the provision of documents and records by any person or organization investigated for possible illegality regardless of registrant status.

But besides providing intelligence about the offense being investigated, investigatory materials also disclose *unrelated* offenses. The intelligence value of the spin-off derives from the assumption that aspects of unrelated offenses are sometimes correlated, an assumption fueled by the complexity of the securities world and the elaborate social networks that develop to implement securities transactions. These networks link stock issuers, underwriters, broker-dealers, investment advisers, attorneys, accountants, promotional or public relations personnel, business associates, suppliers, and investors. Investigation that is centered on any one set of parties may generate information about unrelated behavior of other parties in the network.

One case in my sample began as an investigation of financial problems at a New York brokerage firm. SEC investigators scrutinized most of the firm's transactions and business dealings, including its role as underwriter of a recent stock issuance. Information uncovered in this connection revealed that the previous underwriter of the securities had been involved in stock manipulation, an offense in which the New York brokerage firm played no part. Another investigation of a broker-dealer was initiated to consider allegations that the firm was pressuring clients to switch their holdings and buy mining securities, while making short sales and overcharging clients. The investigation ultimately uncovered information suggesting that the mining company itself had failed to register its securities with the SEC and had issued misrepresentations in promoting them. These misdeeds were not connected with the offenses of the brokerage firm.

Often the direction of spin-off is reversed: investigations of corporations issuing securities uncover unrelated misdeeds by those servicing these companies, such as accountants, brokers, or underwriters. In these cases, intelligence that was gathered about one organization implicated a second on unrelated charges. Sometimes, though, spin-offs link individuals and organizations. For example, investigation of an embezzling employee of a brokerage firm uncovered information implicating the firm itself in unrelated violations.

The previous examples supported the assumption that violation is so pervasive that it is likely that the associates of an offender are involved in illegality themselves. An entirely different assumption may also provide fruitful ground for intelligence spin-offs pertaining not to the distribution of offenders, but to the distribution of victims. Investors, because of gullibility or of the quantity of their transactions, are potential victims of several unrelated offenses. For example, an SEC investigator interviewed an investor about his purchase of stock in a corporation under investigation. In the course of their conversation, the investor mentioned stock in a granite mining company that he had also purchased from his broker. The investigator followed up on this information and discovered that the

securities of the granite company were not registered with the SEC and had been distributed fraudulently. In another case, a questioned investor remarked, "This is nothing. You should have seen what happened to my investment in —— last year."

The investigation, because it permits scrutiny of evidentiary materials and participants at the center of illegal activity and directs attention to actors who may, by personal experience or social relationship, have experienced other illegal activities, is therefore an important intelligence source, especially in generating other spin-off investigations.

THE PROACTIVE STRATEGIES

These examples of surveillance, filings, inspections, and spin-offs reflect the range of strategies employed by SEC staff to ferret out instances of potential illegality on their own initiative. The implementation of proactive methods provides some creative intelligence efforts. Still, these methods have their limitations. Where all elements of illegal activity can be located in private settings, where the magnitude of transactions is small and therefore bypasses market data reporting systems, where participants are not registered with the SEC and are unrelated to those who are associated with the agency through registration or other enforcement, it is unlikely that offenses will be detected through proactive means. Fortunately, parties outside the SEC pick up the slack, referring some of these offenses which seemingly escape proactive intervention.

MULTIPLE SOURCES

The categories of reactive and proactive intelligence and their frequency of use are summarized in table 3.2. Because some offenses are discovered by more than one source, totals exceed 100 percent and subcategory totals sometimes exceed category totals. The duplications derive from multiple detection. A very clear pattern emerges from these data: among the reactive detection strategies, those with greater access to illegality (especially insiders) are the least common sources of investigation; among the proactive detection strategies, those with greater access to illegality (incursions) are the most common investigative sources. This pattern reflects a mixture of different disclosure incentives and ease of access to information.

The last two vignettes in the opening section of this chapter (the whisky and mining frauds) provided a special insight into the investigative process: information travels along the pathways of a complex intelligence network and can be sabotaged at every point of intersection along that network. Virtually every securities offense contains multiple points of vulnerability to detection and therefore multiple opportunities for

Table 3.2. Sources of Investigation

Source	% of cases	(N)	% of cases
Insiders		(39)	9
Participating insiders	3		
Employers	1		
Corporate representatives	5		
Investors		(126)	29
Actual investors	24		
Solicited investors	7		
Securities community		(50)	11
Informants	5		
Professionals	6		
Other social control agencies		(130)	30
Federal agencies	6		
State agencies	14		
Self-regulatory agencies	11		
Surveillance		(55)	12
Market surveillance	5		
Non-market surveillance	8		
Incursions		(167)	38
Inspections	8		
Filings	22		
Spin-offs	9		
Total cases		(440)	

Note: Because some cases were generated by more than one source, percentage totals exceed 100 and subcategory totals sometimes exceed category totals.

detection. The recruitment of investors to buy securities, of brokers to sell them, of accountants to certify financial statements, of employees to staff illicit organizations, the process of registering with the SEC or listing stocks on a national exchange—all these actions generate intelligence about illicit activities. Whether any information or several distinct pieces of information ever reach the SEC is a function of the nature and composition of the intelligence network, access and proximity, investigatory diligence and ingenuity, cover-up, and plain good fortune. Recall the allegations of the Minnesota investor about Scotch whisky investments that reached the SEC by way of the Minnesota attorney general, a postal inspector, and the State Department. One wonders how many other complaints never survive such a precarious journey. Like the fate of a chain letter, with so many links at which the chain can be broken, the successful detection of securities violations by the SEC is a real gamble for which the payoff, though unknown, may be low.

A securities offense may never be discovered by the SEC, may be uncovered just once, or may be detected several times, perhaps in different ways. The first and perhaps the most common outcome is beyond the

scope of my research, which is inherently limited to detected offenses. The second has been assumed throughout most of this book. This assumption is appropriate: almost three-quarters of all offenses in the sample were detected only once; they were docketed after the receipt of one and only one piece of intelligence (a single disclosure, a single inspection, and so on). Still, 15 percent of all offenses in the sample were detected twice, 8 percent three times, 3 percent four times, and 2 percent five times or more. Twenty-two percent of these 121 oft-detected offenses were docketed after receipt of more than one piece of intelligence from the same source, for example, several complaints from different investors. Most of the investigations (78 percent) were generated by different sources of intelligence, for example, a disclosure by an investor and another by a securities professional. It is rare for an investigation to be generated by many different sources of intelligence, however: only 1 percent of all cases in the sample were generated by four or more different sources, 5 percent by three different sources, and 15 percent by two different sources.[11]

Of all detection strategies, incursions are especially likely to be the sole source of detection. Over three-quarters of the investigations generated by incursions were opened after a single incursion with no other supporting intelligence. In contrast, only 32 percent of the investigations generated by disclosures from the securities community and 44 percent of those from investors were detected only once. Investors provide duplicative intelligence; multiple detection derives from the fact that several investors usually disclose a given offense. One quarter of all investor-generated investigations followed several investor disclosures; 4 to 14 percent of the other detection strategies provided duplicative intelligence. For the securities community, multiple detection derives from the fact that other sources are also uncovering the same offense, providing redundant intelligence. Sixty-eight percent of the cases they uncovered were also detected by other sources; this percentage ranged from 21 to 45 for the other detection strategies. This pattern of exclusive intelligence from incursions, duplicative intelligence from investors, and redundant intelligence from the securities community reflects the reliability of intelligence sources, the size of the constituency of a particular intelligence category, and the size of the social network generated by an offense and the spread and diffusion of information about it.

THE SOCIAL ORGANIZATION OF SEC INTELLIGENCE

How are these diverse sources of investigation integrated into the SEC enforcement program? Unfortunately, the exploitation and integration

11. These figures are based on the six-category source classification—surveillance, incursions, insiders, investors, the securities community, and other social control agencies.

of many of these intelligence opportunities is tenuous at best. The SEC has a specific program of broker-dealer and investment adviser inspection (one of the incursive strategies) delegated to its regional offices and a small market surveillance program within the Enforcement Division in Washington. Supposedly, the commission has recently developed a consumer protection program, attentive to the needs and perhaps disclosures of investors.[12] In recent years, SEC enforcers have attempted to induce insiders and securities professionals to disclose incriminating information through threats of prosecution. And training programs for new SEC enforcers have included selected enforcers from other social control agencies, to instruct them in securities offending and enforcement and presumably to cement their ties to the SEC. But, by and large, SEC enforcers do little else to induce or maximize intelligence. The acquisition of information from most other sources—non-market surveillance, filings, spin-offs, insiders, investors, members of the securities community, and other social control agencies—is haphazard and fortuitous. It depends upon the curiosity or imagination of SEC investigators perhaps with extra time on their hands or the anger, vengefulness, good citizenship, conscientiousness, or persistence of outsiders.

Although it is nowhere officially documented, it is clear from the investigative materials I read that certain SEC regional offices have undertaken special intelligence efforts from time to time. Someone at the New York regional office must have met with persons from the telephone company, because there were several disclosures alleging that certain brokerage firms were installing considerable numbers of new telephones or were suddenly experiencing astronomical increases in their long-distance charges. The Seattle regional office must have developed ties with the city's Better Business Bureau. This regional office, which contributed 12 percent of the cases in the sample, contributed 61 percent of those generated by Better Business Bureau disclosures. The San Francisco office must have developed ties with state regulatory agencies. Overall, it contributed 5 percent of the cases in the sample, but 14 percent of those referred by state agencies. In contrast, the New York office contributed 31 percent of all SEC investigations, but only 3 percent of the state referrals.

I also found references in the investigative records to cooperative multijurisdictional securities enforcement conferences held in several regions, in which SEC regional offices, U.S. attorneys, state securities and corporation commissions, self-regulatory agencies, and local law enforcement agencies met to share intelligence and allocate the enforcement

12. No one at the commission was willing to provide me with any information about this program when I persistently inquired during my fieldwork. I suspect that the program is more one of public relations than of systematic intelligence.

workload. But all of these efforts to maximize intelligence were idiosyncratic to particular regions and to particular historical periods. This survey reveals the enormous opportunities for intelligence that are disregarded or unsystematically exploited. The possibilities of better organizing SEC intelligence, better exploiting the diverse sources of information about securities violations, and drawing from the intelligence experiences of others are considered further in chapter 7.

4

Getting Caught: Tactics of Intelligence Contests

The efforts of SEC enforcers to detect the misdeeds of wayward capitalists are not unique. SEC investigators share their search for secret or deviant behavior with many others—other law enforcement agents, spies, private detectives, journalists, researchers, insurance adjusters, credit reporting agencies, blackmailers, gossips, parents, spouses, supervisors.

Oddly, the discipline of sociology, built so fundamentally on a self-conscious methodology for the collection of information about human behavior, has been uninterested in the generic phenomenon of intelligence and has had little to say about the methodologies by which behavioral data are gathered by others.[1] Despite its parochialism, however, sociological research methodology does provide a useful start in thinking about intelligence. It offers three major strategies for gathering valid and reliable data on social behavior: observation, survey, and archival research. Applying these to the work of intelligence organizations, we might label them observation, disclosure, and artifactual methods.

Observation produces data gathered first-hand by the researcher, who is present when the behavior is enacted, disclosure involves information revealed second-hand by participants or other observers, and artifactual methods permit inferences about behavior to be drawn from artifacts or

1. Even the sociological literature on organizational intelligence is not concerned with the process and strategies of intelligence. Harold Wilensky (1967, 1968), who has written the most material on this subject, centers his analysis on the way in which organizations allocate resources to intelligence, the kinds of experts they retain, and the relationship of organizational structure to the blockage or distortion of intelligence. He examines the fate of information once it has reached the organization, with little concern for the process by which information was acquired. Wilensky's analysis of intelligence failures excludes instances in which "the relevant message is not in the system" (1968, 323). This perspective contrasts sharply with one in which the acquisition process is made problematic, in which intelligence failures are fundamentally failures in acquiring information, in assuring that relevant messages are in the system.

byproducts of the behavior. Borrowing from a well-known example (Webb et al. 1966), assume that we are interested in the popularity of a museum exhibit. Observational methods require that researchers be posted around the museum, recording the number of persons at the exhibit, their length of stay, the volume of conversation, repetitiveness of viewing, the sequence in the tour in which persons stop at the exhibit, and the like. A disclosure model might propose that museum visitors or other segments of the population be interviewed or given questionnaires that ask about their own behavior or that of their acquaintances. The examination of the extent of tile or carpet wear around the exhibit relative to other locations in the museum would be one example of an artifactual design.

Each of these strategies, of course, differs in cost, practicality, and validity of the data collected. Observational and disclosure strategies are inherently "reactive":[2] the data collection process may affect the behavior in question (see Webb et al. 1966, 12–22). The presence of observers hovering around the exhibit may create an illusory image of popularity and thus interest persons otherwise unlikely to visit it. Or by crowding the exhibit, observers may deter others from viewing it. Similarly, the act and procedure of questioning museum goers may encourage or discourage them from visiting the exhibit or may elicit false answers offered to impress or satisfy interviewers. These methods, then, may alter behavior or may record false reports of behavior. Artifactual methods, because they are necessarily removed from the behavior and its participants, are not inherently reactive, but they are inferential, and the inferences are often wrong.[3] For example, the floor surrounding the museum exhibit may be worn, not because the exhibit is popular, but because it is near a restaurant, restroom, or drinking fountain.

The diverse activities of intelligence agents—whether they are museum curators evaluating an exhibit's popularity, journalists lusting after a political exposé, anthropologists attempting to tease out the culture and social structure of a primitive tribe, parents seeking to learn of the sexual misconduct of their children, or SEC enforcers searching out wayward capitalism—are simply variations on these themes of observation, disclosure, and artifactual methods. SEC enforcers, for example, use a combination of observational and artifactual methods in their proactive detec-

2. The meaning of the term *reactive* used here is unrelated to that used in the previous chapter. Here, reactive refers to the fact that some research instruments can affect the behavior under investigation. Earlier, reactive referred to detection efforts accomplished by reacting to information provided by others. My apologies for the sociological jargon.

3. Of course, if actors know that the artifacts of their behavior will be scrutinized, they may alter their behavior to create no artifacts or different ones. Drug addicts, for example, may avoid heroin injections on their arms because of their knowledge that narcotics investigators search the arm for needlemarks. Bribes may be paid in cash rather than by check so that investigators will be unable to reconstruct the transactions by examining cancelled checks and bank records.

tion strategies of surveillance and incursions. Their reactive investigative sources derive from disclosures—by insiders, investors, members of the securities community, and other social control agencies.

The intelligence strategies of SEC enforcers differ considerably from those employed by the Kinsey sex researchers, Watergate sleuths Woodward and Bernstein, Allied intelligence during World War II, and more pedestrian intelligence agents such as police officers, insurance adjusters, market researchers, customs agents, and nosy parents. Their work is distinctive and different because each intelligence system shapes itself to the organization of the behaviors it seeks to monitor. Where are these activities located? Are they public or private? Are they secret and concealed, and how so? Are physical props or equipment involved? How frequently do the activities occur? How long do they last? Are they recurrent or episodic? How many persons participate? These features dictate appropriate intelligence strategies.

But the decisive role of behavior in shaping the social organization of intelligence tells only half the story. When the behavior subject to discovery is deviant, secret, or incriminating, its executors may work very hard to insure its immunity to discovery. They strive to insure that their activities remain invisible, protect their misdeeds from the spread of information, guarantee that knowing participants and observers preserve secrecy, and clean up after themselves, avoiding, destroying, doctoring, or distorting the physical evidence of their activities. Hence, the social organization of intelligence also constrains and shapes the social organization of secret behavior. The correspondence between strategies of deviance and detection therefore derive from reciprocal sources.

Enforcers seeking intelligence about deviant or secret behavior are thrust into an eternal tug-of-war. On one side are their targets, attempting to conceal their behaviors and identities from detection. These investigators are, on the other side, attempting to devise new strategies to penetrate these defenses and acquire secret information. Their struggle is a continually escalating one, as each side elaborates and retools its strategies to compensate for the latest innovation in deception or detection that the other has devised.[4] The two worlds of wayward capitalists and SEC enforcers are closely intertwined in an inevitable ritualistic dance, a perpetual game of hide and seek.

4. This notion of enforcement as a conflict over information was captured (though unfortunately not well developed) in a little monograph entitled *Crime and Information Theory.* Its author, M. A. P. Willmer, suggested that illegal activities emit a "signal." Offenders therefore attempt to design their activities to minimize the volume of the signal they broadcast and to cover the signal with "noise" that they create and contrive. The police, on the other hand, are organized to receive and interpret signals. They attempt to increase the volume of criminal emissions and to dispel or silence the noise that surrounds them. See also Cohen (1977, 105) for a discussion of the control of information by criminal organizations.

In this chapter I will discuss this dynamic interplay between deviance and detection. Because the tug-of-war between SEC enforcers and wayward capitalists often lacks the vigor, imagination, and cunning of other intelligence contests, I will often draw on strategies of intelligence and cover-up developed elsewhere. These examples provide a sense of the strategic possibilities available to combatants in the securities enforcement arena and suggest the diverse settings to which findings of correlation between securities deviance and detection may apply.

OBSERVATION

There are essentially two kinds of observational intelligence: participant and nonparticipant. The first requires some involvement of "researchers" in the behavior itself, while the second does not. The line drawn between the two categories is a fine one, reflecting differences in degree rather than in kind.

Nonparticipant observation is a rich and adequate strategy for collecting many kinds of data. Outsiders may observe traffic patterns or children at play or shoppers in a department store and gather reliable data on driving or playing or shopping. Where behavior is deviant, secret, or private, however, opportunities for nonparticipant observation are limited. Observers either are denied access to private settings for observation or their presence tends to decrease the likelihood that the behavior will be enacted when they are present. Despite these impediments, investigators often pursue nonparticipant observation (for example, they go out on patrol or stake-outs in the hope of detecting crimes in progress) and social scientists attempt to observe deviant behavior in its natural settings—streetcorners (Cohen 1980) or police cars (Reiss 1968 for example)—often with some success.

Two alternatives to these methods, which seek to overcome the obvious difficulties of utilizing nonparticipant observation to gather data on deviant acts, include the use of technological surveillance devices—wiretaps, bugs, photographic surveillance equipment, hidden microphones, two-way mirrors—that permit surreptitious observation and the use of undercover observers. By going under cover, parties abandon their observational roles of police officer, journalist, or sociologist and therefore reduce the likelihood that they will deter the activities they wish to observe or be denied access to them. Observers shed their uniforms or other social or physical attributes that identify them. They become bartenders, bar patrons, students, doormen, passengers, shoppers. They do not participate directly in the behavior observed. Rather, they adopt roles contiguous to those directly involved in the behavior, thus facilitating observational access.

Other investigators adopt direct participating roles. Because it binds the observer to the behavior under observation, participant observation insures exceptional data collection opportunities. However, this strategy tends to be much more reactive than nonparticipant methods. Participating observers may deter behavior under observation, encourage it, alter its course, or generate new patterns of behavior.[5]

The social control literature contains a variety of labels for participant observer intelligence roles: decoys, stool pigeons, agent provocateurs, instigators, and field agents (Donnelly 1951; Geraghty 1966; Lundy 1969; Marx 1974; Wilson 1978; Sherman 1978). The labels describe undercover roles taken by parties outside the intelligence organization or "civilians" (decoy, stool pigeon) and by parties inside these organizations (agent provocateur, instigator, field agent). Distinctions based on the kind of roles played by participant observers are more useful than distinctions reflecting the sectors from which undercover actors are drawn. Typically, these include direct participant roles, collusory roles, and victim roles.

Participants, colluders, and victims differ in their ease of gaining entree. Usually, it is most difficult to be accepted as a direct participant in deviant behavior and least difficult to be accepted as a victim. And the degree of specialized role performance and skill is much greater for direct participants and colluders than for victims. The adoption of direct roles is costly—in time, commitment, expertise, and the risk of nonacceptance. Still, sociologists join social movements or move into communes; FBI agents infiltrate and join allegedly subversive organizations like the Ku Klux Klan and Students for a Democratic Society; law enforcement officials occupy positions in criminal organizations; private security investigators obtain routine work in the companies they protect and spy on for management; and journalists secure employment with corporations they are investigating, all for the purpose of covert observation.

Perhaps because of the difficulties of gaining entree, the need for commitment, and the danger of reactivity, the adoption of true participant roles tends to be avoided in most intelligence efforts. The placement of observers in collusory rather than direct participant roles provides a ready compromise. This alternative is particularly suited to consensual forms of behavior that draw parties from different worlds. By posing as one of the colluding parties, the agent can observe the behavior of the other. Police officers and other law enforcement agents pose as "Johns"

5. The literature, both scholarly and journalistic, on the role of undercover agents in shaping and perpetrating illegality is immense. See, for example, Gary Marx's (1974) discussion of the agent provocateur as well as his later work on the unintended consequences of police undercover work (1980). Or see the discussion of Festinger and his colleagues (1956) of the possible contribution of the participating researchers' presence in the response of a small religious group to the failure of prophecy.

to detect prostitution, as fences to detect burglary, as buyers to detect drug pushing, as drug pushers to uncover police corruption. "Observers" may offer bribes to politicians or other public servants to investigate corruption. The Abscam investigations, in which FBI agents posed as representatives of wealthy Arab businessmen, offering substantial bribes to congressmen and other government officials in return for promises that the officials would use their influence to assist the businessmen, provides one notorious example.

Of course, like full observer participation, the adoption of colluder roles also holds the potential for reactivity, or in legal jargon, "entrapment." By enticing potential offenders with attractive illicit opportunities, agents create the very deviance they sought to observe (see especially Marx 1980). And adoption of colluder roles may also require substantial commitment and specialized skills. In the Abscam investigation, investigators—unable to find sufficient expertise or interpersonal contacts within the FBI—had to recruit an experienced confidence swindler from the outside to adopt the central role in the sting operation. In most cases, however, it is considerably easier to gain entree to colluder roles than to full participant ones.

It is easier still for those playing victim roles. A large and diverse set of individuals are eligible victims, and offenders presumably are less fussy about their choice of victims than about their choice of coconspirators. Police officers pose as elderly persons to lure muggers. Investigators of corruption hire actors to play the role of drunken bums, arrest them, and throw them in jail to see whether they will be "rolled" (their money expropriated by jailers) (Sherman 1978, 44). A New York City investigator posed as a patient of a dentist who had been accused of sexually abusing several patients after they had been given nitrous oxide. The investigator, herself immobilized by the gas, was rescued from imminent rape when fellow detectives smashed open two locked doors at the dentist's office (Fried 1982). A Chicago newspaper set up a bar staffed by investigative reporters to see if city officials would attempt to extort bribes (they did; Smith and Zekman 1979). Posing as a potential victim, of course, is also a reactive strategy and provides an easy target for charges of entrapment. The investigator increases the incidence of the behavior under observation, and his or her conduct may significantly affect the pattern of behavior ultimately induced.

THE OBSERVABILITY OF BEHAVIOR

Secret or deviant behavior is vulnerable to detection when it is observable to outsiders. You come home early from work and find a stranger in bed with your spouse. You take a walk through a city park and observe drug dealers openly transacting with their customers. You stand in a

crowded subway car and watch an industrious pickpocket gingerly lifting wallets out of the hip pockets of fellow passengers. Obviously, these behaviors could be protected from observation if they were located in more private or isolated locations where outside observers are not likely or not entitled to go—motel rooms or dark alleys, for example.

As sociologist Arthur Stinchcombe suggested some time ago, legal institutions in modern societies define public and private places and restrict access to private places (1963). These "institutions of privacy" insure that secret or deviant behaviors enacted in private locations are relatively immune from some forms of observation. Those kinds of behaviors that are more likely to occur in public places (for example, drunk and disorderly conduct) are thus more vulnerable to detection than those that typically occur in private places (for example, spouse abuse). Similarly, the offenses enacted by groups in our society that spend a disproportionate amount of their time in public places (that is, the young and the poor) are more vulnerable to discovery than those of persons better able to afford privacy.[6]

Of course, it is not always possible to locate secret or deviant activities in private places. Some secret activities—the deployment of military forces, for example—must necessarily be staged in public places. Offenders often depend on public places to supply their victims. A subway pickpocket, for instance, requires the cover of a crowd and the legitimacy of close physical contact to ply his trade. Even for victimless consensual offenses, the recruitment of consumers, clients, or partners is often facilitated by public conduct. Many prostitutes, drug dealers, and confidence men solicit customers or marks on the streets; those engaged in consumer or securities frauds advertise in newspapers and periodicals. Such public activities can be limited when prostitutes become call girls, customers find drug dealers (Moore 1977) or illicit abortionists (Lee 1969) through a referral process constructed from their social networks, or securities swindlers find marks through the social networks of previous victims. But retreat into private locations often entails substantial sacrifices by offenders, reflected in the diminished profits or opportunities that result from the limitation of victims or clientele.[7]

Public behavior is therefore sometimes unavoidable and often irresistible. Although it may require a bit more ingenuity, secret behavior can still be displayed publicly without necessarily revealing its incriminating char-

---

6. The popular distinction between "crime in the streets" and "crime in the suites" is indeed of consequence, at least in this respect.

7. And some offenders are denied access to lucrative private locations altogether. Presumably, some muggers and robbers would prefer to be embezzlers but are unable to acquire positions of trust inside private organizations and must therefore work their craft in public place°

acter. The art of magic provides perhaps the best example of successfully deceptive public displays (see especially Bowyer 1982, chapter 5). Here, observers are aware that they are about to be deceived and scrupulously watch magicians for any hint of their artifices. Yet through the use of misdirection, distraction, confederates, sleight-of-hand, and special apparatus, magicians are able to enact performances that are other than what they seem. They can behave under close scrutiny without revealing any secrets.

In *Cheating*, J. Barton Bowyer (a pseudonym) describes six strategies of deception (1982, chapter 2). "Masking," "repackaging," and "dazzling" are forms of dissimulation or "hiding"; the other three, "mimicking," "inventing," and "decoying," are types of simulation or "showing." Through some combination of masking, mimicking, repackaging, or inventing, secret behaviors can be camouflaged to blend in with their surrounding environment (Goffman 1969, 17) or packaged to appear to be other than what they really are. And where behaviors cannot be manipulated to blend into the background or to escape notice, dazzling or decoy strategies can be devised to confound, confuse, or distract from true interpretation of the observed activities.

Mark Moore has described the way in which heroin dealers attempt to camouflage or hide the signal of their illicit activities in the background noise of normal daily life (1977, 24–25). Heroin is stored with mothers or girlfriends who are usually visited for legitimate purposes. It is exchanged in a handshake or the purchase of a beer or newspaper. As long as these daily activities usually do not accompany a drug transaction, they can be pursued to increase the amount of noise surrounding the dealer's illicit transactions.

> If a dealer wants to use his mother's apartment as a safe place to store heroin and he wants to be able to have ready access to it, he must become an extremely dutiful son. He must visit his mother on many occasions when he does not bring or take away heroin. Similarly, if a dealer wants to pass heroin on the street through casual encounters, handshakes, and embraces, he must spend a lot of time encountering, handshaking, and embracing when he is not exchanging heroin. In effect, the constant motion, interaction, and hustle that is typical of heroin dealers serves the same function as the incessant wiping, scratching, and arm crossing of major league baseball coaches: an observer attempting to figure out the sign is uncertain about which activity is the real sign [Moore 1977, 25].

Drug dealers frequent areas of the city that are socially disorganized, in which the activities of nondealing residents tend to resemble those typical of the heroin dealer. They locate their businesses in areas with considera-

ble movement and interaction, where people hang out on street corners. Dealers rely on these environments to provide the additional background noise that they do not provide for themselves.

Secret societies are known to create noise and behavioral ambiguity through the use of ritual language or special styles of speech (Brandt 1980; Laguerre 1980). When speaking in the presence of outsiders, Pueblo Indians purge all English or Spanish loan words from their speech and employ "elaborate circumlocutions . . . in the native language to convey information without using a term that might be understood. Some of these circumlocutions have become well-known idiomatic expressions in the native language" (Brandt 1980, 129). (Come to think of it, my parents used to do the same thing!)

Those attempting to preserve secret information may generate noise or ambiguity by creating and disseminating false and misleading information or even physical decoys (Brandt 1980; Andersen 1980). Raoul Andersen has observed that Newfoundland deep-sea trawler fishermen attempt to preserve secrecy and mislead competitors by transmitting deceptive information on supposedly private radio frequencies. In these "private" transmissions to other members of their fleet, fishermen underestimate or overestimate their catch, express false plans to depart from their present location, decry or distort fishing conditions, or manipulate radio silence in the hope of enticing their competitors into unprofitable waters or diverting them from more profitable locations.

Bowyer (1982, 76–81) draws a fascinating example of the use of decoys from World War I. In 1914, Winston Churchill ordered the construction of a dummy fleet of ten vessels, mock-ups of actual top-of-the-line battleships, but built from existing merchant vessels. The reconstruction was achieved through the use of wood and canvas. In order to simulate the silhouette of a warship, the vessels

> were fitted out with broader decks, and were given greater length, warshiplike bows and sterns, fire-control towers, turrets and guns, and the appropriate number of smoke-stacks, ones that belched real smoke from small concealed smoke generators. Because merchantmen without cargo ride higher in the water than warships, each was ballasted down with 9,000 tons of stone [Bowyer 1982, 77].

Some of the phony ships were anchored at British naval bases to draw the first torpedoes from German U-boats; others were sent out as decoys. This dummy fleet enhanced assessments of British naval strength. And even when the Germans discovered the ruse—which they inevitably did when parts of torpedoed ships would float away—they were never sure which of the other ships were real and which were not.

That only one out of numerous identical acts may be in fact related to a

secret or illicit scheme and that the signals emanating from behaviors may be contrived or distorted highlights the problem of relying heavily on Stinchcombe's "institutions of privacy" notion in assessing the vulnerability of behaviors to detection. Even without institutions of privacy, even if all behavior were observable and observational resources substantial, there is so much noise, so much "magic," in the behaviors observed that genuine signals rarely could be isolated from background noise, camouflage stripped or decoy ignored.

And, of course, observational resources are rarely substantial or even adequate. Deviant behavior is so highly dispersed and infrequent that it is unlikely that observers will be at the right place at the right time to observe it. A sense of the futility of this task is provided by some data on police patrol. In a study of several large urban police departments, Albert J. Reiss calculated that less than 1 percent of the time spent on routine preventive patrol yielded a criminal incident worthy of attention (1971a, 96). The Crime Commission Science and Technology Task Force estimated that a Los Angeles patrolman could expect to detect a burglary once every three months and a robbery once every fourteen years (President's Commission 1967, 12). Reiss has argued, though, that as public behaviors become more predictable—frequent, continuing in time, episodic, and socially organized—they become more vulnerable to observation (1974a, 683).[8]

Hence, the problem of observing secret behavior is not simply one of breaking down the institutions of privacy that conceal illicit activities. The problem is also one of allocating observers across a large and highly dispersed social landscape, directing them to seek out very infrequent illicit behaviors that often may not look very different from their licit counterparts.

These insights about the vulnerabilities of behavior to observation and the strategies available to immunize secret activities from discovery explain the insignificance of observational strategies in the SEC intelligence repertoire. SEC enforcers do not utilize technological surveillance apparatus for surreptitious observation. They never send investigators under cover. Their haphazard and fortuitous non-market surveillance efforts generally monitor artifacts rather than actual behaviors. Even the observational opportunities afforded by SEC inspections of broker-dealers and investment advisers are rarely exploited. The difficulties of mounting a program of observational intelligence in the world of wayward capitalism derive from the social organization of securities fraud: it is usually located in private places; it is frequently consummated in faceless computer or market transactions rather than direct interactions;

8. See also Sherman (1978, 42–44) for more elaborate distinctions.

it is rarely "situationally specific" (Katz 1979b) but develops across a patchwork of meetings, decisions, and transactions often years in the making; it is easily masked in the trappings of licit routines and readily camouflaged in noise. Each of these potentialities for cover-up are available to even the most amateur offender. The opportunities to fully exploit the easy invisibility of securities frauds through sophisticated artifices like those described above are immense.

DISCLOSURE

Disclosures provide data on behavior for which observers or observational technology are unnecessary; they are well suited to the discovery of behavior that occurs in private places or impenetrable locations, that is camouflaged or embedded in noise, or that is otherwise very difficult to observe. Reliance on disclosures, then, can considerably expand the access of researchers to behavior. It certainly does so for SEC enforcers. Almost two-thirds of the investigations in the research sample were generated by disclosures.

Because they do not require that an observer be proximate to behavior in order to gather information about it, disclosures permit the collection of data on a broad range of activities. Like observational strategies, those based on disclosure pose problems of reactivity—the act of reporting or soliciting reports of behavior may alter it. And because disclosures are at least one remove from behavior, distortions in information reported are possible and indeed likely.

Like observation, disclosures may be made by behavioral participants and nonparticipants. They may issue from direct participants, colluders, victims, collaborators, or facilitators; those proximate to but not involved in the behaviors; or those who have some incentive to survey the behavior of others. They are often based on direct observation. But often they reflect not observation, but prior disclosures (so-called hearsay) (for example, attorneys who share information revealed by their clients) or inferences about artifacts (for example, auditors who disclose that materials in corporate books and records suggest embezzlement or self-dealing). Sources of disclosure can be arrayed on a continuum that distinguishes their distance from the behavior in question: whether they are participants or nonparticipants, and whether their disclosures are based on observation, prior disclosure, or artifact. Presumably, the accuracy would decrease as one moved along the continuum from reports from participating observers to those from nonparticipants reporting artifactual data.

This presumption, however, assumes that all social actors disclose all information to which they have access and do so with honesty, accuracy, and candor. Such an assumption is, of course, inappropriate, particularly

with respect to the reporting of behavior that is deviant, stigmatizing, or carries negative sanctions.[9] Deviant behaviors therefore pose a dilemma: those whose information is most accurate are least likely to disclose it because of its incriminating, stigmatizing, or embarrassing character; those most likely to disclose such information are at so great a distance from the behavior physically, temporally, and interpersonally that disclosures are unlikely to be accurate.

Those desirous of soliciting disclosures often adopt various strategies to increase the incentives for reporting. Some offer rewards or bounties in exchange for information, positive incentives that are sometimes attractive enough to entice nonparticipants and participants only marginally involved to disclose information. But, given the incriminating nature of the behavior and the fact that the economic stakes are often so high, it is unlikely that many participants will find positive incentives attractive enough to motivate their disclosure. While positive incentives are routinely manipulated to induce disclosure in typical survey research, negative incentives are much more common where the behavior for which disclosure is sought is deviant or incriminating. They include the imposition of negative sanctions, the threat of imposing them, or negotiation over their imposition—embedded in the institutions of plea bargaining, "approval," (Donnelly 1951; Geraghty 1965), torture, immunity, anonymity, and the like.[10]

THE DIFFUSION OF INFORMATION

The vulnerability of deviant behavior to disclosure derives from the fact that information about these activities is often widely diffused. In the rare and trivial case, a single offender who engages in a nonconsensual, often "victimless," offense such as self-dealing contains the incriminating information within himself. But in more complex and ongoing offenses, whether white-collar (such as Watergate, the Equity Funding swindle, or price-fixing conspiracies) or traditional (such as the Brinks robbery or a narcotics smuggling and distribution ring), information is diffused among a number of persons occupying different roles in illicit activities. For white-collar offenses in particular, the size of this informed group can be very large. Recall that perhaps as many as seventy-five Equity Funding insiders were aware of some aspect of that fraud. The possibility that such information may be leaked, intentionally or inadvertently, poses a significant source of vulnerability to detection. Leaks ultimately may alert interested law enforcement agencies to illegal activities or even alert new prospective victims of a continuing scheme.

9. This kind of problem is addressed more fully in the research methodology literature, particularly in data collection strategies based on self-reports of "delicts." See Reiss (1973).
10. See also Wilson (1978), Skolnick (1967), and Currie (1968).

"Hush money" and "cooling the mark" represent strategies to silence two of the many kinds of recipients of incriminating information, in the latter case victims, in the former, participants or observers. In the securities world, three groups are most likely to be the recipients of information about illegality: (1) insiders, direct participants in and executors of illegal or deviant activity; (2) indirect, often unwitting collaborators; and (3) victims.

Participants. "The fact that secrets do not remain guarded forever is the weakness of the secret society. It is therefore said quite correctly that the secret known by two is no longer a secret." So wrote Georg Simmel about the secret society and the problems of maintaining secrets among those who share such knowledge (1950, 346). Simmel suggested that "sociation" was the fundamental strategy for the keeping of secrets (349). Individuals must be bound in social groups to generate mutual secrecy.

> If they were a mere sum of unconnected individuals, the secret would soon be lost; but sociation offers each of them psychological support against the temptation of disclosure. Sociation counterbalances the isolating and individualizing effect of the secret [355].

Within secret societies and other deviant groups, codes of secrecy are developed and enforced with threats of punishment. In addition, new members are carefully recruited and socialized to maintain group secrecy, frequently tested and only gradually entrusted with secret information (Simmel 1950, 349; Cohen 1977, 106; Laguerre 1980; Fidel 1980; Teft 1980; Brandt 1980).

Examples of the concern of secret or deviant groups for in-group loyalty and for limiting the opportunities for disaffection abound. Disclosures may result from vengeance exercised by insiders who feel exploited, double-crossed, unappreciated, or whose services have been terminated.[11] The disgruntled employee who blows the whistle on illegality poses a significant problem for offenders. The Equity Funding bubble, for example, was burst by the disclosures of the vice president of a subsidiary, dismissed during an economy move (Dirks and Gross 1974).

Three common strategies are employed to forestall this problem of insider disloyalty. First, simply keep the staff employed, limiting the possibility of creating embittered whistle blowers. Second, make it dif-

11. Willmer suggests that police sometimes attempt to contribute to or engender conflict among a criminal team after a crime has been successfully completed. One strategy is to plant suspicions in the minds of certain participants that they have been doublecrossed. For example, police may furnish exaggerated reports to the press of the size of the haul. Those participants who were not in a position to see the size of the haul may become distrustful of those participants in such a position (1970, 84–85).

ficult for participants to leave the organization of their own volition. In eighteenth-century Germany, for example, the newly developed process for the manufacture of porcelain was preserved from employee disclosure by confining employees to the factory as prisoners, arresting them if they escaped, and providing for all necessities of life—including a chapel—within factory walls (Bok 1982, 137–38). Less dramatically, some wayward capitalists hire employees who are mediocre or problem-ridden (for example, alcoholics) and then overcompensate them (see McClintick 1977 or Miller 1965). Overcompensation generally results in greater loyalty, a tendency to ask few questions and overlook certain problems, and neither the desire nor the ability to move out of the organization.[12] Third, create employee complicity in the offense or in other illicit activities, so that their culpability reduces their incentive to reveal the scheme (at least prior to its discovery by law enforcement officials) (Cohen 1977, 106). Police officers who do not financially exploit corrupt activities are often silenced by those who do by being entangled in other formal rule violations, such as sexual relations with a prostitute while on duty or the acceptance of Christmas "gifts" from protected businessmen (Sherman 1978, 46).

Structural solutions to the maintenance of secrecy among participants in illegal activities are often available. Many secret and especially criminal organizations utilize centralized power and organizational hierarchies to separate individual participants (Simmel 1950, 367–72). Centralized power is necessary to insure the obedience of group members. Hierarchical arrangements of members help to control the spread of information and to buffer the central leaders from incursions by outsiders. Organizational structure is also used to hide the identities of group members from each other and from outsiders.[13] This use of structural arrangements in the preservation of secrecy is found in many secret societies (Simmel 1950), the American Communist Party (Selznick 1960), conspiratorial groups within the military (Fidel 1980), organized crime families (Cressey 1972), and narcotics distribution rings (Moore 1977).

12. As Katz suggests (1979a, 301), even the fact of resignation by key participants may alert outsiders to the possibility that something is amiss. He cites the Equity Funding case and the response of one of the officers to the resignation of a key insider. First, the officer refused to make the resignation public. Later, he spread the false rumor that the reported resignation of the insider was a euphemism for the fact that he had been fired (Dirks and Gross 1974, 73–74).

13. Simmel cites some fascinating structural solutions, for example an early nineteenth-century secret society, the "Welfic Knights," which worked for the liberation and unification of Italy. Each branch of the society had a highest council of six persons who did not know one another and communicated only by means of an intermediary, "the Visible One" (1950, 372).

Erving Goffman writes about the role of organizational structure in the protection of spy networks:

> Hierarchical organization means that one man "in place" near the top can render the whole establishment vulnerable. In the field, lateral expansion through links means that one caught spy can lead to the sequential entrapment of a whole network. In both cases, the damage that can be done by a disloyal member is multiplied. The usual answer is compartmental insulation and minimization of channels of communication. But these devices, in turn, reduce co-ordination of action and dangerously impede corroboration of information [1969, 99].

Jack Katz also writes about the use of organizational structure and position in cover-up plans: to shield members from charges of wrongdoing (1977) and to permit members to concert their ignorance of wrongdoing (1979a).

The concept of "laundering funds" refers to the process by which money is transferred through a number of conduits—often foreign banks or subsidiaries—to mask its source. The identities of the source of deviance can be laundered in similar fashion, by delegating responsibility for certain illicit activities to more licit actors. This interpersonal distancing, the use of agents, middlemen, nominees, and the like, provides another means of dissociating central offenders from illicit activities.[14] Strategies to mask and launder identities are not restricted to organizational leaders, of course. Efforts to "de-individualize" all members of secret societies are common (Simmel 1950, 372–73; Schaefer 1980; Goffman 1963a). They serve not only to assure secrecy, but to depersonalize secret organizations as well, to supress individuality that is often inimical to group cohesion.

Licit collaborators. Where illegal events are spontaneous or opportunistic, those parties contributing to the offense are usually the direct participating offenders. However, where offenses involve planning and are of substantial duration or complexity, it is likely that goods and services of outsiders may be required. A boiler-room securities operation requires the installation of banks of telephones. Other offenses may need a variety of other services provided by outsiders—advertising, distributing, brokering, warehousing, banking, accounting, legal advising. Or business associates or competitors of illicit organizations may become privy to

---

14. Accounts of the involvement of Gulf Oil Company and the Lockheed Corporation in international bribery provide fascinating illustrations of these contrivances (McCloy 1975; Shaplen 1978).

information as a result of business relationships, physical or social proximity, similar clientele, and the like.

These licit collaborators represent a second group at risk in the protection of secret information. They have variable knowledge of illicit activity. Some may know directly of illegal activities enacted or anticipated; some may suspect such activities; some may be able to guess, only with insight, curiosity, and vigor; others may be truly in the dark. Their disclosure incentives also vary considerably. Some, like competitors, may be eager to share incriminating information and, for offenses such as anti-trust violations, may actually trigger investigations (Weaver 1977). Some, with little stake in the outcome—telephone installers, for example—may be less eager to disclose information, reluctant either to "rat" or to become involved. Other licit collaborators have strong ties with offenders who are clients or important sources of business revenue. They may be unwilling to disclose incriminating information for fear of the economic consequences if their clients' operations go under or their relationships with them are impaired as a result of the disclosures. Or guarantees of professional-client privilege or confidentiality may bind some collaborators to secrecy. For this latter group, only threats of negative sanctions for nondisclosure or for their indirect culpability for illicit acts may prompt disclosure.

The victims of illegality. Victims typically have greater incentives to disclose incriminating information than do participants, colluders, or collaborators. Disclosure may provide an outlet for vengeance or serve as a strategic device to force offenders to cease their victimization, make restitution, pay damages, or in some other way compensate or restore benefits to victims. For victims, disclosure incentives are not especially problematic; disclosure opportunities and the likelihood that they would receive incriminating information are.

At some point in the course of a crime, victims or potential victims usually acquire information about aspects of illegality or themselves become the informing event, the corpus delicti. Sometimes victims actually acquire information prior to the illegal event. In fraudulent schemes, for example, some information is available prior to victimization, when victims are induced to participate in their own victimization. More often, information becomes available only after the offense has occurred. In the case of burglary, this point comes reasonably soon after the event, when the victim returns home. For many white-collar crimes—embezzlement, securities fraud, and so on—this point may occur years after the offense began. And in other offenses victims may remain forever ignorant of their victimization.

As noted in the second chapter, the ability to keep victims unwitting

is a common trademark of white-collar offenses. Because the offenders often occupy positions of trust, they can exploit victims with impunity. They can misappropriate, embezzle, or self-deal with the knowledge that victims are unlikely or unable to scrutinize their conduct. They can pursue secret self-interested transactions that appear and indeed are licit—save the fact that they themselves are the beneficiaries. Since they typically control information that bears on their performance as well, white-collar offenders can deceive victims about their misfortunes and delude them about their actual victimization. They can often use space and time to further conceal their acts from victims and minimize the chance of disconfirmation and therefore diffusion of information. As offenses become more complex, with many transactions, laundering of funds and relationships, creating distance between victims and the commodities they own and the parties with whom they transact, and as offenses endure longer, it is increasingly likely that victims will remain unwitting.

Of course, many persons do learn of their victimization. Even here, offenders endeavor to insure their silence. Confidence swindlers attempt to "cool the mark out," to lessen the likelihood that the mark will express his or her anger by complaining to the authorities (Goffman 1952). The victim usually is encouraged to vent anger safely and may be given another chance to qualify or offered a different status. Cooling the mark is sometimes accomplished by collusory arrangements between offender and victim. The swindler may agree to assist the mark in obtaining recompense for his loss from some external agency (like an insurance company or the government), in passing along the loss to someone else, or in minimizing the public humiliation occasioned by his victimization.[15] A related form of conspiracy between victim and offender involves the payment of "hush money." Victim silence is often bought by providing restitution, settling lawsuits out of court, providing recompense for claims, or repurchasing commodities and cutting the victim out of the transaction.

Although the ability to keep victims unwitting or cool them out or silence them does protect some offenders from victim disclosures, it is a strategic resource for only a minority. Most offenses are vulnerable to victim disclosure. But for many, this intelligence potential is never realized. Empirical data available on victim disclosures of traditional crimes suggest that many crimes go unreported.[16]

15. For example, the chief swindler in the Homestake Oil fraud suggested that victims donate their overvalued securities to a charitable organization and then take income tax deductions to minimize their loss (McClintick 1977).

16. 1979 Justice Department statistics estimate that rates of reporting household victimizations to the police ranged from 14 percent of the larcenies of less than $50 to 87 percent of all completed vehicle thefts, with an overall median of roughly 39 percent. Of the personal victimizations, reporting ranged from 24 percent of attempted purse snatchings to 68 percent of serious assaults, with an overall median of roughly 54 percent (Flanagan 1982, 233).

The circumstances surrounding victim disclosure tend to be associated with the nature of property loss and the desire of victims for recompense. Data on traditional crimes indicate that victims are more likely to report their losses to the police when they are covered by insurance than when they are not (Reiss 1974a, 686). There is some evidence as well that the likelihood of victim disclosures increases with the financial magnitude of victimization. Edelhertz notes, for example, that charity swindles are very resistent to victim complaint because small contributors are unlikely to make the effort to check out representations about the nature of the organization or the use of the proceeds (1970, 17). Although the data gathered in my SEC research are far from conclusive, they disconfirm this hypothesis: the relationship of both the total economic cost of a securities offense and the per capita cost of victimization to investor disclosure is generally random. Lesser factors associated with victim disclosures include the extent of intimacy or the strength of the relationship between victims and offenders, victim attitudes toward law enforcement agencies (Reiss 1974a, 686), and fear of reprisal or embarrassment.

Disclosures from the securities world. The importance of disclosures as a source of SEC investigations suggests that the diffusion of information poses the most significant risk of discovery to wayward capitalists. Securities transactions, whether licit or illicit, are fundamentally dependent on the flow of information. The securities marketplace is staffed by persons who are informational specialists about particular industries and by others who broker information. The tools of this industry include prospectuses, annual reports, trade journals, stock quotations, and tips. The market is a transactional world based on tipsterism, rumor, gossip, and eavesdropping. It is a world where people really do pick up investment tips from overheard steambath conversations, where a television commercial depicts a noisy gathering suddenly silent as a man repeats the advice of his stockbroker to a friend.[17]

Because the securities industry owes its existence to the dissemination of information, the protection of incriminating information presents a problem for wayward capitalists. Many securities violations are implemented by the collaboration of large staffs—whether they are manufacturing phony insurance policies, as in the Equity Funding scheme (Dirks and Gross 1974; Soble and Dallos 1975), shuttling around the world making illicit bribes and payoffs (McCloy 1975; Shaplen 1978), or "stealing from the rich" (McClintick 1977) through a fraudulent oil investment scheme. As the number of culpable participants grows, so too does the diffusion of information about illegal activities.

---

17. The steambath example comes from my research. The commercial: "Well, our broker's with E. F. Hutton, and he says . . . (sudden silence)." The commercial ends: "When E. F. Hutton talks, people listen."

Furthermore, few securities offenses can be contained within a single organization. Most occur in an interorganizational context in which insiders from separate firms—issuers, underwriters, brokers, investment advisers, accountants, attorneys, promoters, bankers, printers, journalists—often conspire in illegality. And finally, information must be diffused to investors if their commitment to a particular securities transaction is to be secured, and to the SEC as well, if registration or other regulatory relationships must be activated to inaugurate the scheme. These recipients of information provide additional detection opportunities.

ARTIFACTUAL METHODS

Social behaviors often leave artifacts—syringes, condoms, corpses, receipts, cigarette butts, and so on—physical or social byproducts of the behaviors. Few byproducts are clear expressions of the behaviors from which they issue and some forms of behavior do not produce byproducts. Although pregnancy, for example, is a byproduct of sexual intercourse, not all intercourse results in pregnancy. And most byproducts are generated by more than one kind of behavior. Pregnancies result from premarital, marital, and extramarital relations, incest, rape, artificial insemination, and in vitro fertilization. The surveillance of social byproducts is a tricky business.

The artifacts of behavior can be examined in attempts to learn about the behaviors that generated them.[18] The examples of artifactual detection strategies abound.[19] The accounting profession and the study of history are both based on the assumption that the examination of archival records provides a meaningful perspective on the behaviors that generated them. In the world of law enforcement, police officers look for needle marks as indicators of previous narcotics use. Insurance inspectors check claims for maternity benefits by those also claiming widow's benefits or make unannounced visits to the homes of persons claiming disability benefits to see if their behavior is consistent with their alleged disability (Rule 1974). In either case, it is possible for widows to be pregnant or for disabled persons to be repairing their roofs. But in most cases, these are not artifacts of the experience of widowhood or disability.

Securities investigators examine telephone billing records for brokerage firms. The installation of many new phone lines or increased long-distance charges may reflect the creation of a boiler-room operation. But it may not. Federal officials sometimes institute a mail cover for a party

---

18. See Erving Goffman's (1969) analysis of "uncovering moves" in "expression games" for a similar perspective.

19. In their book on "unobtrusive measures," Webb and his colleagues (1966) provide some creative examples of artifactual data collection strategies in diverse settings.

under investigation, scrutinizing the senders and return addresses of all incoming mail, which may suggest the addressee's involvement in mail fraud or other illicit activities. But suspicious mail may be generated by legitimate activities as well.

SEC investigators survey the stock market, looking for unusual trading volume, fluctuations in stock prices, and the like—potential indicators of stock manipulation or insider trading. But many suspicious patterns reflect fully licit activities, and many offenses may not generate suspicious patterns at all. Similarly, Bankamericard required merchants to phone in major credit-card purchases so that the computerized buying record of the cardholder could be immediately scrutinized. If a huge volume of purchases occurred on a single day, or if fifty television sets were purchased, officials might suspect that the credit card had been stolen and direct the merchant to confiscate it (Rule 1974). But, of course, this pattern of charges may reflect purely licit (if irrational) behavior.

The notion that crimes leave artifacts or physical evidence relevant to law enforcement is neither new nor unique to this analysis. The field of criminalistics is based upon the premise that the artifacts of criminal behavior are important evidentiary tools in criminal investigation (O'Hara and Osterburg 1972; Saferstein 1977).[20] The examples are endless. What they share is the fact that data collectors are totally removed from the behavioral setting or from those who make disclosures about it. They have access to behavioral *correlates*, not to the actual behaviors. Their behavioral reconstructions are inherently inferential.

Unlike observational and disclosure strategies, artifactual methods, by virtue of their distance from the behavior in question, tend to be less reactive. However, many actors, aware of the potential use to which their behavioral artifacts may be put, intentionally destroy or distort them. Much of what is called cover-up activity is the manipulation of artifacts— destroying or doctoring records, using cash rather than checks, creating slush funds, and so on.

Clearly more central to the validity of these data is the inherent inferential nature of artifactual methods, the fact that many identical behaviors issue different artifacts and different behaviors issue identical artifacts. Nonetheless, this strategy may be the only one available where behaviors

---

20. One gets a sense of the range of activities involved in criminalistics from a partial listing of the contents of a textbook in this field (O'Hara and Osterburg 1972, xvii–xxii): Fingerprints; Foot, Tire, and Tool Impressions; Photographic Optics; Tonal Relations, Fidelity, and Contrast; Direction of Force in Broken Windows; Gambling Machines, Marked Cards, and Altered Dice; Liquor Analysis; Detective Dyes, Fluorescent Powders, and Radio- active Detectors; Detecting Carbon Monoxide and Other Gases; Blood; Semen Examina- tions; Narcotics; Inks; Erasures and Obliterations; The Examination of Documents for Invisible Writings; Microscopy, Photomicrography, Measurement of Refractive Index; Spectrochemical Analysis; X-Ray Diffraction; Color Analysis and the Spectrophotometer.

are highly private (precluding observation) and highly sensitive, incriminating, and well guarded (precluding disclosure).

THE RESIDUE OF ILLEGAL ACTIVITIES

Thomas Gregor provides a fascinating example of the incriminating potential of the byproducts or "residues" of behavior in his study of the Mehinaku, a small Indian tribe in central Brazil (1980, 83). It seems that tribesmen and women are able to recognize the footprints of their neighbors. This ability, coupled with the loose and sandy quality of village soil (which makes good print), means that villagers can construct a rather unambiguous itinerary of the movement and behavior of fellow tribesmen. The print of heels or buttocks on the ground, for example, is taken as an indicator that a couple stopped and had sexual relations along a village path; the surrounding footprints provide identification of the partners.[21]

A nice illustration of the precautions against the incriminating quality of byproducts or residues of offenses is provided by the creative cover-up activities of the notorious price-fixers in the heavy electrical equipment industry who saved and personally destroyed all wastepaper generated by their illicit price-fixing meetings (Smith 1961; Geis 1967). Even the wastepaper, if examined, might have suggested the substance of those meetings. Other byproducts that the price-fixers carefully guarded were the attendance roster for the price-fixing negotiations (labeled the "Christmas card list"), notifications of meetings (sent in plain envelopes and dubbed "choir practice"), the expense account vouchers for travel to and from meetings that could establish that conspirators were in the same cities on the same dates (phony vouchers were provided for different cities and different dates), and long-distance telephone records (calls were made on public telephones).

In some cases, secret behavior is not observable, but related aspects of the behavior are. Erving Goffman (1969, 25) finds an illustration in Theodore Sorensen's account of the Cuban missile crisis. In order to forestall suspicions of crisis, summoned members of the National Security Council arrived at the White House at different times and entered through different doors. Like the electrical equipment price-fixers, members of the National Security Council attempted to conceal the simultaneity of their association. These kinds of physical or behavioral evidence do not directly display secret or illegal activities; rather they reflect residues of that behavior—changes in physical properties or patterns of movement—

---

21. Though perhaps the couple actually stopped only for a rest. Unfortunately, residues rarely provide unambiguous inferences.

that can be examined to make inferences about the behaviors that generated them.

The residue of most white-collar offenses tends to be in the form of records. The vulnerability of such records to surveillance is reflected in some of the most common elements of cover-up jargon: "slush funds," "laundering money," "deep-sixing," "never see the light of day," "the 18-minute gap." Because many white-collar crimes and especially securities frauds are continuing offenses, involve financial transactions, and rely on the use of written or recorded materials to facilitate the illicit transactions, voluminous records and other data are almost always generated, residues likely to further implicate the offenders. Records may simply be nonessential artifacts of illegal activity, for example, long-distance telephone charges that might establish interactions, credit card receipts for hotels, airfare, or gasoline that might establish the location and movement of offenders, or bank records that might establish the timing and magnitude of monetary transactions. Other records are central to the offense itself—receipts, certificates, orders, contracts, documents, memoranda, checks, bookkeeping entries, financial statements, brokerage records, prospectuses, stock market quotations, and so forth. Although these records, in and of themselves, rarely provide conclusive evidence of illegal behaviors, they may nonetheless suggest them.

The modus operandi of many white-collar offenses includes destroying, doctoring, or creating phony records; generating new or supplemental records; back-dating records; maintaining two or more sets of books; creating and utilizing slush funds; laundering money; failing to keep records; bypassing record-keeping systems (by using cash instead of checks); or developing computer software to create, maintain, and manipulate records to conceal certain transactions or to create a façade of normalcy.[22] In addition, offenders often attempt to compromise or control accountants, the major custodians of records, through bribery or corruption. Many of these strategies were evident in the Equity Funding case.

SPIN-OFFS

The SEC investigative spin-off, described in the previous chapter, represents a fourth strategy for gathering information. On occasion, unanticipated and supplemental information comes to light during an investigation of other matters. For example, a police officer checks a car parked

---

22. In the Equity Funding insurance fraud, offenders were able to conceal their activities (creating phony insurance policies) from state auditors by programming the computer to stay a few steps ahead of the investigators, shifting accounts from file to file so that those examined were always flawless and genuine.

illegally and observes statutory rape (Skolnick and Woodworth 1967, 105). Police investigate a break-in at Democratic National Headquarters in the Watergate complex and eventually uncover a political scandal reaching the White House. SEC investigators interview an investor caught in the web of a securities fraud, who discloses other victimizations.

Returning to the research methodology analogy, spin-offs are somewhat akin to "snowball" techniques, sampling strategies based on the selection of a few respondents who then refer researchers to other respondents. Snowball sampling is an informational "pyramid scheme" in which a geometrically increasing pool of research subjects is recruited from only a few initial efforts. The technique is especially valuable where researchers have trouble identifying or locating research subjects. Researchers need only select a few appropriate subjects and then ask them to reproduce themselves.

The detection of secret or deviant behavior poses similar problems of location and identification to which spin-off methods often provide a solution. Spin-off methods are especially suited to the world of white-collar crime: because many offenders are recidivists, they are themselves good predictors of future violators; and because many offenses require collusion and collaboration from disparate social worlds, it is likely that additional deviants will be found in the social circles of known offenders. In short, ongoing investigation processes are more likely to uncover additional offenses than are random shots in the dark.[23]

THE RELATIONSHIP BETWEEN DETECTION AND BEHAVIOR

It has become clear that strategies of intelligence are related to the social organization of deviant or secret behavior and its vulnerability to detection. Except for accidental discoveries, behaviors are vulnerable to intelligence only if outside parties or institutions are organized to respond to their vulnerabilities. If incentives are not provided for disclosures, for example, it is unlikely that many disclosures of incriminating information will be made. It may be that larger groups of offenders have inherent tendencies toward disintegration and individual disloyalty. But this vulnerability and the possibility of insider disclosures cannot be exploited

---

23. Snowball sampling techniques are usually criticized for generating unrepresentative samples without any parameters by which representativeness can be assessed. Whatever biases or idiosyncrasies are characteristic of the initial elements of the sample, they are reproduced endlessly in the pyramid of elements they generate. This same criticism may be leveled at intelligence based on spin-offs. Such strategies, in a sense, overrepresent known offenders and their associates and immunize from detection those who manage to escape association with known offenses and offenders. Although spin-offs unquestionably bias the repository of intelligence data, they nonetheless provide valuable information with relative effortlessness.

unless external systems stand ready with threats of severe punishment for all participants and assurances of leniency to the first to squeal. The necessity of the prostitute to solicit customers in public places does not leave her vulnerable to detection if law enforcement agencies neither engage in surveillance nor send out undercover officers to be themselves solicited. And the executors of bribery schemes need not launder money, create slush funds, and conduct business off the books if their records are never scrutinized or audited. It is the nature and organization of intelligence systems, then, that create vulnerabilities in patterns of behavior.

Of course, this relationship is not a static one. As offenders learn to recognize the vulnerabilities in their behavior and learn of the details of the intelligence process in which they may be entrapped, they redesign their activities. Investigators similarly retool their intelligence strategies as they gather better information about the organization of behavior they wish to detect and about the obstacles that may be placed in their path.

The central agenda of this book is to examine the correlation between intelligence systems and the patterns of deviant behavior that they uncover. An important part of that task involves exploration of the obvious but rarely considered truth that the social organization of intelligence constrains the type and quality of information it uncovers. The empirical materials cited earlier in the chapter suggest that intended offenders or deviants have a vast range of choices in orchestrating their schemes—in the location of illicit activities, the constellation of participants and collaborators, the selection and arrangement of victims, the use of physical devices and records to implement their plans, strategies for the destruction of physical byproducts, and strategies for the creation of noise to mask otherwise observable activities.

These potential decisions each have implications for intelligence; they render offenses differentially vulnerable to discovery and to particular methods of detection. Offenders who cool out victims tend to immunize their activities from victim disclosures; those who restrict their activities to private settings tend to protect them from overt observation; those attentive to internal social control and the management of potential disloyalty and disaffection by participants tend to immunize their activities from disclosure by insiders. And so on.

Intelligence contests in the securities world are no different: the ways that wayward capitalists organize their misdeeds contribute to the way they are ultimately caught. This can be seen in the effect that the scope or scale of offending has on detection. The sources of SEC intelligence—surveillance, incursions, insiders, investors, members of the securities community, and other social control agencies—can be differentiated by their access to the securities world and to the centers of illicit activity. Like the rings of an onion, intelligence sources wrap themselves around the

core of wayward capitalism. Their access to this world determines their distance from the core. The outside rings are occupied by social control agencies (the SEC and others) that are typically excluded from illicit securities activities and avoided by securities swindlers, the inner rings by securities insiders and investors who directly participate in or are touched by these activities, and the middle rings by members of the securities community and SEC incursions.

Were all illicit activities and their artifacts confined to the core, did the odor of wayward capitalism not diffuse to the outer rings, their occupants would be shut out and denied all intelligence. Only those offenses whose observable behaviors, behavioral artifacts, or incriminating information diffuse out or stray from their central locations are vulnerable to detection by outsiders, those occupying the peripheral rings around the securities world.

It is in this sense that the scope of offenses is critical to intelligence, because, with increasing scope, it becomes difficult to confine illegal activities to their central locations, to insulate the core of wayward capitalism, and to shut out more peripheral securities actors and audiences from viewing some piece of these activities. Increasing scope is correlated with the wider diffusion of incriminating information and therefore with improving opportunities for intelligence sources located along the periphery of the securities world.

Compare three of the SEC detection strategies. Surveillance represents a peripherally located intelligence strategy, investor disclosures a centrally located one, and referrals from the securities community an intermediate intelligence location. For investors, directly touched by illegality and located near the center of illicit activities, increasing offense scope affords no special intelligence opportunities. Their rates of disclosure should be unaffected. However, noncomplicit members of the securities community and especially SEC surveillance are positioned at a greater distance from the illicit core. Offenses of greater scope, with their greater diffusion of incriminating information, should afford significant intelligence opportunities for these more peripheral intelligence strategies— particularly for SEC surveillance—and therefore affect their rates of detection.

The scope of securities offenses is expressed by two indicators: the scale of participation and the means by which investments are promoted, information disseminated, and transactions consummated. Where offenders can contrive to limit illicit participation to small organizations and small numbers of conspirators, where they can promote their securities through invisible face-to-face interactions without generating residues, they can protect their activities from scrutiny from peripheral intelligence locations and perhaps even from detection.

These indicators of scope are powerfully related to the means by which offenses are detected. For each of several indicators of the scale of participation—numbers of victims and offenders and the size and diversity of organizations implicated—relationships tend to be weak or nonexistent for investor disclosures, somewhat stronger for those from members of the securities community, and stronger still for SEC surveillance. As the scale of offenses increases, the proportion of offenses detected by surveillance at least doubles (from 9 percent of offenses enacted by one kind of organization to 25 percent by two or more kinds), triples (from 9 percent of offenses enacted by one or two offenders to 28 percent by more than five), increases fourfold (from 9 percent of offenses enacted by small organizations to 35 percent by large ones), and at best increases over eightfold (from 5 percent of offenses with fewer than 26 victims to 42 percent with 500 or more). These proportional differences are quite a bit smaller for disclosures from members of the securities community (from 8 percent of offenses with fewer than 26 victims to 25 percent with 500 or more, and from 8–10 percent increasing to 13–19 percent for the other indicators) and smaller still for those from investors. In short, the enhanced visibility and diffusion of information afforded by larger and more numerous and more diverse offense participants substantially increase the opportunities for peripheral intelligence but have little effect on detection strategies located at the core of wayward capitalism.

The efforts of offenders to promote or effect securities transactions provide another opportunity for outsiders to learn of their actions. The promotional strategies used by offenders affect the distance and direction in which incriminating information diffuses. These strategies fall into three groups: (1) face-to-face promotions, including private conversations, word-of-mouth, professional-to-client communications, and the development of deceptive props and equipment to impress investors; (2) limited promotions, including the use of prospectuses, solicitation letters, investment-related literature, sales brochures, documents, opinion letters, and general correspondence, residues whose dissemination is subject to some control; and (3) global promotions, including use of the press, mass media advertising, and stock market quotations.

Face-to-face efforts consciously control the visibility of promotional activities; the other strategies are far less able to restrict visibility to remote outsiders. The likelihood of investor disclosure is therefore enhanced by face-to-face strategies and relatively unaffected by global and limited ones. The probability of surveillance is patterned in the opposite direction. And that of disclosure by members of the securities community is most affected by faceless promotions of limited distribution typically directed to them.

The proportion of investigations generated by surveillance and members of the securities community is barely affected by the use of face-

to-face promotional efforts, yet those efforts more than double the proportion of investor disclosures (which increase by 25 percent). The proportion of investigations generated by investors and members of the securities community is unaffected by the use of global promotions, yet global promotions increase the probability of SEC surveillance more than fivefold (by 34 percent). And limited promotional efforts, which touch all three intelligence sources—but more subtly and with more restricted access—enhance each of their intelligence capacities, but less dramatically. The proportion of cases generated by the securities community and by surveillance doubles with the use of limited promotional materials; that of investors increases by a factor of 1.5.

These data illustrate half of the reciprocal relationship between deviance and detection: that patterns of behavior affect the means of their discovery. The other half—that because intelligence strategies are each sensitive to different vulnerabilities in the organization of behavior, they therefore uncover different kinds of secrecy—is the theme of the next chapter.

5

Evaluating the Catch: The Output of Intelligence Strategies

Many securities violations represent complex and intricate webs of social behavior, encapsulating or touching in their course numerous organizations and individuals as actual or potential collaborators, facilitators, or victims. The scope and timing of illicit behaviors, their location and modus operandi, strategies for recruiting collaborators and victims or for promoting investments, and contrivances to maintain secrecy and cover up violations vary considerably. Each strategic permutation and combination selected in the orchestration of a securities offense sets up a new range of vulnerabilities to detection.

Each offense, from its inception to its demise, endures a sequence of intelligence risks that emerge and disappear as tasks are undertaken and accomplished, as deadlines approach and are met, and as illicit activities grow and flourish. The Equity Funding offenders, for example, had very different agendas, problems, strategies, secrets, opportunities, raw materials, and an enormously varied scale of violation over the corporation's ten-year history. The intelligence vulnerabilities engendered by securities offenses are therefore neither universal nor static; unique vulnerabilities "fit the crime" and change over its course.

But materials in the previous chapter showed that intelligence strategies are not equally versatile in penetrating these diverse vulnerabilities. Detection strategies possess unique intelligence assets and liabilities that sensitize them to very different qualities of securities offenses. For all but perhaps a few insiders, their purview over the world of wayward capitalism is limited: surveillance can make out only the largest conspiratorial networks and global promotional efforts; inspections can penetrate only those activities that leave ongoing physical artifacts such as records, documents, and banks of telephones; spin-offs are restricted to the illicit activities of known offenders, their associates, or members of their social

networks; investors are likely to see only those activities that directly and dramatically touch them; filings are likely to expose only those actors who choose to register with the SEC; and so on. And since offenses shift and change over time, observable behaviors end, or physical byproducts self-destruct, intelligence opportunities for particular detection strategies may be limited, not only to certain offense scenarios, but to brief periods in the duration of the offense as well.

In short, different intelligence strategies, sensitized to different vulnerabilities, intercept different kinds of offenses at different points in their development. Just as certain kinds of bait, lures, poles, and other paraphernalia are best suited to catch particular kinds of fish, certain intelligence strategies are best suited to catch particular kinds of wayward capitalists or their misdeeds. Novice fishermen can readily learn which lures and bait attract which kind of fish. But the linkages between intelligence apparatus and their catches are considerably more mysterious in the securities world, even to wayward capitalists or SEC enforcers themselves. Which detection strategies are best for snaring an investment scheme? Which are best for hooking big offenses with many perpetrators and victims? Which are best for trapping securities offenders who have failed to register with the SEC? Which discover offenses soon after their inception? Seasoned SEC investigators probably have their hunches about the answers to some of these questions. But I have found that many of these hunches are equivocal, limited to the more obvious linkages, or wrong. Neither these seat-of-the-pants hunches nor more theoretically inspired hypotheses have ever been subjected to empirical inquiry. If SEC investigators were as serious about their securities enforcement as most fishermen are about their sport, they would never remain so ill-prepared, so unfamiliar with the limits, capacities, and risks of their intelligence equipment.

This chapter provides empirical data to demystify the proclivities and capacities of the intelligence strategies available to SEC enforcers. Its analyses differentiate these strategies by the quality of their catch and identify those strategies which net similar offenses and those which do not.

WHICH OFFENSES ARE CAUGHT?

As we empty the nets of the fifteen intelligence strategies, we should expect to find appreciable differences in the species of wayward capitalism caught. Different kinds of securities offenses are organized in very different ways. Offenses such as technical violations or self-dealing usually are located within a single organization, with few participants and few facilitators or colluders. They rarely directly touch investors (since these

offenses do not seek to induce any kind of investment behavior) or require promotional activities or the cooperation of other securities professionals. These offenses are therefore relatively immune from discovery by surveillance, investors, securities professionals, or other outsiders and are unlikely to be found among the catch in these intelligence nets. On the other hand, registration violations often accompany efforts to promote and market investments, activities that touch investors and securities professionals and generate limited or global promotional messages that might inadvertently reach SEC surveillance posts. So these three intelligence strategies, unlikely to catch technical violators or self-dealing, may be much more successful in apprehending registration violators.

Other aspects of securities violations facilitate or impede certain intelligence efforts. The subtlety of stock manipulation or self-dealing undermines investor discovery in a way that most embezzlements or misappropriations of investor monies (eventually) do not. Registration violations are relatively immune from SEC proactive intelligence, which is structured primarily around monitoring aspects of the behavior of agency registrants. Stock manipulation or insider trading generate stock quotations and other public data readily available for surveillance. Boiler-room sales techniques, which rely on high pressure and often annoying sales routines, increase the potential of solicited investor disclosures in a way that more subtle promotions of blue chip stocks would not.

Despite their unique embellishments, specific kinds of violation share common organizational forms that hold similar vulnerabilities. It would be surprising indeed if detected offenses were randomly distributed among the intelligence strategies that are so differentially sensitive to given vulnerabilities. The research data confirm this expectation. The catch of the fifteen intelligence strategies are considerably and significantly different in the kinds of securities violations they represent. For example, 68 percent of the catch of market surveillance involved stock manipulation, in contrast to 5 percent of that of inspections. In 78 percent of the offenses disclosed by securities professionals, stocks were not registered, compared to 21 percent of those discovered through filings. Misrepresentations were found in 88 percent of the offenses uncovered by non-market surveillance but in only 57 percent of those disclosed by corporate representatives. The research data contain dozens of other examples with percentage differences at least as large as those just reported.

But it would be unwise to attach much importance to these findings. Contrasting the violations found by each intelligence strategy is a meaningful exercise only when offenses are structured around a single violation. But this is rarely true of securities offenses. Recall that, on average, cases in the sample investigated more than five separate charges

or allegations of lawbreaking. The Equity Funding scheme, for example, included numerous misrepresentations, registration violations, and misappropriations, as well as self-dealing and insider trading.

Even more commonplace securities offenses are often intricate webs of violation whose diverse elements are structured to conceal as well as to defraud. Included among the registration violators in my sample are fully licit securities organizations that inadvertently failed to register with the SEC and offenders who intentionally avoided registration in order to conceal their calculated fraudulent activities from SEC scrutiny. The class of technical bookkeeping violations includes a brokerage firm whose books and records were not up to date because the firm had just installed a new computer and had not yet gotten the "bugs" out of it and another firm that intentionally doctored its books and records to conceal its involvement in a stock manipulation scheme. Misrepresentations in the sample include the case of a broker-dealer who falsely characterized corporate prospects in order to sell its securities and another who falsely told a client that he was holding stock certificates in safekeeping to conceal the fact that he had embezzled the client's funds.

In short, securities offenses often draw on a number of different violations, assembled to implement the central purpose of the offense, to assist or complement that purpose, or to conceal the other violations. Any single violation represents a heterogenous category of diverse purposes and truly different offenses to which it contributes. It reveals very little about the true nature of these offenses.

In order to appreciate the differences in offenses caught by various intelligence strategies, it is therefore necessary to take all the violations assembled in a given offense and summarize them into an unambiguous designation of the central agenda of illicit activities. For this purpose, the activities that serve to cover up or facilitate other activities or that represent extra illicit opportunities (such as those to misappropriate funds) deriving from some greater illegal accomplishment are ignored. I designated a hierarchy of violations to represent increasing centrality, from technical violations to registration violations, misrepresentations, misappropriation, self-dealing, and stock manipulation. Offenses were characterized by their most central violations, assuming that lesser ones are facilitative, ancillary, or incidental. The procedure generated an eight-category classification in which each offense was assigned only one value:

1. Technical violations only ($N = 84$), for example, improper books or records, net capital violations, disclosure problems, and the like. This category also includes improper sales techniques, boiler rooms, and poor supervision of employees.
2. Registration violations only ($N = 48$), in which stock issuers, bro-

kers, investment advisers, investment companies, or sellers of sub-stantial quantities of securities fail to register with the SEC. These offenders may commit additional technical violations as well but no other violations.

3. Misrepresentations only ($N = 42$), in which stock issuers or profes-sionals falsely characterize their business operations, financial con-dition, prospects, the securities they are promoting, and the like. These offenders may commit ancillary technical violations but no additional violations.

4. Misappropriations only ($N = 39$). Since this category represents offenders who misappropriate funds without committing any addi-tional violations, save perhaps technical ones, most offenses con-tained herein are simple embezzlements, usually by stockbrokers or persons in publicly held corporations.

5. Registration violations with misrepresentations ($N = 80$), the classic securities fraud, in which offenders fail to register investment op-portunities with the SEC and then promote their securities by mis-representing the financial condition of the company, nature of business operations, risks, return on investment, use of the pro-ceeds, and so on.

6. Registration violations with misrepresentations and misappropria-tions ($N = 58$). Offenses in this category often resemble those in the previous one, but offenders here expand their illicit activities by additionally misappropriating the funds fraudulently obtained. (In the previous category, investment monies remain in corporate cof-fers.) Many of the ponzi and other investment schemes are classi-fied here.

7. Self-dealing ($N = 43$), for example, insider trading, scalping, and abuse of corporate resources or opportunities. Offenses may also have elements or combinations of technical or registration viola-tions, misrepresentation, or misappropriation.

8. Stock manipulation ($N = 43$). Offenses may also have elements or combinations of technical or registration violations, misrepresen-tation, misappropriation, or self-dealing.

The relationship of this classification of offenses to detection is pre-sented in table 5.1.[1] Percentages are computed across the rows of the table. Were there no relationship, differences in percentage in each of the columns would be minimal. As the table clearly demonstrates, this is not

1. In this table and others in this chapter, a case is characterized by each of the methods by which it was detected. For example, if an offense was detected by non-market surveillance and investor disclosures, it would be counted twice, reflected in each of these rows in the table. As a result, sums computed down the columns may exceed column totals.

Table 5.1. Detection and Type of Violation

Factor number	Factor loading	Detection strategy	Technical violations only (%)	Registration violations only (%)	Misrepresentations only (%)	Misappropriations only (%)	Registration violations and misrepresentations (%)	Registration violations, misrepresentations, and misappropriation (%)	Self-dealing (%)	Stock manipulation (%)	Total (N)
(1	.95)	Professionals	4	0	4	0	**41**	**26**	15	11	(27)
(1	.93)	State agencies	0	14	10	7	**30**	**19**	10	10	(59)
(1	.90)	Non-market surveillance	0	12	9	0	**38**	15	**18**	9	(34)
(1	.89)	Solicited investors	3	16	12	6	**31**	22	3	6	(32)
(1	.65)	Federal agencies	0	12	16	4	16	**28**	12	12	(25)
(1	.61)	Actual investors	1	10	9	**16**	18	**25**	14	7	(104)
(2	.71)										
(1	.51)	Participating insiders	0	0	13	**20**	20	**33**	7	7	(15)
(2	.63)										
(2	-.83)	Corporate representatives	**24**	19	14	5	10	14	5	10	(21)
(2	-.81)	Filings	**57**	2	12	1	8	6	6	7	(96)
(2	-.74)	Self-regulatory agencies	**26**	13	8	11	15	15	4	9	(47)
(3	.98)	Inspections	**22**	3	5	**22**	16	11	16	5	(37)
(4	.94)	Informants	9	9	4	14	9	9	**18**	**27**	(22)
(4	.91)	Market surveillance	0	0	4	0	0	0	**27**	**68**	(22)
(4	.72)	Spin-offs	8	15	5	10	12	15	**18**	**18**	(40)
		Total	19	11	10	9	18	13	10	10	(437)

Note: Percentages are computed horizontally across the rows.

the case. For many of the offense categories, differences between detection methods exceed 30 percent.

The total displays the distribution of offenses for the sample as a whole. When it is contrasted with other rows in the table, one gets some sense of how different this sample of offenses would look if the SEC pursued only a single intelligence strategy. Market surveillance provides an extreme case: with the exception of 4 percent of its catch committing misrepresentations alone, the remaining 95 percent commit self-dealing or stock manipulation. An enforcement caseload so constructed would have *no* technical or registration violations, misappropriations, or any combination of these violations and misrepresentation—those offenses which comprise 70 percent of the total sample.

Self-regulatory agency referrals contrast sharply with the idiosyncratic catch of market surveillance. With a few exceptions (technical violations only and self-dealing), the distribution of offenses referred by self-regulatory agencies mirrors within 3 percent that of the total sample. This is so perhaps because self-regulatory agencies have access to many of the same intelligence sources available to the SEC. Self-regulatory agencies conduct inspections and market surveillance, compel disclosure from their members and monitor member compliance with regulations, and receive complaints from insiders, investors, and members of the securities community.

The offense distribution of the catch of the other detection strategies falls somewhere between the extremes of market surveillance and self-regulatory agency referrals. In general, however, the departure from the overall sample distribution is more the rule than the exception.

Table 5.1 provides data on how the catches of different intelligence strategies vary from the overall catch. But data also demonstrate how catches of each strategy differ from each other. The table differentiates the catch of each of the refined detection strategies[2] in two ways: by percentage distributions and the results of a factor analysis. (The factor analysis procedure is fully explained later in this chapter.) Briefly, standardized percentages representing the relationship between the eight-category offense classification and the refined detection strategies provided the input for the factor analysis. Its output, four factors that explain 89 percent of the variation in detection strategy, sort the detection strategies into clusters that net similar constellations of offenses.[3] With the

2. Employer disclosures were omitted from the analysis, because of the small number. All four investigations involved charges of embezzlement and possible technical violations.

3. The procedure utilized varimax rotation, but no iteration. Factor analysis procedures based on eight cases are vulnerable to problems of sampling error. However, the results of the factor analysis are consistent with the percentage distributions and are used here to supplement other forms of data analysis, not to replace them. A factor analysis was also performed using the discrete types of violation (summarized in the eight-category classification) as units of analysis. The solution was similar.

exception of actual investors and participating insiders, all detection strategies had relatively high loadings (the correlation between the factor and the detection strategy) on only one factor. That factor number and associated factor loadings are presented in the first column of table 5.1. To facilitate interpretation, detection strategies with similar factor loadings are grouped together in the table; larger percentages have been set in boldface type.

The way in which these clusters of detection strategies differ in the offenses they catch is clear from the percentage distributions as well as from the factor loadings. Investigations generated by referrals from securities professionals, state agencies, solicited investors, and by non-market surveillance all have high loadings on factor 1. Referrals from federal agencies, actual investors, and participating insiders have more modest loadings on the first factor, and the latter two strategies actually have somewhat higher loadings on factor 2. Members of the first cluster of detection methods are especially likely to uncover offenses with both registration violations and misrepresentations (sometimes coupled with misappropriations) and unlikely to detect technical violations. Forty-five percent of the investigations generated by this cluster of strategies (including investors and insiders) discovered offenses with registration violations and misrepresentations (both with and without associated misappropriations), in contrast to 21 percent of the investigations generated by other detection strategies. These proportions for technical violations are 1 percent and 29 percent, respectively.

So this cluster of detection strategies, represented by a member of every general detection category except incursions, is best suited for uncovering the most common kind of securities fraud. These strategies detect offenses that couple misrepresentations with failure to register with the SEC in order to defraud securities investors, and often to misappropriate their funds as well. Over three-fifths of these offenses in the sample were detected by this cluster of strategies.

Disclosures by actual investors and participating insiders had more marginal loadings on factor 1, in part because simple misappropriation (embezzlement) bears a strong negative association with the factor. Yet misappropriation, whether or not it is coupled with other elements of securities fraud, provides the major catch of actual investors and participating insiders. Overall, 41 percent of the offenses uncovered by these investors and insiders involved some form of misappropriation, compared to 17 percent of the catch of the remaining intelligence strategies.

Misappropriations directly victimize investors in a manner that enhances their awareness of victimization and therefore increases the likelihood that they will complain to the SEC. Misappropriation of funds also serves as an inducement for insider tattling, especially when misappropriated monies are not equally shared among insiders or when funds are

embezzled by a participant against the wishes of the others. It is this scenario that seems most ripe for insider disclosure, where the traditional disincentives against self-disclosure are minimized. So the fact of unwilling participation in the misappropriation of securities monies tends to predispose some investors and insiders to confer with the SEC.

The major difference between the cluster of detection methods with high loadings on factor 1 and actual investors and participating insiders therefore pertains to the role of misappropriation. Not only do the former strategies miss simple misappropriation offenses and the latter consistently uncover them, but the coupling of misappropriation with registration violations and misrepresentation increases their likelihood of inclusion in the catch of investors (from 18 percent to 25 percent) and insiders (from 20 percent to 33 percent) and decreases the likelihood of inclusion in the catch of most of the other strategies by about the same proportion.

These differences reflect the distinction between insiders and outsiders. The detection of misappropriation requires close proximity to the centers of illegality, because it is often enacted by a single individual and rarely requires the assistance of co-offenders. The likelihood of substantial offender participation—a factor related to detection by peripheral intelligence locations—is rare. The possibility of misappropriation will not be reflected in the communications or literature disseminated by offenders or in the behavioral artifacts of illicit activities observable to these at a distance. Misappropriations of funds are actions invisible to surveillance or to the scrutiny of nonparticipating members of the securities community. Nor are these activities visible to solicited investors, who differ from actual investors in that they have not yet consummated securities transactions and therefore not yet provided funds available for misappropriation. Because misappropriation is a small-scale, invisible occurrence, it is most vulnerable to detection by parties most proximate to securities offenses, actual investors and participating insiders. All of the other detection strategies in the first cluster are, of course, outsiders to the world of wayward capitalism.

The second factor generated by the factor analysis procedure is defined by very strong positive scores for misappropriations and very strong negative scores for technical violations. Factor 2 differentiates two clusters of detection strategies, those with relatively high positive factor loadings (actual investors and participating insiders) and those with strong negative factor loadings. The latter cluster of detection strategies (filings and disclosures by corporate representatives and by self-regulatory agencies) are especially likely to disclose technical violations alone. Overall, technical violations comprise 44 percent of the catch of these strategies, compared to only 5 percent of the remaining intelligence strategies. In

fact, members of this cluster detect four-fifths of all technical violation offenses in the entire sample. These strategies are particularly unlikely to uncover either misappropriation or self-dealing.

Inspections provide an interesting counterpoint to the five intelligence strategies with high positive and negative loadings on factor 2. Like the strategies with high negative loadings, they catch many technical violations (22 percent of their catch). But unlike those strategies, inspections share a proclivity with actual investors and participating insiders (with high positive loadings on factor 2) to uncover misappropriations (again, 22 percent). Inspections are equally versatile in discovering the technical violations of brokerage firms and the embezzlement of client funds by registered representatives of the firms. Forty-three percent of their catch involves either misappropriation or technical violations, compared to a quarter of that of the other detection strategies. They distinguish themselves from all the other sources of intelligence and alone have high loadings on factor 3.

A fourth factor characterizes the catch of informants, market surveillance, and spin-offs. These detection strategies uncover the most subtle forms of securities fraud, those most likely to leave investors unwitting—self-dealing and/or stock manipulation. Overall, 52 percent of their catch reflects self-dealing or stock manipulation, in contrast to only 15 percent of the catch of the other strategies. Technical violations are unlikely to be detected, as are misrepresentations or nonregistration (whether alone, together, or coupled with misappropriations). Factor 1 strategies uncover the more blatant securities frauds, factor 4 strategies the more subtle ones.

Two of these three investigative sources—spin-offs and informant disclosures—gravitate to the more subtle offenses because of the intelligence resources inherent in their special proximity or access to the centers of illicit activities. Market surveillance lacks this special access, however. Instead, investigators painstakingly monitor stock quotations and other data and then hazard speculations about subtle offenses such as stock manipulation and insider trading, for which these data serve as artifacts. It is ironic that market surveillance, so distant from the center of wayward capitalism, should be such a major source of the offenses of greater subtlety, while referrals from offense insiders, for whom full intelligence is usually available and for whom subtlety is a contrivance, should so infrequently disclose these offenses.

Roughly a quarter of the offenses in the sample were detected on more than one occasion, sometimes through different means. Surprisingly, it is the more complex, subtle, and serious offenses that are most likely to be detected more than once. Thirty percent of the investigations alleged simple technical or registration violations exclusively. But this was true of

only 13 percent of the offenses detected more than once and 6 percent of those uncovered more than once and in different ways. At the more complex end of the continuum, one third of the investigations alleged registration violations coupled with misrepresentations and misappropriation, self-dealing, or stock manipulation. But these violations comprised half of all the offenses detected more than once and 57 percent of those detected by different strategies. With greater complexity, offenses usually increase in scope and generate greater complicity, involvement, and more diffused information that create more opportunities for detection.

WHICH OFFENDERS ARE CAUGHT?

Because the kinds, numbers, and constellations of wayward capitalists assembled in illicit activities pose different vulnerabilities to intelligence, the "faces" of wayward capitalists found among the catches of the different detection strategies vary considerably. Detection strategies catch different kinds of individuals suspected of participation in securities offenses. Overall, most of them (83 percent) represent the organizational "upper class," holding positions as officers, directors, sole proprietors, or control persons of organizations engaged in securities transactions. A much smaller proportion (30 percent) represent the "under class" and serve as employees of these organizations.[4] Detection strategies differ in the likelihood that they will uncover illicit activities by individuals in either class. Non-market surveillance (97 percent of its catch), inspections (94 percent), and participating insiders (93 percent) are most likely to generate investigations of individuals in the corporate upper class. Cases detected by market surveillance (63 percent of them), disclosures by employers (50 percent), informants (74 percent), and federal agencies (67 percent) are least likely to do so. Market surveillance (47 percent of its catch) and spin-offs (55 percent) most often discover the offenses of corporate employees; filings (10 percent) and solicited investors (19 percent) do so least often. The opportunities for committing particular securities violations differ by corporate position. For example, there are few registration or technical violations that can be orchestrated by employees acting alone. So some of these patterns of correlation between detection and organizational position undoubtedly reflect differences by detection method in the kinds of violations they uncover.

Suspect organizations even more than suspect individuals distinguish the catches of the intelligence strategies available to SEC enforcers. As described in chapter 2, most wayward capitalists investigated by the SEC

---

4. Twenty-three percent of all cases involve offenders representing both officer and employee roles. Therefore, the sum of percentages generally exceeds 100.

(88 percent of them) represent or are drawn from stock issuer or broker-age firms. But because intelligence strategies have differential access to the activities of issuers and brokers; because issuers and brokers often commit different kinds of violations, staffed, organized, and implemented in disparate ways; because they transact with and touch investors variably; and because they typically occupy separate locations in the securities world and distinctive business networks; stockbrokers and stock issuers are not equally vulnerable to each intelligence strategy.

Table 5.2 presents the number of offenses enacted by stock issuers, broker-dealers, or both issuers and broker-dealers together found in the catch of each detection method. (Because cases in the latter category are also included in the former categories, totals exceed 100 percent.) The catch of the two proactive intelligence strategies are most different in their representation of stock issuers: a third of the incursions and 87 percent of the surveillance methods uncover the offenses of issuers. As indicated in the table, filings (33 percent) and inspections (11 percent) rarely reveal violations by issuers. Insiders tend also to be less likely to disclose matters involving issuers, though the proportions vary considerably between disclosures by corporate representatives (48 percent) and employers (25 percent), on the one hand, and participating insiders (73 percent), on the other. Self-regulatory agencies are also less likely (51 percent) to refer matters concerning issuers, in part because a significant number of these referrals come from the National Association of Securi-

Table 5.2. Detection and Organization Type

Detection strategy	Issuers		Broker-dealers		Both issuers and brokers		Total
	(N)	(%)	(N)	(%)	(N)	(%)	(N)
Market surveillance	(19)	86	(9)	41	(8)	36	(22)
Non-market surveillance	(30)	88	(9)	26	(6)	18	(34)
Inspections	(4)	11	(36)	97	(4)	11	(37)
Filings	(32)	33	(70)	73	(11)	11	(96)
Spin-offs	(23)	56	(20)	49	(9)	22	(41)
Participating insiders	(11)	73	(5)	33	(1)	7	(15)
Corporate representatives	(10)	48	(10)	48	(1)	5	(21)
Employers	(1)	25	(3)	75	(1)	25	(4)
Actual investors	(74)	70	(42)	40	(15)	14	(105)
Solicited investors	(22)	69	(13)	41	(7)	22	(32)
Informants	(14)	64	(12)	54	(4)	18	(22)
Professionals	(21)	75	(13)	46	(8)	29	(28)
Federal agencies	(21)	84	(4)	16	(2)	8	(25)
State agencies	(47)	80	(10)	17	(2)	3	(59)
Self-regulatory agencies	(24)	51	(22)	47	(2)	4	(47)
Total	(247)	56	(217)	49	(55)	12	(440)

Note: Percentages are computed horizontally across the rows.

ties Dealers, a self-regulatory agency whose members are broker-dealers. Those intelligence strategies most likely to uncover technical violations are also least likely to detect stock issuers.

Those strategies best suited to uncover the misdeeds of stock issuers are generally least likely to detect those of stockbrokers. The catches of incursions and referrals from the securities community contain the highest proportion of broker-dealer suspects, 74 percent and 50 percent, respectively. Government agencies are not particularly interested in or aware of the misdeeds of brokers: only 16 percent of the federal and 17 percent of the state agency referrals pertain to brokers. Non-market surveillance efforts also rarely detect broker-dealers, perhaps because stock issuers are more likely to advertise and promote investments globally than are stockbrokers, who tend to use either professional client contacts or boiler-room telephone solicitations and thereby protect their efforts from outside scrutiny. Only about a quarter of the cases generated by non-market surveillance alleged violations by stockbrokers, and two-thirds of these investigations also scrutinized issuer co-offenders. In contrast, broker-dealer offenders comprised 97 percent of the catch of inspections, 73 percent of that of filings, and 49 percent in the sample overall.

Cases in which investigations inquire about the collusion of stockbrokers and issuers in illicit activities are a relative rarity (12 percent overall). They are most common among the catch of market surveillance (36 percent), spin-offs (22 percent), and disclosures by professionals (29 percent), solicited investors (22 percent), and employers (25 percent). Some of these strategies are best suited to detect more complex forms of violation, which often necessitate a more diverse representation of co-offenders.

So the choice of detection strategy makes a considerable difference in whether the offender pool is primarily composed of stock issuers, brokers, or a combination of both. Not only does the type of offender vary by detection method, but so does its registrant status. The proactive detection strategies are much more likely to uncover offenses of registered stock issuers than are the reactive methods. Among those offenses enacted by stock issuers, 68 percent of the catch of market surveillance was composed of registered issuers, as was 75 percent of that of inspections and 84 percent of that of filings. This proportion for the reactive strategies ranged from 15 percent of the catch of state agency referrals to half of the disclosures of corporate representatives, but it represented less than a third of the catch of most of these reactive strategies. The affinity of SEC registrants to proactive intelligence is readily explained. Market surveillance monitors exchange listed (and therefore registered) securities; inspections are conducted only of agency registrants; and filings are made by actual or anticipated registrants.

Choice of detection strategy is less significant in discovering the of-

fenses of unregistered broker-dealers. Overall, three-quarters of the broker-dealer offenders in the sample are SEC registrants. Percentages of registered broker-dealers among the catch of the detection strategies range from half the federal referrals and three-fifths of the disclosures by participating insiders and securities professionals to 91 percent of the self-regulatory agency referrals and all of the inspections.

In chapter 4 I suggested that greater size increases the likelihood that organizations will be detected by peripherally located intelligence strategies. The catches of detection strategies should therefore vary in the size of organizational offenders represented. Table 5.3 presents data that confirm this expectation. The data discriminate between small ($N = 137$) and medium-to-large organizations ($N = 66$) and also differentiate those cases in which organizational size is unknown, in which several organizations implicated in the same offense differ in size, or in which organizations are bankrupt. The last column presents data only for those cases in which organizational size is known and relevant. It displays the ratio of the number of cases in which organizations are medium or large to those which are small.

The catch of surveillance strategies differs significantly from that of the other detection methods. The ratio of medium or large to small organiza-

Table 5.3. Detection and Organization Size

Detection strategy	Not specified, mixed (N)	(%)	Bankrupt (N)	(%)	Small (N)	(%)	Medium, large (N)	(%)	Total cases (N)	Ratio Medium, large to small
Market surveillance	(6)	32	(2)	11	(2)	11	(9)	47	(19)	4.50
Non-market surveillance	(10)	29	(4)	12	(10)	29	(10)	29	(34)	1.00
Inspections	(10)	27	(11)	30	(10)	27	(6)	16	(37)	0.60
Filings	(26)	27	(25)	26	(35)	37	(9)	9	(95)	0.26
Spin-offs	(15)	39	(9)	24	(7)	18	(7)	18	(38)	1.00
Participating insiders	(2)	14	(4)	29	(5)	36	(3)	21	(14)	0.60
Corporate representatives	(5)	25	(7)	35	(4)	20	(4)	20	(20)	1.00
Employers	(1)	33	(0)	0	(1)	33	(1)	33	(3)	1.00
Actual investors	(23)	23	(30)	29	(33)	32	(16)	16	(102)	0.48
Solicited investors	(10)	33	(3)	10	(11)	37	(6)	20	(30)	0.55
Informants	(6)	29	(7)	33	(3)	14	(5)	24	(21)	1.67
Professionals	(7)	28	(4)	16	(8)	32	(6)	24	(25)	0.75
Federal agencies	(7)	30	(8)	35	(5)	22	(3)	13	(23)	0.60
State agencies	(12)	22	(15)	27	(23)	42	(5)	9	(55)	0.22
Self-regulatory agencies	(9)	20	(12)	27	(18)	40	(6)	13	(45)	0.33
Total	(107)	25	(111)	26	(137)	33	(66)	16	(421)	0.48

Note: Percentages are computed horizontally across the rows.

tions detected is 4.50 for market surveillance and 1.00 for non-market surveillance, compared to an overall ratio of 0.48. Spin-offs are the only other proactive strategy likely to net large organizations (ratio of 1.00)— an expected finding, since spin-offs typically accompany an enlarging scope of investigation, a major source of which is the discovery of sizeable organizational offenders.

Among the reactive detection strategies, informants are most likely to disclose the offenses of large organizations (with a large/small ratio of 1.67), followed by corporate representatives (1.00), employers (1.00), and securities professionals (0.75). Ironically, the reactive strategies most likely to uncover the most serious types of offenses typically reveal the misdeeds of small organizations. The large/small ratio of cases referred by participating insiders, investors, and other social control agencies is less than 0.61.

The important finding apparent in table 5.3, however, is seen in the contrast between detection strategies with little access to illegality (surveillance and the securities community) and those involving participants in the illegal activities (participating insiders and investors) with much greater access. Because of the greater visibility of larger organizations, those strategies with little access are best suited to detect the offenses of large organizations, and strategies with greater access, those of smaller organizations.

Offender constellations provide another indicator of the scope of securities offenses. Like organizational size, the increasing scope of offense participation magnifies and enhances the visibility of illegal activities to peripheral intelligence locations. Two indicators of the scope of participation in illegality are considered here: one counts the number of offenders, another reflects their breadth and diversity. Tables 5.4 and 5.5 present the relationship of these indicators to detection strategy.

A familiar cluster of detection strategies discover illicit activities with the largest number of offenders: participating insiders (a third of whose disclosures pertain to five or more offenders), market surveillance (27 percent of them), non-market surveillance (32 percent), and spin-offs (22 percent). Insider loyalty and controls for the maintenance of secrecy decrease with growing participation and therefore provide greater opportunities for insider disclosure. And small offender groups are insufficiently visible to surveillance personnel located a considerable distance from the center of illegality; increasing participation magnifies illicit activities and therefore enhances visibility.

The detection strategies unlikely to net many offenders also represent a cluster whose catch shares other characteristics: inspections (54 percent of which uncover at most two offenders), filings (60 percent), and refer-

Table 5.4. Detection and Number of Offenders

Detection strategy	One		Two		Three– five		More than five		Total
	(N)	(%)	(N)	(%)	(N)	(%)	(N)	(%)	(N)
Market surveillance	(5)	23	(3)	14	(8)	36	(6)	27	(22)
Non-market surveillance	(1)	3	(12)	35	(10)	29	(11)	32	(34)
Inspections	(5)	14	(15)	41	(12)	32	(5)	14	(37)
Filings	(29)	30	(29)	30	(25)	26	(13)	14	(96)
Spin-offs	(11)	27	(4)	10	(17)	41	(9)	22	(41)
Participating insiders	(1)	7	(4)	27	(5)	33	(5)	33	(15)
Corporate representatives	(1)	5	(4)	19	(12)	57	(4)	19	(21)
Employers	(1)	25	(2)	50	(1)	25	(0)	0	(4)
Actual investors	(6)	6	(33)	31	(45)	43	(21)	20	(105)
Solicited investors	(5)	16	(10)	31	(12)	38	(5)	16	(32)
Informants	(2)	9	(7)	32	(9)	41	(4)	18	(22)
Professionals	(3)	11	(9)	32	(12)	43	(4)	14	(28)
Federal agencies	(3)	12	(9)	36	(10)	40	(3)	12	(25)
State agencies	(6)	10	(13)	22	(28)	47	(12)	20	(59)
Self-regulatory agencies	(11)	23	(15)	32	(13)	28	(8)	17	(47)
Total	(80)	18	(138)	31	(161)	37	(61)	14	(440)

Note: Percentages are computed horizontally across the rows.

rals by self-regulatory agencies (55 percent). The limited scope of participation in offenses caught by these strategies is partially explained by the fact that these offenses predominantly involve technical violations, for which participation is usually limited to a single firm or its principal. Technical violations, which predominate in the catches of inspections, filings, and self-regulatory agency disclosures, rarely involve the large staffs and participation of diverse organizations characteristic of many securities frauds.

A second dimension of the scope of offense participation pertains to the breadth rather than the extent of participation. Do individual offenders represent a single organizational role, corporate officers, for example? Or is individual participation broader, reflecting the conspiracy of officers, directors, managers, employees, inside attorneys and accountants? Do organizational offenders represent a single industry—one or more brokerage firms, for example? Or is organizational participation broader, reflecting the conspiracy of brokerage, law, accounting, and public relations firms, stock issuers, investment advisers, banks, and insurance companies? With increasing breadth of participation, reflected in the diversity of individual and organizational offenders, offenses become more significant, their potential impact more substantial.

The catches of the detection strategies vary in the likelihood that they include offenses with broader and diverse participants. Table 5.5 displays

the relationship of detection strategy to the scope of both individual and organizational offense participation. Those strategies unlikely to detect many offenders are also those most likely to net the offenses of limited breadth, enacted by at most one organizational or individual role. Seventy-one percent of the catch of filings and 68 percent of that of inspections and self-regulatory agencies detect these offenses, compared to less than half of most of the other strategies. At the other extreme, detection strategies do not distinguish themselves as clearly with respect to offenses broad in both individual and organizational participation. Market surveillance (27 percent of its catch) is most likely to uncover offenses of broader scope, but it is followed closely by spin-offs (24 percent), non-market surveillance (21 percent), and disclosures by employers (25 percent), solicited investors (22 percent), and securities professionals (21 percent).

Consideration of the joint scope of individual and organizational participation does not differentiate the catch of detection strategies very well, because those strategies suited to uncover offenses with diverse organizational participants usually are not the same ones suited to uncover offenses with diverse individual participants. The former strategies include market surveillance (55 percent of its catch involve two or more kinds of organizations), spin-offs (41 percent), and referrals from securities professionals (46 percent) and federal agencies (40 percent) (in contrast to 25 percent of the full sample). The latter strategies include disclosures by participating insiders (53 percent of their catch reflect offenses with two

Table 5.5. Detection and Scope of Participation in Offense

| Detection strategy | One type organization | | | | Two or more types organizations | | | | Total |
| | One role | | Two or more roles | | One role | | Two or more roles | | |
	(N)	(%)	(N)	(%)	(N)	(%)	(N)	(%)	(N)
Market surveillance	(8)	36	(2)	9	(6)	27	(6)	27	(22)
Non-market surveillance	(14)	41	(8)	24	(5)	15	(7)	21	(34)
Inspections	(25)	68	(6)	16	(3)	8	(3)	8	(37)
Filings	(68)	71	(6)	6	(10)	10	(12)	12	(96)
Spin-offs	(14)	34	(10)	24	(7)	17	(10)	24	(41)
Participating insiders	(7)	47	(6)	40	(0)	0	(2)	13	(15)
Corporate representatives	(8)	38	(7)	33	(2)	10	(4)	19	(21)
Employers	(1)	25	(1)	25	(1)	25	(1)	25	(4)
Actual investors	(43)	41	(36)	34	(9)	9	(17)	16	(105)
Solicited investors	(17)	53	(3)	9	(5)	16	(7)	22	(32)
Informants	(11)	50	(5)	23	(2)	9	(4)	18	(22)
Professionals	(12)	43	(3)	11	(7)	25	(6)	21	(28)
Federal agencies	(10)	40	(5)	20	(7)	28	(3)	12	(25)
State agencies	(28)	47	(19)	32	(3)	5	(9)	15	(59)
Self-regulatory agencies	(32)	68	(9)	19	(4)	9	(2)	4	(47)
Total	(236)	54	(90)	21	(54)	12	(55)	13	(435)

Note: Percentages are computed horizontally across the rows.

or more individual roles involved), corporate representatives (52 percent), employers (50 percent), actual investors (50 percent), spin-offs (49 percent), state agency referrals (47 percent), and non-market surveillance (44 percent) (in contrast to a third of the full sample).

The essential difference between those strategies best suited to uncover offenses with diverse organizational participation (*inter*organizational scope) and those with diverse individual participation (*intra*organizational scope) is that the former are outsider strategies, the latter insider strategies, each with differing access to the central locations of illicit activities. Offenses of intraorganizational scope are most characteristic of the catch of insiders and actual investors, those centrally involved in and accessible to illicit activities. Indeed the increasing spread and diversity of participation within a deviant organization is usually accompanied by a greater diffusion of information to noncomplict insiders and by fewer disclosure disincentives. Offenses of interorganizational scope are most characteristic of the catch of market surveillance, spin-offs, securities professionals, and federal agency referrals, strategies all located at the periphery of illegal activities. Intelligence opportunities are quite limited when illicit activities are contained (and more readily concealed) in a single organization. Detection is facilitated for those strategies with only a peripheral perspective on illegality by the greater magnification and visibility of illicit activities occasioned by the addition of new organizational coconspirators.

WHAT IS THE IMPACT OR SIGNIFICANCE OF THE OFFENSES CAUGHT?

Many fishing expeditions yield no catch. Sports enthusiasts deploy their elaborate fishing apparatus, only to find their bait untouched, their hooks, traps, or nets empty, or their catch too small, below the legal limit. In the securities world, intelligence strategies may likewise accumulate a catch below the legal limit—offenses so small, trivial, or inconsequential, generating insignificant victimization or economic consequence—while truly big fish, offenses of substantial impact and social harm, swim freely by. These strategies net offenses that are ultimately tossed back, not so much because they fall short of some *actual* legal or prosecutorial criteria, but because their impact is trivial and unworthy of further enforcement attention.

Intelligence technologies are differentially likely to detect securities violations with substantial impact. Data presented in chapter 4 demonstrated that an increasing scope of victimization facilitates detection from peripheral intelligence locations. They also documented the linkage between intelligence and strategies to promote investment—that face-to-face strategies facilitate investor discovery and global promotional efforts enhance surveillance opportunities. But promotional strategies create not

only qualitative offense differences; they also produce quantitative differences. Face-to-face strategies, requiring costly and time-consuming interactions, can recruit relatively few investors and therefore few investment dollars relative to global mass-media promotions that can touch literally thousands of potential investors and millions of investment dollars in one fell swoop. So intelligence strategies that rely on diffuse global promotions are more likely to snare offenses with significant impact than are those sensitive to the vulnerabilities inherent in limited or face-to-face promotions.

The catch of detection strategies varies in its significance or impact as well because strategies catch different types of violations. And impact is at least modestly correlated with offense type. Technical violations, for example, rarely have any or many investor victims or associated economic costs. Embezzlements rarely net as much money (or victims) as classic stock swindles in which investment monies in some illicit, often unregistered, enterprise are fraudulently collected. Of course, offenses structured around the same violations differ enormously in their success and therefore their impact. The Equity Funding fraud has had many precursors and imitators, few of which were able to endure so long, touch so many investors, or accumulate so many ill-gotten gains. But the range of possible impacts is at least somewhat constrained by the type of illicit act undertaken.

The catches of the intelligence strategies vary significantly in their impact, measured by the scope of victimization and magnitude of economic injury or cost.[5] Table 5.6 presents data on numbers of victims as a percentage of those offenses for which victims could be specified and counted. The last two columns describe the cases that are omitted from this analysis, either because the offense did not generate victims or because they could not be enumerated. Percentages in these columns are based on the total number of investigations generated by each detection strategy. The enormous variability by detection strategy in the proportion of cases in which victims or victimization data are absent is striking. For 45 percent of the surveillance cases, victims could not be enumerated, in contrast to about a quarter of the other strategies. Problems of enumeration were highest (59 percent) for market surveillance. This is to be expected, since market surveillance's characteristic catch of stock manipulation and insider trading violations generate diffuse victims, who are not always easy to specify.

Table 5.6 also reveals considerable variability by detection strategy in

5. Chapter 2 described the data available to this research on victimization and the economic magnitude of violations. For both of these variables, data were sometimes unavailable, or where available, biased or inaccurate. Still, the data are reliable enough to provide some sense of the differential impact of offenses detected by different methods.

Table 5.6. Detection and Victimization

Detection strategy	Victims									No victims (%)	Victims not enumerated (%)
	1–25 (N)	(%)	26–100 (N)	(%)	101–500 (N)	(%)	501+ (N)	(%)	Total (N)		
Market surveillance	(0)	0	(2)	67	(1)	33	(0)	0	(3)	27	59
Non-market surveillance	(3)	18	(5)	29	(4)	24	(5)	29	(17)	15	35
Inspections	(7)	78	(1)	11	(1)	11	(0)	0	(9)	38	38
Filings	(2)	18	(5)	45	(3)	27	(1)	9	(11)	74	15
Spin-offs	(7)	54	(3)	23	(2)	15	(1)	8	(13)	27	39
Participating insiders	(2)	22	(1)	11	(4)	44	(2)	22	(9)	7	33
Corporate representatives	(2)	33	(3)	50	(0)	0	(1)	17	(6)	43	29
Employers	(3)	75	(1)	25	(0)	0	(0)	0	(4)	0	0
Actual investors	(26)	39	(19)	29	(13)	20	(8)	12	(66)	10	27
Solicited investors	(2)	14	(6)	43	(4)	29	(2)	14	(14)	25	31
Informants	(2)	22	(2)	22	(4)	44	(1)	11	(9)	41	18
Professionals	(3)	20	(7)	47	(3)	20	(2)	13	(15)	18	25
Federal agencies	(5)	50	(2)	20	(1)	10	(2)	20	(10)	20	40
State agencies	(10)	26	(16)	42	(9)	24	(3)	8	(38)	12	24
Self-regulatory agencies	(9)	39	(4)	17	(10)	43	(0)	0	(23)	36	15
Total	(65)	38	(57)	34	(35)	21	(12)	7	(169)	36	25

Note: Percentages are computed horizontally across the rows.

the likelihood that any victims, whether or not specifiable, were generated. Fewer than half of the offenses uncovered by incursions (especially filings) generated victims, in contrast to 87 percent of all offenses disclosed by investors and 82 percent of those derived from surveillance. If the creation of any victims bears on the impact of an offense, the data indicate that employers (100 percent victims), participating insiders (93 percent), actual investors (90 percent), state agencies (88 percent), non-market surveillance (85 percent), professionals (82 percent), and federal agencies (80 percent) uncover offenses of greater impact. Those with least impact are detected by filings (26 percent) and disclosures by corporate representatives (57 percent) or by informants (59 percent).

However, the fact that the catch of a detection strategy includes offenses that touch some victims does not insure that its impact is significant in terms of the number of victims generated. Indeed, for many strategies, there seems to be a trade-off between the universality of victimization in the offenses they net and the number of victims typically touched by these offenses. For example, all offenses referred by employers involve victims, but none of them involves more than one hundred victims. For informant

disclosures, the trade-off is reversed: relatively low proportions of victimizing offenses (59 percent) and very high proportions of offenses with more than one hundred victims (56 percent, relative to 28 percent overall). A similar relationship is found between actual and solicited investors. Actual investor disclosures are more likely than those of solicited investors to disclose victimizing offenses (90 percent versus 75 percent), but less likely to disclose those touching more than one hundred victims (32 percent versus 43 percent). For other strategies, though, especially non-market surveillance (85 percent victimization, 53 percent more than 100 victims) and participating insiders (93 percent victimization, 67 percent more than 100 victims), the high likelihood of victimization is coupled with a high likelihood of substantial victimization. In any event, participating insiders, non-market surveillance, informants, and solicited investors uncover offenses with the largest number of victims. And perhaps market surveillance and federal agency referrals do so as well, if the many unspecified victims in their catch were too numerous to be counted by investigators.

The relationship of detection to the economic impact of an offense mirrors that of victimization. Just as offenses may not create victims, they may not carry an economic price tag. Some technical or registration violations, for example, may involve illegal procedures unrelated to economic transactions—keeping records, for example. As shown in table 5.7, inspections, filings, and disclosures by corporate representatives are most likely to uncover those offenses which have no associated economic costs. This is true of half to three-quarters of these cases, compared to proportions of less than a quarter for non-market surveillance, participating insiders, employers, actual investors, and state agencies—the same strategies most likely to generate victims.

And like the victimization analysis, those strategies whose catch disproportionately includes offenses with an economic price tag still differ significantly in the likelihood that they will detect offenses with substantial cost. The larger offenses in economic terms are most likely to be uncovered by non-market surveillance and participating insiders. In 27 percent of the catch of both strategies, sums in excess of $500,000 were at stake, in contrast to 9 percent of the overall sample. Employers (25 percent), actual investors (18 percent), solicited investors (16 percent), professionals (18 percent), and state agencies (15 percent) are next in line as sources of the more costly offenses. The magnitude of victimization and of cost bear similar relationships to detection method. Offenses that generate victims also tend to incur monetary damage, and a major contributor to high economic cost is the large number of investors. These findings of powerful correlations between mode of intelligence and the significance or

Table 5.7. Detection and Offense Cost

Detection strategy	Offense cost														Total cases
	None		$1–$5,000		$5,001–$25,000		$25,001–$100,000		$100,001–$500,000		$500,001–$1,000,000		$1,000,001+		
	(N)	(%)	(N)	(%)	(N)	(%)	(N)	(%)	(N)	(%)	(N)	(%)	(N)	(%)	(N)
Market surveillance	(8)	36	(0)	0	(4)	18	(3)	14	(4)	18	(2)	9	(1)	5	(22)
Non-market surveillance	(8)	24	(2)	6	(2)	6	(5)	15	(8)	24	(4)	12	(5)	15	(34)
Inspections	(18)	49	(1)	3	(8)	22	(3)	8	(6)	16	(1)	3	(0)	0	(37)
Filings	(72)	75	(2)	2	(2)	2	(5)	5	(12)	12	(2)	2	(1)	1	(96)
Spin-offs	(17)	41	(1)	2	(3)	7	(6)	15	(10)	24	(0)	0	(4)	10	(41)
Participating insiders	(3)	20	(0)	0	(0)	0	(4)	27	(4)	27	(3)	20	(1)	7	(15)
Corporate representatives	(10)	48	(0)	0	(2)	10	(5)	24	(2)	10	(0)	0	(2)	10	(21)
Employers	(0)	0	(0)	0	(1)	25	(0)	0	(2)	50	(0)	0	(1)	25	(4)
Actual investors	(18)	17	(4)	4	(16)	15	(31)	30	(17)	16	(9)	9	(10)	10	(105)
Solicited investors	(13)	41	(1)	3	(5)	16	(4)	12	(4)	12	(3)	9	(2)	6	(32)
Informants	(8)	36	(1)	5	(2)	9	(5)	23	(3)	14	(2)	9	(1)	5	(22)
Professionals	(9)	32	(1)	4	(3)	11	(4)	14	(6)	21	(2)	7	(3)	11	(28)
Federal agencies	(11)	44	(1)	4	(3)	12	(2)	8	(6)	24	(1)	4	(1)	4	(25)
State agencies	(13)	22	(1)	2	(5)	8	(16)	27	(15)	25	(5)	8	(4)	7	(59)
Self-regulatory agencies	(18)	38	(4)	9	(3)	6	(8)	17	(8)	17	(4)	9	(2)	4	(47)
Total	(184)	42	(18)	4	(42)	10	(77)	18	(78)	18	(21)	5	(20)	5	(440)

Note: Percentages are computed horizontally across the rows.

impact of victimization have obvious policy implications for the SEC's enforcement program. They are considered later in chapter 7.

THE QUALITY OF INTELLIGENCE

OFFENSE DURATION

The longevity of securities offenses varies considerably. Some take longer to implement, to recruit investors, and so on. Some frauds are better able to protract the ultimate point of disconfirmation when the pyramid collapses, the bubble bursts, the wells yield no oil, the dividend checks never arrive. Some offenses are better able to escape or prolong discovery by the authorities. One explanation for differential offense impact, therefore, derives from variable longevity or duration of offense. With increasing time, offenders can recruit ever larger numbers of investors/victims and accumulate a greater sum of investment monies.

Does the duration of securities offenses, like their impact, vary by intelligence strategy? Table 5.8 presents data on this relationship. Detection strategies likely to uncover the offenses with greatest impact are also most likely to catch those of greatest duration. Three-quarters of the disclosures of employers, 53 percent of those of participating insiders, 47 percent of those of actual investors, 50 percent of those of professionals, and 45 percent of those of state agencies, in contrast to one-third of the sample overall, revealed offenses ongoing for more than two years. The

Table 5.8. Detection and Duration of Offense

Detection strategy	Less than 8 months (N)	(%)	8 months– 2 years (N)	(%)	More than 2 years (N)	(%)	Total cases (N)	Mean duration (years)
Market surveillance	(12)	60	(6)	30	(2)	10	(20)	1.12
Non-market surveillance	(8)	25	(12)	38	(12)	38	(32)	2.28
Inspections	(9)	26	(14)	40	(12)	34	(35)	1.80
Filings	(30)	33	(32)	36	(28)	31	(90)	2.58
Spin-offs	(5)	14	(18)	49	(14)	38	(37)	2.45
Participating insiders	(2)	13	(5)	33	(8)	53	(15)	2.61
Corporate representatives	(10)	48	(7)	33	(4)	19	(21)	1.14
Employers	(1)	25	(0)	0	(3)	75	(4)	5.28
Actual investors	(17)	17	(35)	36	(46)	47	(98)	2.47
Solicited investors	(9)	31	(11)	38	(9)	31	(29)	2.09
Informants	(6)	32	(9)	47	(4)	21	(19)	2.10
Professionals	(7)	27	(6)	23	(13)	50	(26)	2.24
Federal agencies	(6)	26	(9)	39	(8)	35	(23)	2.10
State agencies	(8)	14	(23)	41	(25)	45	(56)	2.32
Self-regulatory agencies	(15)	37	(17)	41	(9)	22	(41)	1.45
Total	(121)	30	(151)	37	(134)	33	(406)	2.06

Note: Percentages are computed horizontally across the rows.

very shortest offenses were detected by market surveillance or disclosures by corporate representatives, 60 percent and 48 percent of which continued for less than eight months, respectively.

Of course, the catches of detection strategies vary in the violations represented, which are in turn correlated with offense duration. For example, a simple stock manipulation, embezzlement, or a nonfraudulent but unregistered stock distribution may take considerably less time to be enacted than a shell corporation investment scheme, which requires the acquisition of controlling shares of stock in a defunct corporation from scattered investors, gradual manipulation of the price of these securities, and then the reselling of stock at manipulated prices. So the relationship between detection and offense duration may simply be an artifact of that between violation and duration.

TIMELINESS

However, this relationship may be explained by a different reason altogether. Each of the analyses of detection and offense impact or significance have implicitly assumed that detection is a static process. They take for granted that there are numerous offenses in the real world, some more significant than others, and that detection strategies simply pick and choose. Such an assumption would be reasonable if detected offenses had all been completed and therefore their victimization or monetary impact fully realized. But at least three-quarters of the offenses in the sample were still ongoing at the time of detection.[6] If detection has some impact on subsequent offense duration by shortening and forestalling illegal activities, then the point at which detection intervenes in the sequence of these activities is a critical factor in offense significance. A more realistic assumption, then, would suggest that detection strategies play a dynamic role in the making or unmaking of significant offenses. Those detection strategies associated with large numbers of victims, huge monetary costs, and long duration may be responsible for these very characteristics in their inability to quickly uncover and stop illegal activities before their effects are felt.

The contrast in the duration of offenses disclosed by actual and solicited investors is especially telling. Recall that cases generated by actual investors tend to involve more money and a higher proportion of victimizing offenses of longer duration than those generated by solicited investors. Assume that their catches contain similar violations. What differs is

6. There is some variation by detection strategy in the likelihood that offenses ended prior to detection. Although the proportion of ongoing offenses is greater than 80 percent for most strategies, it is only 25 percent for employer disclosures, 57 percent for filings, 64 percent for informants, 67 percent for market surveillance and participating insiders, and 72 percent for actual investors.

that solicited investors notify the SEC when they first learn of investment opportunities before making an investment; actual investors wait to notify the SEC until after they have made the investment and then realize that they have been victimized. For actual investors, impact in terms of money and victims is generally greater, because their "untimely" detection permitted greater offense duration. Those detection strategies associated with insignificant offenses may be of greatest enforcement value because of their timeliness, their ability to intercept illegalities early and foreclose their significant possibilities.

These speculations can be evaluated empirically with data on the interval between the inception of illegal activities and the time that suspicions or allegations of illegality develop or reach the SEC. This relationship is displayed in table 5.9. In this table, the unit of analysis is the detection strategy and not the case, so the number of cases is somewhat larger than in most other tables (recall that some offenses were detected more than once).[7]

Table 5.9. Detection and Recency of Offense

Detection strategy	Less than 2 months (N)	(%)	2–6 months (N)	(%)	6 months– 1 year (N)	(%)	1–2 years (N)	(%)	More than 2 years (N)	(%)	Total cases (N)
Market surveillance	(6)	33	(8)	44	(1)	6	(3)	17	(0)	0	(18)
Non-market surveillance	(6)	18	(11)	32	(4)	12	(5)	15	(8)	24	(34)
Inspections	(8)	24	(6)	18	(8)	24	(7)	21	(4)	12	(33)
Filings	(25)	30	(15)	18	(7)	8	(14)	17	(23)	27	(84)
Spin-offs	(1)	5	(4)	21	(5)	26	(3)	16	(6)	32	(19)
Participating insiders	(0)	0	(0)	0	(3)	21	(4)	29	(7)	50	(14)
Corporate representatives	(6)	29	(3)	14	(4)	19	(5)	24	(3)	14	(21)
Employers	(0)	0	(0)	0	(1)	25	(0)	0	(3)	75	(4)
Actual investors	(7)	7	(11)	11	(21)	20	(24)	23	(40)	39	(103)
Solicited investors	(11)	37	(6)	20	(7)	23	(2)	7	(4)	13	(30)
Informants	(0)	0	(4)	21	(6)	32	(7)	37	(2)	11	(19)
Professionals	(3)	12	(6)	24	(4)	16	(8)	32	(4)	16	(25)
Federal agencies	(2)	9	(4)	18	(4)	18	(4)	18	(8)	36	(22)
State agencies	(6)	11	(5)	9	(13)	24	(15)	27	(16)	29	(55)
Self-regulatory agencies	(6)	16	(10)	27	(6)	16	(8)	22	(7)	19	(37)
Total	(89)	17	(94)	18	(95)	18	(110)	21	(136)	26	(524)

Note: Percentages are computed horizontally across the rows.

7. This is essential because offenses with multiple investigative sources have multiple dates of detection for each source.

Overall, these data document some significant differences. An unusually high proportion of offenses detected by surveillance (23 percent) and incursions (25 percent) had been ongoing for less than two months, in contrast to unusually high proportions of insiders (35 percent) and investors (33 percent) who disclosed offenses continuing for more than two years. Data displayed in table 5.9 confirm earlier speculations about the contrast between actual and solicited investors. Thirty-seven percent of the offenses disclosed by solicited investors, in contrast to 7 percent of those by actual investors, were ongoing for less than two months; 13 percent of those by solicited and 39 percent by actual investors had already continued for more than two years.

In addition to solicited investors, some of the most rapid detection methods include market surveillance, filings, and disclosures by corporate representatives. Indeed, whereas about a third of the offenses in the sample had been ongoing for less than six months, this was true for more than three-fourths of those uncovered by market surveillance. In addition to referrals by actual investors, some of the slowest detection methods include disclosures by employers, participating insiders, and federal agencies. More than a third of the offenses they each detected had been initiated more than two years earlier.

As offenses unfold, they generate different kinds of information and involve additional parties in facilitator or victim roles. If we generated a hypothetical time line or chronology of typical securities violations, noting the time when a corporate structure and physical plant are assembled, conspirators are recruited, stocks are registered, advertising is issued, stock market quotations are manipulated, brokers and investors are solicited, actual investments are made, investors realize that they have been victimized, and so on, we would have a series of predictions about the timing of intelligence opportunities. And these predictions are generally validated by the available data: surveillance, solicited investors, and professionals, with access primarily to activities scheduled early in offense chronologies, intervene earlier than do actual investors and the other intelligence strategies. Just as detection strategies are constrained by the diffusion and visibility of information and activities, they are limited by the timing of offense elements to which they are most sensitive.

The one major empirical exception to this predictive scheme is found in the insider category—comprising those presumably first to know and last to tell. Insiders (corporate representatives, employers, and participating insiders) provide an interesting case. Where the offender is the organization itself, disclosures by corporate representatives are rapid. When the employer is excluded from illegality (and perhaps even is its victim), he or she is one of the last to know and last to tell. Where the offender is an individual participant, presumably first to know, disclosure is very slow,

perhaps because events must unfold sufficiently for him or her to be disaffected, disaffiliated, or fearful enough of increasing culpability to make disclosure a likelihood.

These findings lend support to the speculation that detection strategies make and unmake significant offenses by their speed in uncovering newly instituted illegal activities, which raises the question of whether the relationship of other indicators of offense impact or significance to detection is simply an artifact of differential duration. Perhaps offenses are significant merely because untimely intelligence allowed them to endure too long. Both the number of victims and the economic cost of an offense are positively related, though weakly, to offense duration. So it is possible that the relationship of these indicators of impact to detection strategy may disappear when offense duration is controlled.

Table 5.10 presents the data that bear on this question. Because of small Ns, duration, victimization, and economic cost are all dichotomized. The percentages in boldface type highlight those detection strategies most likely to uncover offenses with many victims and large economic costs. For many of the detection strategies with greatest impact, controlling for

Table 5.10. Detection and Offense Impact
(controlling for offense duration)

Detection strategy	Less than 1 year % more than 100 victims	More than 1 year % more than 100 victims	All cases % more than 100 victims	Less than 1 year % more than $100,000	More than 1 year % more than $100,000	All cases % more than $100,000
Market surveillance	0	100	33	60	33	50
Non-market surveillance	50	54	**53**	56	69	**65**
Inspections	33	0	11	22	50	37
Filings	0	50	36	33	79	62
Spin-offs	33	25	23	44	64	58
Participating insiders	100	62	**67**	0	73	**67**
Corporate representatives	50	0	17	0	67	36
Employers	0	0	0	0	100	**75**
Actual investors	33	31	32	32	48	41
Solicited investors	50	56	**43**	33	70	47
Informants	0	71	**56**	67	40	43
Professionals	25	44	33	33	64	58
Federal agencies	33	33	30	57	67	57
State agencies	18	38	32	50	53	52
Self-regulatory agencies	33	50	**44**	54	53	48
Total	24	31	28	37	54	47

Note: Percentages are computed horizontally across the rows.

duration makes no difference. Non-market surveillance still nets multiple-victim, high-cost offenses regardless of duration. And this is true of participating insiders, solicited investors, and self-regulatory agencies with respect to victims.

But for informants with respect to victims and participating insiders and employers with respect to money, proportions are high only for offenses that continue for more than one year. Furthermore, other detection methods that overall do not detect large proportions of high-impact offenses do so for their longer-lasting ones. Among offenses that continue for more than one year, filings, disclosures by corporate representatives, solicited investors, and federal agencies detect proportions of costly offenses as high, for example, as non-market surveillance. It appears, then, that although duration does not account for the impact of an offense entirely, it does contribute to the opportunities for impact. And to the extent that detection strategies can limit duration, they can limit the impact of offenses as well.

ACCURACY

Some detection methods provide more timely intelligence. Because they are most sensitive to the vulnerabilities to intelligence that typically occur early in the unfolding of a securities violation, they are able to intercept offenses before they have had time to amass considerable profits, victims, or impact. But do the sources of this timely and therefore high quality intelligence also contribute accurate intelligence? Or, in their zest to nip wayward capitalism in the bud or to develop suspicions based on the first fragmentary evidence that an illicit scheme is being assembled or implemented, do these detection strategies generate erroneous suspicions? Solicited investors, for example, who immediately contact the SEC when they first learn of attractive investment opportunities hazard a considerably greater risk of unwarranted suspicions than do actual investors who may have several opportunities to discover and validate incriminating information during the course of their investment experience. By waiting out the course of an illicit scheme, intelligence disclosed by actual investors is less timely, but perhaps more accurate.

But intelligence may be inaccurate for reasons other than overeagerness. As observed earlier, intelligence strategies have differential access to the loci of securities violations. Some intelligence sources—insiders, for example—have an unobstructed view of securities violations. If they choose to disclose intelligence, they have few structural impediments to accuracy (though there may be other incentives to distort information for purposes of self-protection).

Other intelligence strategies, such as surveillance, are located at such a distance from the center of securities offenses that they can make out only

the faintest outlines of these behaviors. Surveillance strategies are inherently inferential; they collect vague inconclusive artifacts or ancillary pieces of illicit activities and attempt to reconstruct the full offense. These inferential exercises are much like attempting to reconstruct the skeleton of an unfamiliar prehistoric creature from the discovery of a single bone. The reconstruction is bound to be less accurate than one in which all the bones have been found. And so, too, are inferences derived from the fragmentary evidence accessible to SEC surveillance outposts. With increasing access, detection strategies should generate more accurate intelligence.

The correspondence between the suspicions or allegations of illegality that generate investigative work and the characterization of the offense, if any, at the conclusion of investigation may be rather limited. But what precisely constitutes accurate intelligence? Are partial characterizations of a complex set of activities inaccurate? Are characterizations broader than the actual offense inaccurate? How does one treat allegations of offenses that do not exist but that alert investigators to other violations? The data gathered in this research on initial allegations are not substantial enough to resolve questions of this kind. Data are available, however, on those SEC investigations in which no violations of any kind were found, regardless of the nature of initial suspicions. Detection strategies can be compared by the proportion of investigations they generate for which no violation was ultimately discovered.

Unfortunately, a methodological caveat is necessary. The docketing of SEC investigations—a designation that defines my sample—is a highly discretionary process. Decisions about whether or when to docket an investigation upon the development of suspicions of illegality generally are left to the judgment of individual investigators rather than determined by formal procedures (at least during the period of my research). It is quite possible that investigators are more reticent to docket allegations from what they presume to be less trustworthy intelligence sources. Therefore, research findings may be counterintuitive: the least trustworthy sources may appear most accurate because greater discretion is used in docketing their allegations than those of more trustworthy sources.

In any event, whether because of access, the point at which intelligence becomes available, the greater expertise and sophistication of certain intelligence sources, or the structure of disclosure incentives, some detection strategies should amass more accurate intelligence than others. But these alternative explanations generate sometimes contradictory hypotheses about the accuracy of the catches. Actual investors should disclose relatively accurate intelligence because they have considerable access to illicit activities and generally wait out an offense, thereby amassing considerable incriminating intelligence. But actual investors are also unsea-

soned; they often lack experience in the securities arena and knowledge of the technical details of securities law. Often investors complain when they have been stung by misfortune in speculative but fully licit investment deals. So one would also expect the substance of their disclosures to be relatively inaccurate. Surveillance strategies, on the other hand, because they have marginal access to the securities world, should generate relatively inaccurate intelligence. But because surveillance is conducted by SEC investigators, its discoveries should be more accurate than those of investors. And insiders, by virtue of access, are often capable of disclosing the most accurate intelligence. But fear of complicity or insiders' use of disclosure opportunities to protect themselves or to manipulate co-offenders often leads to distorted intelligence. So it remains unclear what patterns of candor and accuracy actually should be found.

Table 5.11 provides data on the relationship of detection to the finding of a violation. The least accurate strategies include surveillance, incursions, and referrals from the securities community; the most accurate include investor and insider disclosures. Specifically, the strategies of market surveillance (36 percent), filings (27 percent), and informants (32 percent) are most likely to result in findings of no violation; those least likely include non-market surveillance (6 percent), inspections (3 percent), all insider categories (0−7 percent), investors (5 percent, 9 percent), and state agencies (5 percent). And since they involve fuller initial evidence, investigations generated by more than one intelligence strategy

Table 5.11. Detection and the Finding of a Violation

Detection strategy	No violations (N)	(%)	Total cases (N)
Market surveillance	(8)	36	(22)
Non-market surveillance	(2)	6	(34)
Inspections	(1)	3	(37)
Filings	(26)	27	(96)
Spin-offs	(5)	12	(41)
Participating insiders	(1)	7	(15)
Corporate representatives	(1)	5	(21)
Employers	(0)	0	(4)
Actual investors	(5)	5	(105)
Solicited investors	(3)	9	(32)
Informants	(7)	32	(22)
Professionals	(3)	11	(28)
Federal agencies	(3)	12	(25)
State agencies	(3)	5	(59)
Self-regulatory agencies	(8)	17	(47)
Total	(65)	15	(440)

Note: Percentages are computed horizontally across the rows.

are more likely to result in the finding of actual violations than those detected only once.

Data in table 5.11 confirm some expectations. Insiders and investors, those detection strategies with greatest access to securities violations, do disclose the most accurate intelligence. Among the proactive strategies, incursions (with greater access than surveillance) generate more accurate intelligence. Actual investors, with greater access and time to confirm their suspicions than solicited investors, are more likely to disclose information that leads to the finding of a violation. Participating insiders, with the greatest incentives to distort information, disclose less accurate intelligence than the other insider strategies. Market surveillance and filings, more likely to generate timely intelligence, are also among those strategies more likely to gather inaccurate intelligence.[8]

But closer examination of the data also reveals inconsistent, contradictory, or unexpected findings. Many refined detection strategies that should share equal opportunities for accurate intelligence in theory are dissimilar in practice. Over a third of the intelligence generated by market surveillance leads to findings that no violation had occurred, in contrast to only 6 percent of that uncovered by non-market surveillance. Of the disclosures from the securities community, 11 percent of those from securities professionals were inaccurate, compared to 32 percent of those from anonymous informants (many of whom may actually be insiders with considerable access to accurate information). Among the other social control agencies, the referrals of federal agencies are inaccurate 12 percent of the time and those of self-regulatory agencies 17 percent of the time, while only 5 percent of the disclosures of state agencies fail to uncover actual violations. Among the incursive strategies, 27 percent of the filings generate unfounded suspicions, compared to only 3 percent of the inspections. And spin-offs are relatively inaccurate (12 percent) despite the fact that they are outgrowths of considerable previous investigation.

These contradictory findings may derive from several sources. Perhaps the most important pertains to differential docketing procedures. Some of the detection strategies associated with more accurate intelligence may benefit from slow and cautious docketing practices, in which only the most

8. Some readers might interpret this finding of the correlation between timely and inaccurate intelligence quite differently. Since many white-collar offenses are not "situationally specific" nor do they generate "presumptive evidence" (Katz 1979b), a pattern of irregular activities must be accumulated before it is possible to differentiate illicit from licit schemes. Timely intelligence, by quickly aborting an offense, precludes the possibility that subsequent activities can be scrutinized, patterns established, and true violations conclusively identified. In short, many of these apparently licit schemes are actually violations as well. My scrutiny of the full investigative history of hundreds of SEC cases finds little support for this interpretation.

credible suspicions result in formal investigation. Market surveillance, for example, represents an organized intelligence program with special staffing and uniform procedures. Whenever a computer subroutine isolates a deviant trading pattern, it may be automatically docketed for further investigation. Non-market surveillance, on the other hand, is haphazard and fortuitous, deriving from the curiosity of individual members of the staff. When enforcers notice suspicious conduct, they may make preliminary inquiries, follow up leads, and gather a fair amount of evidence before they share their suspicions with superiors and request that a docketed investigation be opened. Similar differences in anxiousness or reticence to docket a formal investigation, based on ongoing enforcement programs and established procedures or the presumed trustworthiness of intelligence sources, may explain other contradictions in the data.

Other explanations for these unexpected findings may derive instead from the incentives or reasons various SEC outsiders have for disclosing information or from the correlation between types of violation and detection. Some securities violations—such as stock manipulation, insider trading, or self-dealing—are subtle and sophisticated and difficult to ascertain conclusively without considerable investigation. Detection strategies, like market surveillance or informants, that are most likely to discover these more subtle offenses are also likely to generate more erroneous initial suspicions.

Table 5.11 reveals that the most accurate of the detection methods are the reactive rather than the proactive strategies. A hasty policy decision might suggest that since proactive detection strategies often require greater agency resources and are less likely to uncover actual securities violations, proactive strategies—or at least their inaccurate members—be curtailed. Such a policy decision would be reasonable if all detection strategies uncovered the same kinds of offenses and offenders. It is clearly inappropriate in this setting, however, where detection methods vary not only in the kinds of offenses and offenders uncovered, but in the seriousness or impact of these offenses as well. This is particularly true for the least accurate strategies that typically uncover some of the most subtle, complex, and distinctive kinds of offenses in the sample and do so most quickly, reducing their potential impact.

The tension between allocating resources between predominantly accurate and less accurate detection methods is similar to that between Type I and Type II errors in statistical analysis. In one case, the confidence limits in testing a hypothesis are set so narrowly that it is unlikely that researchers would ever err by not rejecting a hypothesis that was false. Accuracy is assured, but true hypotheses may be rejected in the process. In the other case, the confidence limits are set so broadly that false hypotheses are not rejected. The setting of limits has associated costs. In

one case, all detected offenses will prove to be prosecutable violations, but many significant offenses will never be detected. In the other case, a broader set of offenses will be detected, but many will later prove unworthy of prosecution.

Policy trade-offs will be addressed more fully in the concluding chapter. It should be noted here, however, that the generation of prosecutable violations is not the only purpose of an enforcement program. Deterrence may represent another aim. It may be necessary to attempt to detect a broad spectrum of offenses and offenders, whatever the prosecutorial outcome, to assure potential offenders that they are not immune from detection and the enforcement process.

PULLING IT ALL TOGETHER

I hope that the eleven tables in this chapter have provided a real sense of the patterns, clusters, and uniqueness of the catch of the intelligence strategies available to SEC enforcers. But the big picture to which each discrete piece of information contributes can seem uncomfortably remote. That big picture, derived from a statistical procedure used to summarize these data, is presented here. It takes the form of a map on which each of the detection methods is plotted. The location of each intelligence strategy on the map and its proximity to other strategies is determined by its catch. Strategies plotted near one another net offenses with similar characteristics; strategies plotted far apart net very different catches.

The plotting formula for the map is derived from a factor analysis. Through factor analysis, the full array of detection strategies can be reduced to a smaller number of factors that summarize the interrelations of these strategies with respect to their catch. The catches of detection strategies with high loadings on a particular factor share common attributes. Factor loadings for each detection strategy (which represent the correlation between the detection strategy and a given factor) are the coordinates according to which strategies are plotted on the map.

Data utilized in the factor analysis procedure pertain to the relationship between the refined classification of detection strategies and each of fifty-three attributes of offenses or their detection—characteristics such as types of offenses and offenders, strategies for promoting investment, victimization, wittingness, cost, scope of participation, offense duration, timeliness and accuracy of intelligence, and the like.[9] The analysis yielded

9. The percentage of the catch of each of fourteen refined detection strategies that possess each of the fifty-three attributes was calculated. (A fifteenth strategy, employer referrals, was omitted from the analysis because its N of four was prohibitively small.) Each of the fifty-three cases therefore had scores ranging from 0 to 100 on fourteen detection

a two-factor solution, which accounted for 84 percent of the variation in detection strategy.[10]

Figure 5.1 presents the rotated factor loadings generated by this procedure. The considerable spread of the plots of detection strategies provides visual proof that strategies differ in their catches, some of them substantially. The figure also displays the proximity of detection methods defined by their catch. Offenses typically detected by SEC scrutiny of filings and those detected by referrals from federal agencies are as different as offenses uncovered in any other way. These two detection strategies net very different offenses. Other detection strategies plotted more proximately—state and federal agencies or actual and solicited investors, for example—uncover offenses that share many common characteristics. And the figure reveals other strategies whose coordinates are not especially proximate to those of any other—market surveillance, for example. These isolated strategies net a more distinctive catch. The diversity of the SEC investigative caseload would be more seriously impaired by abandonment of isolated strategies such as market surveillance than by abandonment of closely surrounded strategies such as disclosures by solicited investors.[11]

Figure 5.1 helps to summarize the many dimensions on which the catch of the detection strategies vary and to assemble the narrow perspectives they provide into a larger portrait. The detection strategies are arranged pretty much as we might have predicted. Plotted across the top of the figure, with high loadings on factor 2, are the detection strategies of filings, inspections, and disclosures by corporate representatives and self-regulatory agencies. These strategies share more than statistical similarity. They tend to uncover offenses that violate SEC technical regulations, engaged in primarily by broker-dealers and by offender participants limited in number and in scope (reflecting the involvement of a single individual role and single kind of organization). The offenses so detected are unlikely to victimize directly or to incur any economic costs and tend to be short in duration. Finally, these strategies often intercept

variables. These percentage scores were standardized and used to compute a correlation matrix between the fourteen detection variables, which was entered into the factor analysis. The output of the analysis therefore provided factors that reduced the set of fourteen variables and provided loadings and factor scores for each detection strategy. The factor analysis procedure utilized iteration and varimax rotation.

10. A third factor, which explained an additional 5 percent of the variation, had high factor loadings only on market surveillance.

11. The reactive/proactive intelligence distinction bears no relationship to the arrangement of detection strategies in figure 5.1: proactive strategies are plotted at both ends of the distribution as well as in the center. Previous analyses have demonstrated that it is not the locus of initiative—whether intelligence originates inside or outside the SEC—that determines the catch, but rather the locus of intelligence and its access to the securities world (among other factors).

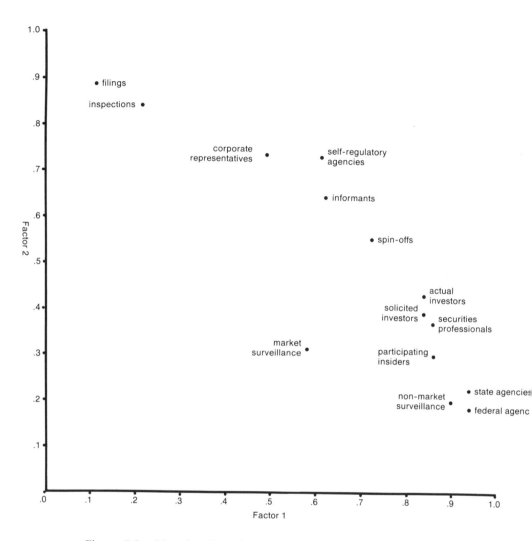

Figure 5.1. Mapping Detection Strategies (Factor Loadings)

offenses soon after their inception, generating a catch of relatively recent offenses. The catch of this cluster of strategies is distinctive. It includes substantively different offenses of limited impact engaged in by a different category of offender. Were these strategies abandoned, the SEC would by and large lose all access to the nonfraudulent offenses of broker-dealers and to all violations of the regulations it has developed to control its registrants.

The remaining detection strategies generate offense catches that primarily involve securities fraud, with at least limited victimization and economic cost. But strategies within this group differ significantly in their respective catches. Some (actual investors and participating insiders) are most likely to uncover misappropriations, others (solicited investors, securities professionals, non-market surveillance, and referrals from state and federal agencies) to uncover fraudulent schemes that couple registration violations with misrepresentations, and still others (disclosures by informants, market surveillance, and spin-offs), with somewhat lower loadings on factor 1 and higher loadings on factor 2, to uncover the more subtle offenses of self-dealing and stock manipulation. Because of the subtlety of these offenses, the latter strategies are also more likely to generate inaccurate intelligence.

The catches of these strategies plotted in the lower right-hand corner of figure 5.1 differ in other significant respects as well. With regard to offenders, some strategies uncover the misdeeds of the corporate upper class and others those of its under class, some those of stock issuers and others of stockbrokers, some registered issuers and others unregistered issuers, some larger organizations and others smaller ones, and some offender constellations of substantial scope and others constellations of limited scope. Some strategies uncover offenses that usually victimize investors and others that rarely do, some that touch significant numbers of victims and others relatively few victims, some that incur substantial economic costs and others for which cost is minor or nonexistent, some that continue for a substantial period of time and others of relatively short duration. These strategies vary as well in the accuracy of their intelligence and in their capacity to nip offenses in the bud.

These ancillary offense attributes are distributed in some predictable ways. Surveillance strategies are more likely to uncover offenses larger in scope and therefore more visible—with larger organizations, registered offenders, diverse organizational involvements, and larger numbers of victims and economic costs. Violations detected by offense participants— actual investors and participating insiders—are quite different and generally smaller in scope (such as misappropriation) and they inhere in smaller and usually single organizations.

Intelligence derived from actual involvement—that is, referred by ac-

tual investors and participating insiders—tends to be accurate. Intelligence generated by market surveillance—based on marginal access to illegality—is considerably less accurate. Because surveillance involves public disclosure of securities information, usually stock quotations or advertisements in the mass media to induce investor participation, this strategy tends to uncover illegality relatively early. The circumstances that permit investor and insider disclosures come much later—after investors discover they have been victimized or after insiders have had time to develop feelings of betrayal, fear, or disenchantment. Offenses referred by these investigative sources tend to be old and stale.

Although the contrast between surveillance and actual investors or insiders is most interesting theoretically, there are other contrasts among the detection strategies that are empirically real and significant. The catches of two detection strategies may be virtually identical in almost every respect, but one may detect offenses of stockbrokers and another stock issuers, one registrants and the other nonregistrants, one offenses with substantial impact and another those of limited impact. Few of the strategies, however proximate on figure 5.1 and however similar on more qualitative offense indicators, are easily replaceable or their catches truly redundant. Each provides a unique perspective on the world of illicit securities transactions. Each fills a different cell (or series of cells) on some hypothetical matrix defined by the diverse offenses and offenders over which the SEC has enforcement jurisdiction.

The overall catch of some of these strategies is, of course, more significant than the catch of others and is therefore more worthy of enforcement priority. But there are important tensions in features of the detection strategies, even among those with more significant output, that create serious trade-offs and require difficult choices. Before evaluating these trade-offs and choices, however, we need to learn what happens after securities violations are first discovered—how they are investigated, how SEC enforcers exercise discretion in taking legal action, how offenses are prosecuted, and what the outcomes of legal action are.

6

SEC Enforcement: From Detection to Prosecution

Previous chapters have focused attention on securities offenses and on their earliest encounter with SEC investigators—their detection. But the history of a securities offense rarely ends there. Rather, detection inaugurates a new stage in the course of an offense and a new sequence of encounters with investigators. These encounters range from investigatory activities to the delivery of sanctions, experiences sometimes of greater duration and complexity than those of the illicit activities themselves. It is these postdetection activities for which the Securities and Exchange Commission is known and on which its reputation is largely based.

The strategies of observation, disclosure, and artifactual exploration, which identify the opportunities for detection, also delimit investigatory tactics. Just as the orchestration of securities offenses (the choice and number of co-offenders, patterns of victimization, the social location of illicit activities, the development of promotional strategies, and so on) affects opportunities for different detection strategies, it shapes the investigative process as well. It determines which members of the securities world—suspected offenders, business associates, or investors—are likely to be good sources of evidence, which records or documents should be subpoenaed, which kinds of artifacts that might implicate offenders should be pursued and examined. And it affects the scope and success of investigatory effort. Many of the correlates of SEC detection strategies—types of violation, scope of the offense, characteristics of offenders, offense timing and duration, offense impact—are also related to the style, techniques, and scope of investigation.

Many of these offense characteristics are also related to case disposition and decisions about whether to take legal action, what form it should take, and what sanctions, if any, should be imposed. But the basis of the

correlation of offense organization to disposition is different from that to investigation. The latter relationship is derived from constraints on information and hence on intelligence imposed by the organization of behavior. The former derives from the fact that differential organization is also related to offense seriousness, impact, staleness or urgency, inferences about the intent, willfulness, or connivance of offenders or about the innocence or gullibility of victims—factors central to decisions about the appropriateness and severity of punishment.

THE NATURE OF INVESTIGATIVE WORK

Federal securities statutes authorize the SEC to conduct investigations to determine whether these laws have been violated. In most cases, investigations are private and the materials gathered confidential to insure the cooperation of witnesses and to protect persons about whom unfounded or unsubstantiated charges have been made. The SEC institutes and dockets an average of 313 investigations annually, ranging from 145 in 1947 to 674 in 1935, the latter figure of somewhat questionable reliability. In recent years, the investigative caseload has hovered just over three hundred.[1]

Surprisingly little is known about the conduct of SEC investigations. The SEC is a low-profile agency. Its annual reports and assorted publications reveal little about the organization of its work. The agency has had few scandals and the attendant journalistic and congressional scrutiny that follow in their wake. Its current and former employees have been sufficiently loyal or insufficiently literary or entrepreneurial to generate the exposés common in other regulatory agency settings.[2] Of course, some popular accounts of notorious securities offenses have been written, for example, concerning the Equity Funding and Homestake Oil frauds, which include in their narratives (usually to heighten the suspense) some accounting of the involvement of SEC investigators in the latter stages of these swindles.[3] But we should distrust these accounts provided by agency outsiders, in part because of their outsider status and incomplete access to information, in part because of their often self-interested relationship to the narrative. Even if accurate, they are clearly not representative of everyday investigative practice. Unfortunately, there is little in the public domain from which we can learn about the nature of SEC investigative work.

1. These figures are derived from SEC annual reports. In contrast, the Internal Revenue Service opened over nine thousand tax fraud investigations in the fiscal year 1979 (U.S. Department of the Treasury 1979, 175).
2. But see Ferrara (1971) and Mathews (1975).
3. See, for example, Jones (1938), Patrick (1972), Dirks and Gross (1974), Soble and Dallos (1975), Maxa (1977), and McClintick (1977).

The description provided here is derived from several sources: (1) systematic observation of the headquarters and one of the SEC regional offices for about six weeks in the summer of 1976 and less systematic observation for ten months the following year; (2) interviews and informal conversations with then present and former agency personnel; (3) participation in a week-long Enforcement Training Program for new SEC staff; and (4) materials in non-public SEC investigative records. Several hundred persons across the country work on SEC enforcement matters at any one time, and several thousand others have done so over the past half-century. I have observed or spoken with only a small portion of them, though I have indirectly witnessed the work of hundreds of others while scrutinizing the memos, briefs, and documents they prepared.

THE OFFICES

Investigations are conducted by the Division of Enforcement in SEC headquarters as well as by nine regional offices located in New York, Boston, Washington, Atlanta, Chicago, Fort Worth, Denver, Los Angeles, and Seattle and by six branch offices. With over two hundred staffers (about 11 percent of all SEC personnel), the New York regional office is by far the largest. Six percent of all agency staff work in the Chicago regional office, 5 percent in Los Angeles, 4 percent in Washington, and 2–3 percent in the other regional offices.[4]

Very little is known about the SEC regional offices. Annual reports, for example, list only the names of administrators and addresses of the regional offices. They do not even enumerate their staff (my estimates were derived from non-public records) or their budget, let alone furnish information on their workload, problems, or priorities. Because of the informational blackout surrounding the regional offices and the prominence, visibility, and drama of the activities of the SEC headquarters office, outsiders often fail to recognize the existence of the regional offices or fail to differentiate between regulatory activity arising from the regions and from the headquarters. But, at least with respect to the historical legacy of enforcement, most of the activity has been in the regions. The popular image of the SEC as being almost synonymous with its Division of Enforcement, and of Washington, D.C., being the site of all the action in securities regulation—whatever its accuracy with regard to contemporary practice—truly fails to characterize the historical record.

Older SEC annual reports as well as other documentary material read like a broken record: "The regional offices form the front line of

---

4. These estimates were derived from a 1977 SEC in-house telephone directory. I have been unable to find any public documents presenting regional office staff allocations.

enforcement work" (*The Work of the Securities and Exchange Commission* 1941, 9) or "The primary responsibility for investigation rests with the Commission's regional administrators whose investigators conduct most of the field work" (Annual Report 1951, 154). Prior to the 1960s, enforcement activities conducted by the regional offices were supervised and coordinated by a skeleton staff in the headquarters Division of Trading and Exchanges (which also had responsibility for the regulation of broker-dealers, supervision of the stock exchanges and other self-regulatory agencies, and market surveillance).

The home office, as this unit of enforcement coordinators was called, served primarily as a clearinghouse. Its staff tracked regional office cases, kept the commission apprised of regional enforcement activities and secured commission authorization of enforcement action, assigned personnel to assist in substantial regional office investigations, and spent a considerable amount of time answering letters from the public. In contrast to the prestige accorded to contemporary SEC enforcers, attorneys in the early 1950s took positions with the home office hoping that they would lead to more prestigious positions in the SEC Division of Corporation Finance.[5]

Material in annual reports suggests that where matters of public interest or urgency dictated, the home office would initiate its own investigation. The rarity of this practice is shown in table 6.1, which displays investigative caseload by regional office over time.[6] Prior to 1958, the home office had docketed 91 investigations, in contrast with figures in the regional offices ranging from 417 in Atlanta to 3,035 in New York. Home office investigations constituted at most only 1 percent of all docketed investigations during this period.[7]

Although the data clearly demonstrate the relative unimportance (quantitatively) of the home office in investigative conduct, it also portrays an important trend. The office dramatically and consistently increased its relative caseload from 1 percent prior to 1953 to 15 percent after 1972. Annual reports and interview materials document this trend as well. Beginning in 1958, reports refer to a "Special Investigations Unit" in the

5. Interview with SEC enforcement attorney, December 16, 1977.
6. These data were drawn from a nonpublic SEC computer file created for administrative purposes.
7. Indeed, this figure and that characterizing the overall caseload of the home office are actually inflated. In many instances, joint investigations conducted in several regional offices were consolidated into a single case and assigned a home office docket number, despite the absence of any direct involvement of the home office staff in investigative work. Fifty-three percent of the home office cases in the sample pertained to matters assigned other regional office docket numbers as well. Probably only about half to two-thirds of all investigations allocated to the home office actually involved investigative work conducted by that office.

Table 6.1. Regional Office Investigative Caseload[a]

Regional Office	Pre–1948[b] (N)	(%)	1948–52 (N)	(%)	1953–57 (N)	(%)	1958–62 (N)	(%)	1963–67 (N)	(%)	1968–72 (N)	(%)	Post–1972[b] (N)	(%)	Total 1934–76 (N)	(%)	Total 1948–72 (N)	(%)
Atlanta	(299)	4	(51)	5	(67)	6	(95)	4	(87)	4	(114)	6	(85)	13	(798)	5	(414)	5
Boston	(398)	5	(37)	4	(57)	5	(109)	5	(119)	6	(119)	7	(29)	5	(868)	5	(441)	5
Chicago	(1365)	18	(132)	13	(88)	8	(182)	9	(191)	9	(186)	11	(67)	10	(2211)	14	(779)	10
Denver	(677)	9	(101)	10	(156)	15	(156)	7	(217)	10	(127)	7	(35)	5	(1469)	9	(757)	9
Fort Worth	(811)	11	(135)	13	(108)	10	(143)	7	(153)	7	(157)	9	(47)	7	(1554)	10	(696)	9
New York	(2466)	33	(316)	30	(253)	24	(817)	38	(624)	30	(393)	22	(85)	13	(4954)	30	(2403)	30
Seattle	(432)	6	(113)	11	(142)	14	(231)	11	(245)	12	(200)	11	(45)	7	(1408)	9	(931)	12
San Francisco/ Los Angeles	(559)	7	(67)	6	(69)	7	(163)	8	(143)	7	(130)	7	(75)	12	(1206)	7	(572)	7
Washington	(490)	6	(80)	8	(75)	7	(123)	6	(144)	7	(159)	9	(76)	12	(1147)	7	(581)	7
Home office	(55)	1	(14)	1	(22)	2	(104)	5	(181)	9	(183)	10	(96)	15	(655)	4	(504)	6
Total	(7552)		(1046)		(1037)		(2123)		(2104)		(1768)		(640)		(16,270)		(8078)	

Note: Percentages are computed vertically down the columns.
a. Based on a listing of closed docketed investigations.
b. Unreliable.

Division of Trading and Exchanges, called the "Office of Special Investigations" (1961), "Branch of Special Investigations, Trial and Enforcement" (1961), and "Office of Enforcement" (1962) in subsequent years. This unit was involved in some special investigations of boiler-room operations in the New York area, followed by a major investigation of a scandal that erupted at the American Stock Exchange (AMEX) in the late 1950s and early 1960s. It became clear from these investigative efforts that the SEC lacked the capacity for quick response to pressing matters, offenses of national scope, or offenses of depth, complexity, and breadth that were not being picked up by the regional offices. The home office was the natural setting for developing such an investigative capacity; the investigation of the AMEX scandal provided the impetus.

Shortly thereafter, home office personnel were involved in the preparation of the "Special Study of the Securities Markets," a massive investigation of the adequacy of the national securities exchanges and associations in protecting investors, ordered by Congress in September 1961 and completed in mid-1963. A staff of about sixty-five persons was assembled for the special study. Many of them were subsequently available for enforcement work. By many accounts, the completion of the study marked the emergence of the home office as a significant contributor to SEC enforcement.[8]

In the ensuing years, a staff of specialists assembled in the home office to take on investigations of more complex patterns of violation (for example, those with complicated accounting irregularities), multiregional or international violations, offenders with connections to organized crime, or offenses reflecting novel interpretations of the securities laws or novel enforcement targets. By the late 1960s, half of the home office's Division of Trading and Markets (as the Division of Trading and Exchanges was later called) staff were involved in enforcement. A formal reorganization of the SEC in 1972 acknowledged this development and strengthened the home office's enforcement role by setting up a separate enforcement division. By 1976, the Division of Enforcement staff comprised about 15 percent of the staff of the headquarters office of the commission.

In a period of less than ten years, the home office developed from a small, reactive, caretaker office to a large, specialized, proactive, self-initiating office, constantly expanding the boundaries of enforcement policy and serving as a leader and model for the enforcement activities of the regions. Even so, home office enforcement activity is overshadowed by that of the regions.

The regional offices have been a significant force in the definition and shaping of SEC enforcement policy, both qualitatively and quantitatively.

8. Interviews with SEC enforcement attorneys and a commissioner, August 10, 1976; August 16, 1976; December 16, 1977.

SEC enforcers liken the regional office to the cop on the beat, taking in anything and everything encountered in the region.[9] Thus, regional office conduct is a reflection of the norms, concerns, and activities of regional constituencies. One SEC observer has noted, for example, that "aggressive sales practices which are standard in Los Angeles would evoke cries of horror in Boston. Trading practices in penny mining stocks that are considered a normal aspect of speculation in the Northwest would probably be looked upon as outright manipulation in other parts of the country" (Ratner 1971, 590). In addition to their norms and business practices, regional constituencies are unique and idiosyncratic because of geographical patterns in the distribution of securities professionals and public corporations. For example, most of the investigations of oil and gas companies are conducted in the Fort Worth regional office, gold and silver mining companies in Denver or Seattle, real estate and land-related securities in California or Atlanta, and brokerage firms and stock exchange listed securities in New York.

SEC regional offices are so distinctive that after several months of coding SEC investigations, I was usually able to guess the regional office conducting an investigation from characteristics of the alleged offenders under investigation, their modi operandi and styles of violation, their strategies for recruitment of victims and the kinds of victims they touched, and especially by the kinds of investigative strategies and practices adopted and enforcement priorities articulated by regional office personnel. Sometimes the trademarks were more esoteric, for example, the involvement of other law enforcement or self-regulatory agencies in investigative activity, the way in which an offense was detected, the kind of evidence gathered, the amount of time it took to complete the investigation, or the quality of care taken in documenting investigative activities. Even though these investigations span twenty-five years and reflect the efforts of hundreds and perhaps thousands of individuals, regional offices and their constituencies leave such a distinctive mark on investigative caseload that they can often be blindly identified.

THE INVESTIGATORS

SEC enforcers are an odd breed to the criminologist, familiar with their counterparts in other law enforcement agencies—police officers, FBI agents, vice squads, drug enforcement agents, and the like. In many respects, SEC investigators more closely resemble their adversaries than their colleagues in other agencies. The investigators are predominantly attorneys. Many of those I encountered were young, briefly passing through the agency on their way to private practice. They dressed like the

9. Interviews with SEC enforcement attorneys, April 30, 1976; August 10, 1976; March 21, 1977.

individuals they regulated, the men in three-piece-suits, the women in conservative attire. They enforced the law primarily from their offices, pouring over documents, scrutinizing stock data, negotiating on the telephone, writing memos, meeting constantly with coworkers and supervisors. Their law enforcement technology included books, telephones, word processors, calculators, and computers. Their cramped offices and the hallways that surround them were piled high with boxes of subpoenaed documents and work papers. Enforcers occasionally ventured from their offices to take testimony, gather documents, or make a court appearance. But, with the exception of a group in the regional offices who are always out routinely inspecting brokerage and investment advisory firms, most enforcers remain in their offices, passing their days with their compatriots rather than their adversaries.

At any one time, the attorneys might be working on a half dozen investigations, with responsibilities shared with several other attorneys and sometimes a non-lawyer investigator or accountant. On occasion, their investigative caseload is generated by their own inquiries, discoveries, leads, or detection efforts, but usually cases are assigned by superiors— branch chiefs, assistant or associate directors, regional office administrators, or the deputy director or director of the Division of Enforcement in Washington. The typical investigation continues for many months, sometimes years, with the amount of investigator involvement varying, as enforcers await "stonewalling" and subpoena compliance or litigation. It is rare for investigators to be working on their full caseload at any one time. Rather, most investigations sit on back burners while one or two are actively pursued. Most attorneys work their cases from beginning to end, from investigation through litigation. The SEC has a small special trial unit, but routine litigation is handled by the investigative attorneys themselves. Where investigations are long and complex, there may be some investigator turnover and greater specialization.

The SEC investigators I got to know during the mid-1970s were hardworking and committed. Their dedication was dramatically underscored by the eerily empty Washington streets—deserted by a far less devoted group of government employees rushing out of the city at the earliest possible moment—I would discover after SEC enforcers called it a day. Staff morale was extraordinarily high. The vigorous enforcement program had captured the interest and imagination of investigators. Conversations over lunch, coffee, and after-work drinks were filled with the exploits of newly discovered offenders and the legal strategies and maneuvers that were being developed to control them. SEC enforcers were often heady from their newfound power (Karmel 1982, 71). These young attorneys, many of them only a few years out of law school, were dictating to the top executives of major corporations. They had the reputation of

being young, bright, serious, ambitious, "hot-shot kids out of Harvard" (Bruck 1980, 18) who could be "rigidly and even arrogantly moral" (Karmel 1982, 73). They made the SEC exciting, energized, frenetic, and unique in a lethargic federal bureaucracy.

THE GATHERING OF EVIDENCE

When parties regulated by the commission, particularly broker-dealers, are the subject of investigation or possess relevant evidence, SEC investigators have the power to inspect their offices and compel delivery of books and records. This power is not available, however, for other members of the securities world, offenders and nonoffenders alike, with no formal regulatory relationship to the agency. And one can imagine that because of fear of incrimination, embarrassment, betrayal of friends and business associates, or simple inconvenience, these other evidentiary sources may not be inclined to cooperate with SEC investigators.

It is for this potential disinclination that the formal order of investigation is a corrective. With the formal order, SEC commissioners empower designated investigators to issue subpoenas for the production of documents and the appearance of witnesses and to take sworn testimony. Formal orders are restricted to a particular investigative matter and granted only when necessary evidence cannot be obtained in any other way. In 32 percent of the cases in my sample, the commission issued a formal order of investigation. Since SEC investigators can compel the cooperation of broker-dealers without a formal order, this proportion was lower when only broker-dealers were the subject of investigation (18 percent) than when stock issuers and their principals were investigated (41 percent). With the greater complexity of SEC investigations in recent years, formal orders have been increasingly used. In the fiscal year 1980, formal orders were issued in 58 percent of all investigations opened.

During their training, SEC enforcement staff are introduced to a diverse list of evidentiary sources: traditional corporate books and records; records of stock transactions; bank and tax records; testimony of informants, offenders, their associates, and their victims; SEC records and filings; records of other state, federal, and self-regulatory agencies (that is, Justice Department, FBI, CIA, State Department, Social Security Administration, Postal Service, congressional committees, state securities commissions, police departments, stock exchanges, National Association of Securities Dealers, and others); court, real estate, credit card, hotel, airline, and marriage records; newspaper and periodical materials; *Who's Who* and other directories; exposés; wills; and the like.[10]

10.   This list is derived from lectures I attended during the SEC Enforcement Training Conference, Washington, D.C., July 26–30, 1976.

In fact, investigatory files reveal a smaller list of evidentiary sources typically pursued by agency investigators. Most frequently (in 77 percent of all cases), the subjects of investigation themselves and their coconspirators are questioned, or their books, records, and minutes inspected (61 percent of all cases). Almost as frequently (59 percent), their customers, clients, investors, or victims are questioned, either through direct interview or mailed questionnaires. And testimony from business associates of the subjects of investigation—corporate officers, directors, employees, brokers, attorneys, consultants—is also solicited (53 percent). Somewhat less frequently, previous SEC records and filings are examined (48 percent), other social control agencies are consulted (42 percent),[11] or the premises and books and records of brokerage firms are examined (36 percent). Although many less obvious sources of evidence may be pursued—bank, tax, telephone, mail, and credit card records, stock market trading data, newspapers and magazines, journalists, mining engineers and other specialists—they are pursued infrequently, none of them employed in more than 15 percent of the cases. The sum of these percentages considerably exceeds 100 because most investigations (90 percent) rely on more than one evidentiary source. About half of the investigations examined more than four different kinds of evidence.

As is to be expected, different kinds of evidence are pursued in the investigation of different kinds of violations. For example, the questioning of business associates is much more common in the investigation of stock manipulation, self-dealing, and offenses coupling misrepresentation with nonregistration than in other violations. Investors are questioned and corporate books and records examined most often when offenses with some combination of misrepresentation, registration violations, and misappropriation are investigated. Corporate books and records are also scrutinized during investigations of self-dealing. Brokerage records are examined when there are allegations of misappropriation or stock manipulation; bank records for self-dealing and misappropriation alone or coupled with misrepresentation and nonregistration; tax records

11. The social control agencies consulted and the percentage of investigations in the sample in which each agency was consulted include: other federal regulatory or criminal justice agencies (7 percent); state securities commissions (9 percent); other state regulatory or criminal justice agencies (5 percent); self-regulatory agencies, such as stock exchanges, the National Association of Securities Dealers, Better Business Bureaus (6 percent); foreign agencies (2 percent); corporate receivers (2 percent); and a mixture of these sources (9 percent). The nature of this interagency collaboration varied considerably. It ranged from SEC staff simply asking these agencies for information, records, or filings, to requests to self-regulatory agencies to make independent investigations, to agencies turning over an extensive investigatory record to SEC enforcement staff, to full investigatory collaboration between the SEC and other agencies. In most cases, interagency investigatory relationships were superficial, informal, and only marginally important to the full scope of investigatory effort.

for self-dealing; SEC records for technical violations. Other social control agencies are most often consulted for investigations of stock manipulation, self-dealing, misappropriation, misrepresentation coupled with registration violations, and both coupled with misappropriation. The pursuit of evidence also varies by characteristics of the offenders under investigation.

THE SCOPE OF INVESTIGATIVE EFFORT

Most investigations are located within a single SEC office. But for 26 percent of the cases in the sample, investigation was conducted multi-regionally (usually in two different regions). Multiregional investigation is often required by securities violations that are national in scope. The perpetrators of an offense may be located in Florida and their victims in the Pacific Northwest. Or the offenders may be moving around the country. Or the manipulated stock of a Texas corporation may have been traded on the New York Stock Exchange. In order to fully and expeditiously investigate offenses of this kind, interoffice cooperation may be necessary. Among cases in the sample, regional offices most often collaborated with the New York office, undoubtedly because of its proximity and easy access to the country's major stock exchanges and brokerage firms. Collaboration between the home office and the New York regional office was particularly common. Most other collaborative relationships primarily involved offices in adjacent regions, reflecting the way in which patterns of illegality and of victimization spread geographically.

Interregional collaboration provides one perspective on the scope of SEC investigation. Another is the extent of actual investigative effort expended on a given case. Three different indicators of investigative effort can be derived from the data. The first measures the sheer number of types of evidence (that is, offenders, business associates, investors, books and records, and so on) pursued in the investigation. About one fifth of the investigations in the sample pursued one or two evidentiary sources, 30 percent three or four, 32 percent five or six, and 17 percent seven or more sources.

A second indicator measures the time interval from the institution of investigative activities to their completion.[12] Docketed investigations in the sample ranged in length from one day to more than eleven years. The mean length of investigation was 469 days, the median, 287 days. Twenty-eight percent of the investigations were completed in less than three

---

12. It was impossible to devise a refined temporal measure—for example, some estimate of investigators' hours—from records in investigative files. The measure of duration is a gross and sometimes misleading proxy measure. An investigation of longer duration may not always indicate more substantial effort. On occasion, it may reflect a low-priority investigation that has spent considerable periods of time on investigators' back burners.

months, 57 percent within one year, 80 percent within two years. Seven percent of the investigations were still ongoing after four years.

A third indicator of the scope of investigative activity reflects such factors as the number of investors interviewed, the number of books and records subpoenaed, the amount of testimony taken, the range of evidentiary materials pursued, and an estimate of the number of attorneys, accountants, and other investigators utilized. The measure differentiates between tremendous (2 percent of the cases), significant (9 percent), average (60 percent), and minor (27 percent) investigations and those based on no investigative activity at all, simply extensions of other cases (2 percent).[13]

Just as the quality of investigative effort varies by offense characteristics, so too does its quantity. The differences are clear and powerful. Securities violations, arrayed in increasing order of investigative effort on all three indicators, include technical violations, registration violations alone, misrepresentations alone, misrepresentations coupled with nonregistration, misappropriations alone, misappropriation coupled with both misrepresentation and nonregistration, self-dealing, and stock manipulation. Not surprisingly, this ordering mirrors that of the typical degree of subtlety and complexity of these offenses. Seven percent of the investigations of technical violations pursued six or more evidentiary sources; 5 percent continued for more than a year and a half; and 1 percent were judged significant. In contrast, the figures for stock manipulation were 58 percent, 38 percent, and 22 percent, respectively.

The greatest amount of effort (reflected in all three indicators) was expended investigating stock issuers, especially those conspiring with brokers, six or more offenders representing different organizational positions, the conspiracy of several kinds of organizations, offenses enduring for more than four years and those ongoing at the time of detection, and offenses touching more than one hundred victims with costs exceeding $1,000,000. Offenses of greater complexity, greater scope, and greater impact are those that require the largest expenditure of investigative resources.

---

13. Despite the weaknesses of each of these indicators—the number of evidentiary sources, the duration of investigatory activity, and judgments of scope of effort—they tell much the same story. The measures are highly intercorrelated. Six percent of the investigations judged minor pursued six or more evidentiary sources, in contrast to 78 percent of those judged tremendous or significant. Seven percent of the investigations judged minor continued for more than one-and-a-half years, compared to 62 percent of those judged tremendous or significant. Finally, 18 percent of the investigations completed in less than three months, in contrast to 56 percent of those spanning more than one-and-a-half years, also scrutinized six or more sources of evidence; 46 percent of the investigations with less than three sources of evidence, compared to 12 percent of those with six or more sources, were completed in less than three months.

THE DISPOSITION OF SEC INVESTIGATIONS

THE DECISION TO TAKE FORMAL LEGAL ACTION

At some point in the course of an investigation, a determination of the likelihood that violations did occur and, if so, of the desirability of taking formal legal action is made. For 15 percent of the docketed investigations in the sample, no violations were found. Suspicions of market manipulation or investor complaints, for example, were simply unfounded. These investigations were closed without formal action. Another 40 percent of the investigations were closed without formal legal action despite the discovery of violations.

It would be impractical and counterproductive if every instance in which some violative conduct was uncovered was subject to formal proceedings. It is for that reason that the securities laws vest the commission with discretion in the decision to proceed formally against securities violators. Among the alternatives to formal proceedings, the commission may refer the matter to other agencies (it did so in 9 percent of the unprosecuted violations) or it may secure informal remedies (25 percent). About a third of the cases referred were sent to self-regulatory agencies, about two-thirds to other government agencies. The informal remedies secured include public admissions of violation by offenders (4 percent of the unprosecuted violations); agreements either to register with the SEC or to withdraw or cancel registration (12 percent); disclosure-related agreements (amended or supplemental reporting or conducting special inquiries or audits) (2 percent); the undertaking of remedial behavior by offenders (instituting new internal corporate procedures, restricting business practices, suspending or barring business activity, dismissing employees, appointing a receiver) (6 percent); actual dissolution of the offending firm (1 percent); and disgorgement of profits, rescission, or restitution (8 percent).

In some of the cases in which formal legal action *was* taken, SEC enforcers also secured informal remedies or referred information to other social control agencies. But these outcomes were much less typical of the prosecuted offenses (found among only 16 percent) than of the unprosecuted ones (34 percent).[14] It would appear that undertaking informal remedies does protect some offenders from formal prosecution. The data indicate that voluntary admissions of violation, undertaking of remedial behavior, and disgorgement, rescission, or restitution of illicitly

---

14. The term *prosecution* is used in this context to describe the decision to take formal legal action of any kind (civil, administrative, or criminal) against securities violators. It is not used here in its more narrow and common legal usage pertaining exclusively to criminal dispositions.

secured monies do spare some offenders from prosecution. Of course, many of these unprosecuted offenses differ from their prosecuted counterparts in more significant respects than the presence of informal remedies. Whether the undertaking of informal remedies is a strategic device employed by offenders to insulate themselves from prosecution or a strategic lever employed by enforcers to compel corrective action by marginal offenders involved in otherwise unprosecutable violations is an open question, for which data are not available.

Whatever the significance of informal undertakings for prosecutorial immunity, it accounts for only a minority of cases spared formal legal action. About two-thirds of these violations were not prosecuted despite the absence of any referrals or informal agreements. Annual reports and instructional materials developed for new SEC staff discuss some of the factors considered in the decision to take formal legal action against securities violators. These include whether the activity is continuing or likely to recur, the recency of the violations, the nature of the offense, whether it is the kind of scheme that poses the greatest threat to investors, whether offenders are about to abscond with victim funds, the need for remedial action, the impact of illegality on the public, the number and type of investors, the amount of money lost, the willfulness, inadvertence, and culpability of offenders, other offender characteristics (whether they are still in the securities business, chronic violators, associated with organized crime), concern for legal precedent, and whether the case would be a suitable vehicle for the clarification of existing rules.

A more realistic perspective on the issues is provided by an examination of actual SEC investigations. Data were gathered on the justifications for the decision not to take formal legal action against securities violators. The justifications found in investigative records may in some cases be incomplete or inaccurate. But in only 3 percent of all cases were no justifications given or was it impossible to ascertain the rationale for nonprosecution. On average, investigators articulated two and a half justifications for nonprosecution per case. Therefore, the sum of percentages reported below exceeds 100.

Most often, SEC enforcers decline to prosecute securities offenses because of informal settlements or legal action taken elsewhere. In 45 percent of the cases, offenders were subject to private civil suits or legal action by some federal, state, or self-regulatory agency. For another 14 percent, the offense was being resolved by restitution, other corrective behavior, or other kinds of settlements. And for another 14 percent, jurisdictional problems dictated that the matter be proceeded against elsewhere; at least two-thirds of these cases were subsequently referred by the SEC to other agencies.

Another common justification (44 percent of all cases) for the decision

against legal action pertained to matters of equity and other temporal features of the offense and its investigation—staleness of the offense, expiration of the statute of limitations, the cessation of the illegal activity, and so forth. Three other justifications, each used in about a fifth to a quarter of the cases, pertained to (1) characteristics of the offenders— they were defunct, dead, elderly, or naive—or of their victims—they were sophisticated or somewhat culpable (together reflecting 27 percent of the cases); (2) problems of evidence—its insufficiency, the exhaustion of investigatory resources, the lack of good witnesses, or the difficulty of proving fraud or willfulness (24 percent); or (3) the seriousness, extent of victimization, or cost of the offense (22 percent).

Some of the less common justifications pointed to the fact that the offense was not willful (10 percent), that offenders did not personally benefit from their conduct (3 percent), that the legal issues involved were technical, ambiguous, or novel (6 percent), that the case had little jury appeal or little appeal to the U.S. attorney responsible for criminal prosecution (3 percent), or that the decision to take formal action would constitute an inappropriate drain on agency investigative resources (5 percent). In three cases, the SEC commissioners refused to approve staff recommendations for formal proceedings, the rationale for which could not be ascertained.

Although the justifications intuitively make sense and correspond to other formal statements of the rationale for prosecution, the question remains whether justifications actually correspond to the characteristics of these offenses. Are cases that are prosecuted or sanctioned elsewhere really less likely to be subject to formal legal action by the SEC? How about stale cases, those of limited severity, those with particular constellations of offenders and victims? These questions can be answered by looking beyond the justifications and comparing the characteristics of prosecuted and unprosecuted violations.

For cases in the sample, the decision not to take formal legal action was most common where offenses were small in scope—with few offenders, representing a single organizational role, few victims, and little money at stake.[15] Justifications for nonprosecution based on staleness or equity

15. About three-fifths of the offenses involving a single offender were not prosecuted, in contrast to about a quarter of those with more than six alleged offenders. Forty-eight percent of the cases whose offenders all represented the same individual role were not prosecuted, compared to 37 percent where two or more roles were represented. There were no differences in prosecutorial likelihood, however, by diversity in the kinds of offending organizations represented. Seventy-six percent of the offenses with aggregate costs of $5,000 or less were not prosecuted, in contrast to 30 percent of those with costs exceeding $1,000,000. Forty-eight percent of the offenses generating five hundred or fewer victims were not prosecuted, compared to 28 percent of those touching more than five hundred victims.

were borne out by the data as well. Legal action was not taken against 47 percent of all offenses still ongoing at the time of investigation, compared to 58 percent of violations that had already ceased. However, data supporting the hypothesis that non-SEC proceedings and sanctions diminish the likelihood of formal legal action are inconclusive.

Finally, prosecutorial likelihood is related to qualities of the offense and offenders. The undertaking of legal action varied considerably by violation committed. Technical violations were significantly less likely than the other offenses to be spared legal action. Only 17 percent of these offenses were not prosecuted, in contrast to 40 percent of the misappropriations, 47 percent of the stock manipulations, 52 percent of the self-dealing schemes, 55 percent of offenses with both registration violations and misrepresentations, 60 percent of the misrepresentations alone, and 72 percent of the registration violations alone. With the exception of technical violations, offenses increase their vulnerability to prosecution as they increase in complexity. Only a quarter of the offenses with one or two discrete violations were subject to legal action, in contrast to more than three-quarters of those with more than ten discrete violations.

Because the violation of SEC technical regulations (which primarily pertain to brokerage firms) is so vulnerable to legal action, broker-dealers are considerably more likely to be prosecuted than other kinds of offenders. Twenty-eight percent of the offenses committed by broker-dealers acting alone were not prosecuted, compared to 57 percent of all other offenses. Surprisingly, the prior record of investigated offenders—a powerful explanatory variable in much criminal justice research—is unrelated to the likelihood of SEC prosecution.

UNDERTAKING LEGAL ACTION

From justifications articulated in the investigatory record and empirical patterns in the data, it appears that the nature of the violations committed, their magnitude, impact, and timing best account for the decision *not* to take formal legal action. For about half of those cases in which violations were uncovered by investigation, some formal legal action is taken, however. Where staff investigators determine that such action is appropriate, they prepare a detailed memorandum, stating the nature of the offense, the evidence, the recommended form of legal action and its justifications. The memorandum passes through the various hierarchies of supervision and oversight among regional and headquarters enforcement personnel and eventually is presented to the SEC commissioners, who make final prosecutorial decisions.

As noted earlier, in three cases the commissioners refused staff recommendations for prosecution, and the cases were closed without formal legal action. This figure is misleading, however. First, it understates the

number of cases in which this occurs. Justifications in investigative records probably often restate the explanations given by commissioners when they refuse prosecution—staleness, the scope of violations or their impact, and so on. Second, although commissioners may approve staff recommendations that some formal action be taken, they may substantially alter the nature of the recommended action. They may decide to include different parties in the action than those recommended by staff (for example, drop the inside counsel, add the chief executive officer) or to invoke different forms of legal action (for example, respond civilly rather than criminally).

The deliberative conduct of regulatory agency commissioners, particularly surrounding enforcement matters, is shrouded in secrecy. It is therefore difficult to characterize this critical juncture in case disposition. My comments are based on my observations of this process during a brief period of several weeks in the half-century of SEC enforcement. These observations may be atypical of other SEC commissions that presided over the cases in this study.

SEC commissioners spent several hours every day considering staff enforcement recommendations for formal orders of investigation, legal action, or settlement arrangements. Memoranda and related documentation supporting the recommendations are distributed to commissioners prior to the private hearings. Documents supporting any single recommendation typically range in length from fifteen to thirty pages (but often number into the hundreds). Commissioners often enter the hearing room with foot-high stacks of documents related to the day's agenda.

During the period that I observed, an average of eight separate investigations were considered each day, though only two or three were discussed in any great detail. Enforcement attorneys and their branch chiefs or assistant directors would appear before the commissioners at these daily sessions and make a brief presentation of the matter under consideration.[16] Then debate ensued—with differences of opinion not only between the commissioners and enforcement staff, but often between commissioners and staff members themselves. Staff recommendations were rarely rubberstamped by the commission I observed. They generated complex, thorough, often heated discussions pertaining to details of particular offenses and of enforcement policy.

The degree of attention given to the minutiae of the individual case and the pertinent evidence was truly impressive. An entire morning might be spent scrutinizing stock market trading data or the accounting work

---

16. One of the branch chiefs in the Division of Enforcement was responsible for representing regional office enforcement matters before the commission. Only on rare occasions did regional office investigators themselves appear before the commission (usually for very complex and difficult decisions).

papers pertaining to a single offense. Commissioners sometimes posed hypothetical problems to get at the important distinctions or policy implications latent in the details of a particular case. Determinations pertaining to all aspects of a given case often continued over days, weeks, or months.

The kinds of issues articulated over and over again in commission deliberations of prosecutorial discretion are familiar ones. Commissioners scrutinized the available evidence for weakness or inadequacy, instructing enforcers to drop the more tenuous charges. A great deal of deliberation pertained to matters of intent, knowledge, direct involvement, culpability, negligence, or inadvertence. Commissioners might ask whether a particular corporation should be held culpable for the actions of its employees and would ultimately examine corporate structure to determine, for example, whether a vice president is high enough in its hierarchy to implicate the entire organization. Commissioners evaluated the deterrent or prophylactic effect a prosecutorial decision might have on potential lawbreakers. And they explored other potential impacts of their prosecutorial discretion as well: will commission attempts to punish corporate insiders further harm their victimized investors? Will their decision affect the willingness of offenders to make restitution? Insure that illicit activities will be terminated quickly enough? Have an adverse effect on subsequent litigation?

Commissioners considered the impact of prosecutorial decisions on the development of policy: is this the perfect set of circumstances to retry an unfavorable court decision? Is this the right scenario to extend the definition or boundaries of a given statute or regulation? Discussion pertained to the concern or desire to maintain consistency with previous decisions or precedents. Less frequently, deliberation turned to questions of costs and benefits: is pursuing this investigation/prosecution worth the effort?

Although other SEC commissions might have relied on votes or more formal decision-making strategies, the one I observed made its prosecutorial decisions by consensus, with commission preferences emerging after discussion. Of course, I was not privy to the discussion and politicking that occurred outside the commission chambers, the impact—on enforcement policy generally, as well as on particular enforcement matters—of which may be substantial.

LEGAL REMEDIES

SEC commissioners determine not only whether legal action should be taken against the perpetrators of a particular offense, but also the nature of the action to be taken. They have three formal legal options: civil proceedings, administrative proceedings, and referrals to the U.S. Department of Justice for criminal prosecution. For any given offense, any combination of these three alternatives may be imposed.

Civil actions are inititated by SEC staff in the federal district courts. Typically, they are injunctive proceedings, the successful outcome of which enjoins offenders from future violations of the securities laws. In some instances, other forms of ancillary relief may be secured, for example, the appointment of receivers or supplemental investigation or disclosure. Injunctions are imposed where violations are ongoing or have a high likelihood of recurrence. Through temporary restraining orders and preliminary and permanent injunctions, civil actions seek to halt illegal activities. In an emergency, a temporary restraining order can be obtained in a matter of hours, thereby freezing corporate assets before they are pilfered.

Although contested proceedings may involve protracted litigation, injunctive actions frequently are resolved by consent, in which offenders neither admit nor deny any wrongdoing, but agree that they will not violate the securities laws in the future. Failure to abide by an injunctive decree can result in criminal contempt proceedings. There is no other sanction attached to the injunction, although it may serve as a bar from future activities in the securities industry or as the basis for revocation of registration with the SEC. There are no restrictions on the characteristics of the parties subject to civil remedies. They may be individuals or organizations, securities issuers, professionals, or ordinary citizens.

The administrative proceeding is a public or private hearing, ordered by the commission, and presided over by an SEC administrative law judge. Some are lengthy and complex, with the presentation of numerous documents and witnesses; others are settled by consent or default without formal hearings. Administrative law judges recommend a disposition to the SEC commissioners, who render the final disposition in the case. Respondents can request oral argument before the commission and can appeal its decision to the federal courts. Although the law concerning the utilization of the SEC administrative proceeding has changed somewhat over the years, it is generally available for persons or organizations bearing some kind of relationship to the SEC, either as registrants or their employees or as professionals who practice before the agency (that is, attorneys or accountants).

The most severe sanction in an administrative proceeding terminates this relationship—the registration of a broker-dealer or investment adviser is revoked or the professional is barred from practice before the commission. Less radical sanctions and ancillary remedies associated with administrative proceedings include temporary suspensions of business, employment, association with a regulated firm, or trading; expulsion or suspension from self-regulatory organizations; censure; alterations in the management or supervisory structure of the organization; restrictions on business practices; and the voluntary withdrawal of the party from the

securities business. Unlike civil proceedings, remedies ancillary to administrative sanctions are generally not available unless a respondent voluntarily consents to it.

Criminal prosecutions are instituted in the federal district courts by the U.S. Department of Justice. In most cases, SEC staff determine that criminal prosecution is appropriate, and the commission formally refers the case to the Justice Department. On occasion, the Justice Department requests SEC records while investigation is still underway. In either case, the decision to refer investigative files must be made by the SEC commissioners. Criminal referrals are assigned to local U.S. attorneys who have the discretion to accept or decline the case for criminal prosecution. Although SEC staff frequently contribute to the preparation of an indictment and to the eventual criminal trial, criminal prosecution and discretion over its outcome is vested in the U.S. attorney.

Criminal sanctions for the violation of the securities laws and the mail fraud and conspiracy statutes (often included in these charges) during the period covered by my study include imprisonment of up to five years, fines of up to $10,000 (and up to $500,000 for securities exchanges), and probation. Conditions of probation sometimes include a bar from engaging in the securities business or an order to make restitution to victims. There are no restrictions on the kind of parties liable for criminal prosecution.

Table 6.2 displays the constellation of legal proceedings invoked for offenses and offenders in the sample. Numbers of proceedings are presented as a percentage of the number of alleged offenses/offenders in which formal legal action was taken, the number of cases in which violations/violators were confirmed by investigation, and the total number of alleged offenses/offenders in the sample. As shown in the "Offense" portion of the table, 83 percent of the prosecuted offenses were subjected to only one kind of proceeding, 15 percent to two kinds of proceedings, and 2 percent to all three. Civil and administrative proceedings are equally likely (48 percent and 47 percent, respectively) to be imposed, and referrals for criminal prosecution are only about half as likely (25 percent).[17] Although civil and criminal proceedings are appropriate for any securities violator, administrative proceedings are available only where

17. The distribution of instituted proceedings against individual offenders (see table 6.2) closely mirrors that pertaining to offenses. Even the ratio of the number of persons proceeded against to the total number investigated (46 percent) is the same as that of the number of prosecuted offenses to the number of investigated offenses (45 percent). The only major difference between the offenses and offenders pertains to the frequency of multiple proceedings. The likelihood that a single offender will be subjected to more than one kind of proceeding (11 percent) is lower than that for a particular offense (17 percent). This follows from the fact that multiple offenders in a single offense may be subjected to single but different kinds of proceedings.

Table 6.2. Types of Legal Proceedings

Offense	N	% of total proceedings[a]	% of total violations[b]	% of total cases
Civil proceedings only	(78)	33	17	15
Administrative proceedings only	(80)	34	18	15
Criminal referral only	(37)	16	8	7
Civil and administrative	(20)	8	4	4
Civil and criminal	(11)	5	2	2
Administrative and criminal	(5)	2	1	1
Civil, administrative, criminal	(5)	2	1	1
All civil	(114)	48	25	22
All administrative	(110)	47	24	21
All criminal	(58)	25	13	11
Total (N)	(236)	(236)	(449)	(526)

a. Excludes 290 cases that were closed without formal proceedings, regardless of whether investigation uncovered violations.
b. Excludes 77 cases in which no violations were uncovered. Includes 213 cases in which violations were uncovered but were closed without formal proceedings.

Offender	N	% of total offenders proceeded against[c]	% of total violators[d]	% of all parties investigated
Civil proceedings only	(346)	39	20	18
Administrative proceedings only	(304)	34	17	16
Criminal referral only	(149)	17	8	8
Civil and administrative	(58)	6	3	3
Civil and criminal	(15)	2	1	1
Administrative and criminal	(9)	1	1	0
Civil, administrative, criminal	(12)	1	1	1
All civil	(431)	48	25	22
All administrative	(383)	43	22	20
All criminal	(185)	21	11	10
Total (N)	(893)	(893)	(1754)	(1934)

c. Excludes 1041 parties that were not proceeded against, regardless of whether investigation uncovered violations.
d. Excludes 180 parties that were not proceeded against because investigation did not uncover violation. Includes 861 parties not proceeded against for whom violations were uncovered.

offenders are SEC registrants or bear some special relationship to the agency. If only those cases are considered in which administrative remedies are available ($N = 186$), the proportion of cases disposed by administrative proceedings (59 percent) is even higher. Thus, if prosecutorial opportunity or availability is taken into consideration, administrative proceedings are the most common legal response to violation and criminal referrals, the least common.

Civil proceedings. As noted in table 6.2, 431 offenders (22 percent of the total sample) were the subjects of civil injunctive proceedings. Slightly less than two-fifths of them were organizations; 45 percent were officers or directors of these organizations. On average, about 3.75 parties were named in each injunctive proceeding. Ninety-one percent of them ultimately were enjoined with a permanent injunction. Of the remainder, 2 percent were named in a temporary restraining order and 3 percent were also named in a preliminary injunction, but charges were either dismissed or not supported after litigation. The experience of litigation was relatively rare for these offenders: 80 percent settled charges by consent, 12 percent litigated, and 8 percent were enjoined by default. Only thirty-six parties (8 percent) appealed their injunction, and only a tenth of them succeeded with a reversal or alteration of the remedies originally imposed. The civil proceeding is a relatively efficient dispositional alternative for SEC investigators: of 100 parties named in injunctive proceedings, at least 90 are permanently enjoined, at a cost of litigating with only about 12 of them.[18]

The outcome of injunctive proceedings can include more than simply enjoining offenders from future lawbreaking; ancillary relief can be secured as well. However, despite the considerable talk of the importance of ancillary relief in SEC injunctive proceedings by the SEC (1976 Annual Report, 108), its staff (Levine and Herlihy 1977; interview with enforcement attorneys, March 21, 1977), and by legal scholars (Treadway 1975, Farrand 1976), these remedies rarely were imposed on civil proceedings in the sample. The discrepancy between talk and action probably reflects the greater use of ancillary remedies in recent years, a period underrepresented in my research.

For only 17 percent of the offenders in the sample named in civil proceedings (23 percent of the offenses) were ancillary remedies imposed. The most common forms of relief are traditional ones, used for the more severe and blatant forms of fraud: disgorgement, rescission, or restitution of illicitly acquired monies (7 percent of all proceedings and 30 percent of all remedies) or the appointment of a receiver to replace

---

18. These ratios are about the same when the case rather than the individual is the unit of analysis.

incumbent management (5 percent of proceedings, 20 percent of remedies). Some of the more novel and presumably current remedies, which shift the cost of investigation to the offender and attempt more subtle changes in corporate operations (supplemental reporting, special audits, restrictions on business practices, reorganization of management) are just not very common among cases in the sample. These remedies were imposed on only sixteen parties, representing 4 percent of all proceedings and 15 percent of all remedies. Other uncommon forms of ancillary relief, each secured in less than 3 percent of the injunctive proceedings, include amended filings, orders pertaining to proxy solicitations, freezing of assets or records, suspensions or bars to professional or business activity, and the liquidation of offending organizations.

Administrative proceedings. Most offenders in the sample subject to SEC administrative proceedings were registered broker-dealers, investment advisers, and their principals or employees. Many of the administrative proceedings available to SEC enforcers—suspension or revocation of the registration of securities exchanges or associations, stop orders, trading suspensions, and the like—rarely arise from docketed agency investigations. Rule 2(e) proceedings against securities professionals (usually accountants and attorneys) that challenge their privilege to appear or practice before the commission were invoked in only three cases (involving a total of 5 individuals).

In the sample, 360 offenders were involved in administrative proceedings concerning the revocation or suspension of their SEC registration, 23 in proceedings concerning the denial of registration.[19] On average, 3.5 parties were named per proceeding. Thirty-seven percent of them were registered securities organizations, 45 percent were officers or directors of these organizations, and 18 percent held roles of employee or affiliated person. Coincidentally, these percentages mirror exactly those pertaining to the subjects of civil proceedings.

About two-thirds of these administrative proceedings were instituted publicly. For about a third of the parties named in these proceedings, charges were litigated through hearings before administrative law judges; 61 percent settled charges by consent, and 7 percent by default. The outcomes of administrative proceedings were favorable to SEC enforcers. Whatever the response of defendants to SEC charges, 89 percent of them were found in violation, 1 percent were found innocent of charges, and proceedings against the remaining 10 percent were dismissed or discontinued. Only 3 percent of the defendants appealed the disposition rendered. All dispositions were affirmed on appeal. Like civil ones, adminis-

19. Revocations/suspensions pertain to parties already registered, denials to those applying for SEC registration.

trative proceedings are often successful, though as a result of more litigation. Of 100 parties named in administrative proceedings, 89 were found in violation, at a cost of litigating with 32 of them.

About 5 percent of the parties found to be in violation or consenting to charges of violation were not sanctioned. Sanctions imposed on the remaining 326 parties ranged in severity from censure (22 percent) to denials of registration applications (6 percent) to suspensions from association with SEC registrants (8 percent), from stock exchange membership (2 percent), from membership in the National Association of Securities Dealers (NASD) (5 percent), and of SEC registration (7 percent)[20] to permanent measures such as revoking SEC registration (35 percent), barring association with an SEC registrant (13 percent), barring future SEC practice (1 percent), or expelling them from the NASD (11 percent). Revocation of SEC registration coupled with expulsion from the NASD is the most common combination of sanctions, imposed on three-quarters of all defendants subject to two or more sanctions. Severe sanctions were imposed more than twice as often as less severe sanctions: permanent sanctions were imposed on 64 percent of all parties sanctioned, suspensions on 23 percent.[21]

Remedies ancillary to administrative sanctions are rarely imposed. Only 41 parties, 13 percent of those found in violation and subject to administrative sanctions, were also subject to ancillary remedies. And like the civil remedies, the incidence of the more innovative remedies, attempting subtle changes in corporate conduct or disclosure, was quite low. The most common ancillary remedy (representing 31 percent of all remedies) involved the agreement of parties to withdraw their SEC registration. The remaining remedies were of three kinds: (1) disclosures (10 percent of all remedies) requiring amended filings, supplemental disclosure, or special audits; (2) instituting new controls or restricting business practices (13 percent); and (3) restrictions on the employment possibilities of individuals (40 percent), either barring them from the securities industry, permanently or subject to SEC approval, or limiting them to nonsupervisory roles in the industry.

Some ancillary remedies in fact appear to substitute for administrative sanctions. For defendants subject to ancillary remedies, the likelihood that other sanctions will be imposed is 73 percent; for those not subject to ancillary remedies, the likelihood is 98 percent. This trend is especially pronounced for defendants who agreed to withdraw registration, restrict

20. Suspensions generally ranged in length from one day to one year, with the median length of ten days for SEC registration suspensions and twenty-five days for other suspensions.

21. For a more detailed analysis of SEC administrative sanctioning practice between 1967 and 1969, see Thomforde (1975).

business practices, refrain from acting as brokers without SEC approval, or stay out of the securities business, of whom 44, 33, 50, and 0 percent, respectively, were sanctioned. Although it is unlikely that administrative charges will be dropped without some response, it does appear that some charges may be dispensed without formal sanctions where parties consent to the imposition of ancillary remedies. Of course, sanctioned and un-sanctioned offenders differ in other ways, which may account for the disposition of proceedings against them.

Referrals for criminal prosecution. A third legal response to the discovery of violations by SEC investigators involves the referral of the case to the U.S. Department of Justice or directly to a U.S. attorney for criminal prosecution. A comprehensive criminal reference report, usually exceeding fifty pages in length, is prepared by SEC investigators, outlining the nature of the offense and its victims, describing the conduct and background of offenders, coconspirators, and other participants, reviewing the available evidence, witnesses, and the like, and usually recommending for which of the participants criminal proceedings are appropriate.

Fifty-eight cases, or 11 percent of the sample and 25 percent of all cases subject to some formal legal action, were referred for criminal prosecution. In these criminal reference reports, 185 parties were named (165 individuals, 20 organizations), representing 10 percent of all parties investigated and 21 percent of those subject to some legal proceeding. Recommendations for criminal prosecution named a smaller number of offenders per offense (less than 3.2) than did civil (3.75) or administrative (3.5) proceedings. Subjects of criminal referral also differed from those subject to civil and administrative proceedings, where 37 percent were organizations, 45 percent officers or directors of these organizations, and 18 percent other individuals. These figures for criminal referrals were 11, 44, and 45 percent, respectively. Criminal proceedings emphasize the individual over the organizational offender and members of both the corporate under class and upper class.

U.S. attorneys are not required to prosecute all matters referred by the SEC. They declined prosecution for 16 percent of the cases and 26 percent of the parties recommended for criminal prosecution by the commission. The latter percentage is larger than the former because, in some instances, the prosecution of one or two among several proposed defendants in a given case was declined.

It is not always possible to determine the reasons for case declination by Justice Department officials. Even where the actual notification of declination letter to SEC officials is included in investigative records or where its contents are summarized by SEC enforcers and noted in the file, it is possible that stated justifications do not reflect actual justifications. And in some instances, declination is simply reported without explanation.

Many of the reasons offered for declination of SEC cases by U.S. attorneys resemble those utilized by SEC investigators and commissioners to justify their own decisions not to take formal action against securities violators in other cases. In some instances, U.S. attorneys deemed other prosecutions or convictions of offenders on related matters sufficient. In other cases, they argued about the appropriateness of federal jurisdiction. In two cases, U.S. attorneys referred matters to the states and deferred declination until successful state prosecutions were completed. Other justifications concerned evidentiary issues, the fact that witnesses were uncooperative, not credible, or self-serving, that offenders derived no benefit from their conduct, or the difficulty of demonstrating intent. Others noted the magnitude of the offense—that the take was small, the extent of injury minor—and problems of staleness or expiration of the statute of limitations. Less frequently, declination was based on more general policy concerns. One justification, perhaps more typical of Justice Department declinations than of SEC nonprosecutions, pointed to issues of marginality or ambiguity of the alleged illegal conduct. U.S. attorneys argued that conduct reflected puffing and not misrepresentation, that statements were general, that accounting documents were questionable but not improper. The intentional cover-up of an offense by its perpetrators sometimes served as a justification for declination as well, based on the difficulty of proving fraud.

Where cases were not declined but the prosecution of particular individuals was declined, U.S. attorneys frequently pointed to the role of individuals in the illegal activity—that they were marginal and not the principal cause of the fraud, that the extent of their participation was small, that they were subordinates. These justifications were particularly likely where the main perpetrators were not subject to criminal prosecution because of death or plea bargaining. As observed in the discussion of SEC justifications for nonprosecution, it is unclear whether these Justice Department justifications have any empirical reality—whether declined cases were really weaker, more trivial, more ambiguous, the evidence more lacking than cases prosecuted.

Whatever the rationale, a substantial number of cases and defendants were ultimately subject to criminal prosecution. Since criminal prosecution is not conducted by SEC attorneys, the data available in SEC investigative files to document this process are more limited. For example, I was unable to learn anything about plea bargaining, grand jury presentations, and the like from investigatory records. Nonetheless, information in these records does document the outcome of the criminal cases.[22]

Table 6.3 sorts the different outcomes of SEC criminal referrals. In

---

22. But see Mathews (1971).

Table 6.3. Outcomes of Criminal Referral

	(N)	% of total referrals	% of total prosecutions
Prosecution declined	(48)	26	—
Charges dropped	(33)	18	—
Acquitted	(20)	11	19
Convicted	(85)	46	81
Pleaded innocent (29)			
Pleaded guilty (45)			
Pleaded nolo contendere (11)			
Total parties referred	(186)		
Total parties prosecuted	(105)		

addition to those for whom prosecution was declined, another 33 offenders in the sample were spared criminal prosecution when charges against them were dropped (nolle prosequi). The rationales for dropping these charges were diverse, including ill health, death of the defendant before trial (including suicide), fugitive status, and other pending charges for which the offender was awaiting trial. Thus, only a little more than half of the original subjects of criminal referrals eventually were subject to criminal prosecution. Forty-seven percent pleaded innocent; only 20 (19 percent of those prosecuted) were acquitted. Rates of litigation are much higher for criminal than for civil or administrative proceedings and, perhaps as a result, success (that is, conviction) rates are somewhat lower. Twenty defendants appealed their convictions, all of which were affirmed.

Available criminal penalties for securities violations include actual or suspended prison sentences, probation, and fines. The most common sanction was a prison sentence, imposed on more than half of the convicted defendants. Still, of 1,211 persons investigated for securities violations, fewer than 50 spent any time in prison. Twenty-six percent of the others received suspended prison sentences, 36 percent probation, and 18 percent fines. These latter three sanctions are not usually imposed alone. Suspended sentences are most often accompanied by fines, fines by probation, and probation by a fairly even number of each of the others.

Prison sentences ranged from less than three months (4 percent of the defendants) to more than three years (27 percent), with sentences as high as eight years. The median prison sentence was two years in length. Suspended sentences ranged from nine months (14 percent) to more than three years (27 percent), with a sentence as high as 34 years. The median suspended sentence was two to three years. The most common length of probation (45 percent) was more than three years, with only 3 percent of the convicted offenders receiving less than one year's probation; the median was two to three years. Fines ranged in magnitude from $1 to $36,000. A third of the defendants were fined less than $1,000, and a

quarter more than $10,000. The median fine was $2,700 and the mean $6,446. Formal sentences sometimes included additional requirements to make restitution, to stay out of the securities business, or never to hold a position with a public corporation.

THE CHOICE OF FORMAL LEGAL REMEDIES

The distinctive features of offenses predispose them to one kind of proceeding over another. Most unambiguous are the criteria that predispose an offense to an administrative disposition. Overall, prosecuted offenses have a 47 percent chance of being proceeded against administratively. But various offender groups considerably increase their chances for this outcome. Eighty-one percent of all prosecuted registered broker-dealers acting alone are named in administrative proceedings; when they conspire with stock issuers in illicit activities, they reduce their chances for administrative proceedings to 57 percent. Still they are more vulnerable to administrative dispositions than other categories of violators. A second correlate of administrative disposition is offense-related: the commission of technical violations increases the likelihood of such an outcome from 47 percent to 79 percent.

Registered broker-dealers acting alone and involved primarily in the violation of SEC technical regulations (if they are unable to immunize themselves from legal action) are extremely vulnerable to administrative proceedings. Still, the offenses of registered broker-dealers are occasionally disposed with civil or criminal action, either to the exclusion of administrative (19 percent) or coupled with administrative proceedings (23 percent). They render their activities vulnerable to civil or criminal prosecution by designing more complex offenses of greater scope. The likelihood that registered broker-dealers will experience civil or criminal prosecution grows from 5 percent to 50 percent by increasing the number of co-offenders from one to more than one, from 34 percent to 74 percent by increasing the number of organizations involved from one to more than one, from 37 percent to 74 percent by conspiring with stock issuers, from 25 percent to 57 percent by increasing victimization from fewer than five investors to more than twenty-five, from 15 percent to 65 percent by increasing the economic cost of violation from none to more than $5,000. Registered broker-dealers increase the likelihood of civil or criminal prosecution from 38 percent to 83 percent by their involvement in stock manipulation activities and from 26 percent to 51 percent by being or conspiring with repeat violators.

The time frame of offenses is associated with the choice between administrative and civil/criminal dispositions for registered broker-dealers. The invocation of administrative proceedings is greater for stale, completed offenses. Almost half of their continuing offenses experienced civil or

criminal prosecution, in constrast to about a fifth of those already completed, as did 65 percent of those offenses of less than nine months' duration, in contrast to 18 percent ongoing for more than four years. When an urgent, continuing technical violation—for example, a net capital violation—is discovered, enforcers will seek an immediate legal response in the form of an injunction. When less pressing violations are encountered, slower administrative proceedings are adequate.

Of course, civil and criminal forms of legal action are available to all securities violators, not only registered broker-dealers. Although 43 percent of the registered broker-dealers who were prosecuted were subjected to civil or criminal proceedings, this proportion was 92 percent for all other prosecuted offenders. The choice between civil and criminal remedies is determined primarily by offense substance, impact, timeliness, and offender characteristics.

Civilly prosecuted offenses are likely to be less serious. Twenty-two percent of the offenses proceeded against civilly involved only technical or registration violations without more serious elements of fraud or cover-up. None of these violations were subject to criminal prosecution. Criminal offenses had elements of misappropriation (46 percent of them, compared with 27 percent of the civil cases) or reflected greatest complexity—investment schemes, self-dealing, stock manipulation (characterizing 65 percent of them, in contrast to 38 percent of the civil cases). The greater seriousness of criminally prosecuted offenses is seen in their impact as well: 43 percent of the criminal cases, compared to 23 percent of the civil ones, touched more than one hundred victims; 21 percent had economic costs exceeding $1,000 (64 percent exceeding $100), compared to 10 percent of the civil cases (41 percent of them exceeding $100). Criminal prosecutions were more likely where offenders were repeaters. Eighty-four percent of the criminal prosecutions charged offenders with a prior record, in contrast to 70 percent of the civil prosecutions.

So the choice of criminal prosecution is more likely for serious offenders whose more complex and significant offenses generate more victims and incur greater costs. Because a civil injunction can be obtained quickly and utilized to halt or freeze illicit activities, its leverage is greatest when offenses are still ripe, when there are ongoing violations that can be intercepted or halted. Civil proceedings therefore include the fresher, more threatening offenses. Ninety-six percent of the civil caseload pertained to offenses still ongoing at the time of SEC detection, compared with 82 percent of the criminal caseload; 39 percent versus 22 percent of their cases, respectively, had been ongoing for less than nine months.

Consistent with the same logic (civil proceedings intervene to alter the course of an offense, criminal proceedings when the damage has already been done), criminal proceedings are more common where of-

fending organizations are bankrupt (53 percent of its caseload, as compared to 26 percent of the civil caseload), civil proceedings where they are viable. Indeed the fact that civil proceedings nip recent offenses in the bud and criminal proceedings respond to older, staler violations may partially explain the lesser impact of civilly prosecuted offenses. These offenses presumably were halted with civil injunctions before their full victimization (in human and monetary terms) could unfold. If these offenses were not so quickly terminated, perhaps their impact would be as considerable as that of offenses subject to criminal prosecution.

Finally, the affinity of criminal prosecutions to the offenses of individuals rather than those of organizations is reflected in these data. It is rare for the activities of individuals acting alone or organizations acting alone to be the subjects of SEC investigations. Still, none of the investigations of organizations acting alone were subject to criminal prosecution; 82 percent of the offenses (for which the SEC took some legal action) in which individuals acted alone resulted in criminal prosecution. In part, this is true because individuals acting alone are usually embezzlers, an offense for which criminal prosecution is common. In part, it reflects the fact that civil and administrative proceedings are better suited to controlling the conduct of organizations than of persons acting outside an organizational context.

OTHER OUTCOMES OF INVESTIGATED OFFENSES

A discussion of the dispositions of SEC investigations cannot close without some consideration of the legal responses to these offenses occurring outside the agency, specifically, legal actions taken by other social control organizations or jurisdictions and private litigants.[23] Most SEC investigations (60 percent), including those which result in formal legal action by the agency (54 percent), do not experience any other legal proceedings pursued by parties outside the agency. Due to underreporting, however, these percentages are probably inflated. Private civil suits instituted by the investors, shareholders, clients, or victims of securities violators represent the most common legal action reported in SEC investigative records. Twelve percent of all investigations in which SEC enforcers uncovered violations resulted in investor suits. Almost as common were civil suits instituted by state agencies for violation of state statutes usually similar to the federal securities laws (10 percent of all violations). Another 5 percent of the violations were subjected to state criminal prosecution. Nine per-

___

23. Since these phenomena occur outside of the purview of the SEC, the likelihood that they will be fully or even superficially documented in SEC investigative records is not high. Therefore, the data upon which this consideration is based are among the least reliable in the study. They clearly underreport the incidence of other legal responses to illegality, and there may be some reporting biases as well.

cent of the violators were sanctioned by self-regulatory agencies (6 percent by the National Association of Securities Dealers, 2 percent by one of the stock exchanges) for violation of their regulations. Civil or criminal prosecutions by federal agencies (2 percent of all violations) or foreign agencies (1 percent) or civil litigation in connection with bankruptcy or receivership proceedings against offenders (2 percent) was much less common. For at least 12 percent of the violations, more than one of these legal remedies was instituted.

CONCLUSION

Regulation by Prosecution, the title of a recent book written by a former SEC commissioner (Karmel 1982), echoes the widespread reputation of the SEC as preeminantly a prosecutorial agency. But this prosecutorial mystique requires reexamination. Prosecution is a minority outcome of the agency's enforcement work. Less than half of those suspicions of securities violation serious enough to warrant opening a formal docketed investigation ultimately are subject to legal action. Less than a third of these investigations were disposed of with civil proceedings or a referral for criminal prosecution. Rather than opting for indiscriminate prosecution as a knee-jerk response to illegality, SEC enforcers exercise considerable discretion in selecting legal responses to wayward capitalism. Indeed, what is distinctive about the SEC is not its overreliance on prosecution to discharge its regulatory responsibilities, but rather its prosecutorial restraint.

This finding is not surprising, given the circuitous and often fortuitous route by which intelligence travels to the agency. Because the acts of wayward capitalists are often subtle and complex and are made even more so by diverse strategies of cover-up and deception, the offenses that victimized investors disclose to the SEC are often obvious, amateurish, small-scale, trivial crimes that rarely warrant formal legal action. The often self-serving reasons that disaffected insiders have to "squeal" (to save their own skins, seek revenge against former coconspirators, or increase their leverage in a power struggle) often generate tainted intelligence (exaggerated or distorted allegations or noncredible witnesses) and offenses for which prosecution is inappropriate or problematic.

Inferential intelligence strategies—like surveillance—pose different problems. Activities detected in this way often do not merit prosecution, because investigation proves the inferences to be false or trivial. Many investigations derived from the inquiries of wary investors solicited to participate in investment opportunities are not prosecuted, because the schemes turn out to be wholly legal or, if illegal, are nipped in the bud before significant damage is done. These offenses often do not merit legal

action, because their impact is insignificant and the activities have ceased.

It is important to remember that the purpose of an enforcement program is not only to find the most wayward offenders, who have done the greatest harm, and then escort them through the courts. It also includes gathering intelligence about incipient illicit schemes and shutting them down before significant harm can be done. And it includes using detection strategies and the fear of being caught as deterrents to illegal activity in the first place. The next and final chapter therefore reconsiders the role of intelligence in the enforcement process.

7

Detection and the Enforcement Process

The central finding of my research reveals that the social organization of illicit activities determines the way they are detected and, therefore, that different strategies of intelligence catch different kinds of securities offenses. Figure 7.1 summarizes this relationship between deviance and detection, differentiating intelligence strategies by the characteristics of their catch. Detection strategies plotted proximately catch securities offenses with very similar characteristics overall; those with the most dissimilar catches are plotted farthest apart. The figure also specifies the clusters of strategies that detect similar violations: the first cluster, which typically detects misrepresentations coupled with registration violations, occupies the necktie shape in the lower right-hand corner of the figure; the two members of the second cluster, more likely to detect misappropriations alone or coupled with misrepresentation and nonregistration, are linked by the half-circle to the left of the first cluster; the third cluster of strategies, which catch technical violations primarily, span the narrow gray triangle across the top of the figure; the fourth, which uncovers both technical violations and embezzlement, is occupied only by inspections, circled at the top of the figure; and the fifth cluster of strategies, defined by the triangle in the center of the figure, detects self-dealing and stock manipulation.

These data can assist SEC policymakers to systematically develop an intelligence program that generates a caseload consistent with enforcement priorities. For example, current SEC officials indicate that they favor policing the securities marketplace more than corporate oversight as the agency's major enforcement priority (Gerth 1981a, 1981b; Crock 1981). They emphasize the control of securities violations such as stock manipulation and insider trading over other kinds of securities fraud or registration or technical violations. Data presented in figure 7.1 suggest

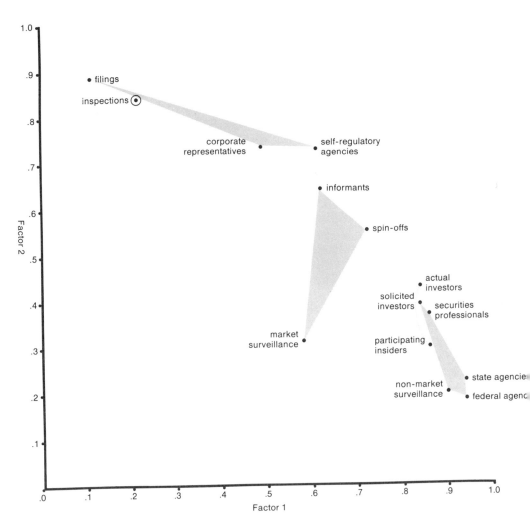

Figure 7.1. Differentiating Intelligence Strategies

that only a small number of detection strategies readily uncover these marketplace offenses: informants, market surveillance, and spin-offs, located in the center triangle of the figure. Indeed, these three strategies, which generated less than a fifth of the investigations in my sample, detected 60 percent of all stock manipulations and 50 percent of all insider trading violations. Therefore, enforcement officials might be wise to allocate greater resources to this triad of intelligence strategies, develop more sophisticated computer surveillance programs, more actively exploit the intelligence insights available from ongoing investigations, and attempt to locate and provide greater disclosure incentives to anonymous informants.

But agency policymakers should also be aware that retooling intelligence techniques and reallocating resources to better uncover fraud in the securities marketplace come at a price. First, many other kinds of securities violations are radically underrepresented in the catch of this triad of intelligence strategies, especially technical violations and offenses with elements of misrepresentation (the latter contributing the most common and often most insidious form of securities fraud). Second, the three strategies are among the least prolific in the sample. Agency enforcers would be hard pressed to generate an adequate investigative caseload from this triad alone. Third, these strategies tend to provide the most inaccurate intelligence of all detection strategies currently in use by SEC enforcers. Many of the few intelligence leads these strategies are capable of discovering will prove to be erroneous after investigation, even further diminishing the size of their catch and wasting enforcement resources.

Instead of shoring up particular detection strategies, SEC policymakers might consider streamlining their intelligence technologies so that enforcers are not encumbered by redundant strategies. An examination of figure 7.1 reveals that, despite the considerable dispersion of many detection strategies, several share almost the same coordinates, plotted so near as to be almost indistinguishable. Since these strategies therefore uncover similar catches of offenses, their pursuit represents a duplication of effort. Policymakers might allocate more resources to a single, selected representative of each cluster of proximate strategies and harness intelligence efforts to more efficiently and systematically focus on the disparities rather than the redundancies of their catch.

For example, each cluster in figure 7.1, defined by the kinds of violations detected, has at least one reactive member: corporate representatives and self-regulatory agencies in the upper triangle, informants in the center triangle, and everything but non-market surveillance in the two clusters in the lower righthand corner. So perhaps SEC enforcers could abandon the redundant proactive strategies that expend so many scarce resources and simply wait for agency outsiders to hand a presumably

similar catch over to them. Even inspections, the one proactive strategy with no reactive counterpart, could be abandoned as well, since its catch is duplicated by that of two other clusters of strategies. Its catch of technical violations is also provided by corporate representatives and self-regulatory agencies, its catch of misappropriations by actual investors and participating insiders.

The problem with undertaking these efficiency measures is that the catches of proximate strategies, though statistically similar, are often not qualitatively similar. And minor differences in a statistical sense may be major when applied to policymaking. Take, for example, two proximate strategies, non-market surveillance and state agency referrals. The distribution of violations detected by these strategies is almost identical. Both are most likely to uncover registration violations coupled with misrepresentations and detect other kinds of offenses at similar rates. But in almost every other way, the offenses they detect are different. Compared to the catch of state agencies, offenses uncovered by non-market surveillance are substantially more likely to have been committed by broker-dealers, to involve larger numbers of offenders, a more diverse set of organizational offenders, larger organizations, more substantial victimization and monetary impact, and to be of shorter duration. Although constructing an intelligence system around either non-market surveillance or state referrals may make no difference with respect to actual violations detected, it would make a substantial difference with respect to other qualities of these offenses. Substituting the effortless reactive strategy of state agency referrals for proactive non-market surveillance would generate an enforcement caseload *considerably* more trivial.

Comparisons of other pairs of strategies reveal similar findings. Corporate representatives and filings both uncover technical violations. But their catches differ significantly in almost every other respect: the proportion of issuers, SEC registrants, or members of the corporate upper class represented, the size of organizational offenders, the number of victims, economic impact, offense duration, and the timeliness and accuracy of intelligence. Informants and spin-offs both discover self-dealing and stock manipulation. However, informants are more likely to discover more serious offenses with many victims and to do so in a timely fashion, but, unfortunately, with considerably less accuracy.

Although both participating insiders and actual investors disclose misappropriation, insiders expose offenses with more substantial and costly victimization. But participating insiders delay longer and therefore disclose more stale intelligence than do actual investors. And they are considerably less prolific; for every investigation generated by a participating insider, actual investors generate seven.

Solicited and actual investors also disclose similar offenses and share

similar coordinates. But solicited investors typically make their disclosures in the earliest stages of an offense; intelligence from actual investors
typically arrives at the agency late in offense development, after the illicit
activities have victimized countless investors and incurred substantial
economic costs. It would not be desirable for the SEC to lose the opportunity to forestall incipient offenses (by dropping solicited investor disclosures) or the opportunity to sanction the perpetrators of serious offenses
that victimize substantial numbers of investors (by dropping disclosures
by actual investors).

Streamlining these presumably redundant detection strategies requires
some very difficult choices—between snaring stock issuers and brokers,
registrants and non-registrants, offenders from the corporate upper
class and under class, offenses with diverse individual or diverse organizational participation, fresh incipient violations and stale violations with
considerable impact—and some unfortunate trade-offs between timely or
accurate intelligence and between strategies that uncover the most complex, subtle, and significant offenses but are often slow, inaccurate, and
not very prolific and strategies whose intelligence about more commonplace offenses is timely, accurate, and considerable.

Even some of the easier choices are not so easy to make. Inspections, for
example, discover some of the least serious forms of securities violations
that other strategies detect anyway. They rarely discover offenses of stock
issuers or of non-registrants. Offenses in their catch are relatively small in
scope with few offenders, few victims, and insignificant cost. They are not
especially prolific. And inspections are enormously expensive—probably
considerably more SEC personnel do inspections than are involved in all
other intelligence activity combined. But, though their intelligence capacity is small, their enforcement capacity—as a deterrent to illegality—may
be considerable. There might be substantially greater numbers of stockbrokers and investment advisers among the ranks of the wayward capitalists if they knew that their business operations, books, and records would
never be scrutinized by inspectors. So the power of inspections as an
enforcement tool is related to its limitations as an intelligence strategy.
Presumably, fewer significant violations are found because they were
deterred.

These data on the relationship of deviance to detection suggest that
none of the detection strategies available to SEC enforcers is stellar in the
quantity, quality, significance, or diversity of its catch. Each strategy,
sensitive to different vulnerabilities of securities offenses, makes its own
unique intelligence contribution, constrained by its own limitations of
access or perspective. Some detection methods are more versatile in the
range of offenses they uncover than others, but no single method or small
set of methods can uncover them all. The intelligence available to SEC

enforcers is timely, accurate, relevant, diverse, significant, and considerable only in its aggregation. In order to assemble an investigative pool that represents some of the most significant offenses and the full range of offenses and offenders over which the SEC has enforcement responsibility, it is necessary to strive for balance, not exclusivity. As enforcement priorities fluctuate, the allocation of resources or the balance of intelligence effort may shift from one cluster of strategies to another, but the wholesale abandonment of particular detection methods would have disastrous consequences, inconsistent with original policy goals.

EXPANDING INTELLIGENCE TECHNOLOGIES

The suggestion that no detection strategies be dropped does not necessarily imply that these existing strategies are fully exploited, adequately or creatively implemented, or that there are no additional detection methods that would make important contributions to SEC intelligence. Non-market surveillance strategies, for example, often uncover significant securities frauds of considerable scope quickly and accurately. But SEC enforcers have no formal or even informal non-market surveillance program. Participating insiders and securities professionals provide intelligence often unavailable from other sources, but they do so very rarely. Only forty-three investigations, 8 percent of the cases in the sample, were derived from either source. And much of the most valuable intelligence, disclosing the most serious securities frauds, is inordinately stale, launching investigations of illicit activities that have been underway for years. Indeed, much of the evidence suggests that SEC intelligence is passive, haphazard, and fortuitous. SEC enforcers may be so preoccupied with the power and drama of their investigative and prosecutorial responsibilities that they have disregarded and abdicated creative responsibility for detecting and selecting the violations they will subsequently enforce.

In this section, the possibility that existing strategies can be expanded, invigorated, or expedited or that new intelligence strategies can be adopted is considered. The focus here is on changes that have implications for *intelligence,* not changes that are designed to lower the incidence of lawbreaking. Although the latter concern is clearly an important one, it is beyond the purview of this study.

DISCLOSURES

As demonstrated by the significant proportion of SEC investigations that are generated reactively, a major intelligence vulnerability of securities violations derives from the diffusion of incriminating information to parties who then disclose it to the SEC. The vulnerabilities of securities offenses to disclosure can be enhanced if (1) the diffusion of information

about illicit activities is increased; (2) disclosure incentives are expanded; and (3) current disclosure mechanisms are improved.

Increasing the diffusion of information. The diffusion of information about illicit activities poses a serious risk. It is for this reason that many offenders carefully attend to matters of cover-up, cooling out their victims, and recruiting, assembling, and organizing a staff of perpetrators and facilitators who are loyal, quiet, and ignorant. They attempt to reduce the flow of information to insiders within the offending organization(s), outside members of the securities community, investors, and especially social control agencies. SEC enforcers must devise strategies to expose cover-ups, engender disloyalty, and facilitate the spread of information inside and outside deviant organizations.

Intelligence reform might attempt to limit the opportunities for intraorganizational cover-up and other efforts to insure the ignorance of both culpable and nonculpable members of deviant organizations. A number of observers have alluded to the role of organizational structure (hierarchy, centralization, specialization, overlapping responsibilities and jurisdiction, collaboration, turnover and rotation of personnal, and so on) and governance on the blockage, distortion, and cover-up of information within organizations (Wilensky 1967; Stone 1975; Katz 1979a; Clinard and Yeager 1980). Some have proposed changes in corporate governance, expanding the responsibilities and accountability of corporate boards of directors, increasing the ratio of outside over inside directors, increasing the representation of the public in the choice of outside directors, and the like (see, for example, Stone 1975). Voices in support of corporate governance reform have indeed been raised within the SEC itself (Karmel 1982, chapter 5). Reorganization of the governance of securities firms and publicly held corporations is presumed to create greater critical scrutiny of company operations by more disinterested overseers. New governance structures might expand the diffusion of information and reduce the disincentives for disclosing incriminating information.

These proposals reflect a somewhat naive assumption that solutions to the blockage of information can be secured by those at the top of corporate hierarchies. Undoubtedly, radical changes in corporate governance at the highest level will have some effect on the diffusion and disclosure of information. But more substantial solutions may derive from tinkering with organizational structure—the recruitment and distribution of personnel, the degree of centralization, the steepness of hierarchical structure, the degree of specialization and interchangeability of personnel, the role and responsibilities of managers, the networks of authority, supervision, and accountability, and the like—the real sources of informational blockages and cover-ups. However, changes in structural features of organizations, because they are so deeply entrenched in organizational

history and so strongly related to the nature of organizational tasks and their profitability, are even more difficult to successfully implement (perhaps even impossible) than changes in corporate governance. But without structural changes throughout the corporate pyramid, changes at its top will have mostly cosmetic results.

A different solution to the blockage of information involves providing the occasion rather than the structure for the diffusion of information within deviant organizations. In recent years, several corporations have created special audit committees, usually composed of outsiders, with responsibility to investigate and report on violations of law and other improper or questionable conduct engaged in by corporate personnel.[1] Most of these special audits were required by the terms of settlement of SEC injunctions alleging securities fraud, and their reports subsequently filed with the federal district courts. Why restrict the use of "deviance" audits to those firms caught and charged with securities violations? Just as brokerage firms and corporations subject to SEC regulation must expend funds for annual financial audits by outside accounting firms, so might they be required to perform similar "deviance" audits as well. Certainly the law-abiding capacity of corporations is as material as their financial condition to investment decisions. By requiring public corporations and brokerage firms to routinely examine themselves for possible violations or for structures or relationships that are ripe for illegality, some cover-ups may be penetrated, some information diffused, and perhaps some offenses forestalled or halted.

Of course, astute offenders simply devise more sophisticated cover-up techniques to dupe financial auditors, and they can do the same with deviance auditors. Still, an atmosphere of self-scrutiny and institutionalized structures for informational dissemination engendered by an audit program may considerably reduce the level of actual or concerted ignorance (Katz 1979a) in public corporations and brokerage firms. The costs, both in money and staff time, and the disruption incurred by such audits would be considerable and should be weighed seriously before implementing a reform of this kind.

Unfortunately, these proposed reforms, however successful, cannot touch wayward capitalists who choose not to register with the SEC and who commit many of the most egregious securities frauds. Therefore, in addition to loosening up informational blockages within deviant organizations by facilitating the flow of information to organizational insiders, intelligence reforms should also be directed to its dissemination to outsiders—members of the securities community, social control agencies,

---

1. See McCloy (1975), one of the earliest and finest special audit reports, concerning the participation of Gulf Oil Corporation in domestic and international bribery.

and investors. Increasing the amount of incriminating information possessed by these outsiders requires educational efforts. Outsiders must be trained to recognize and appreciate the meaning and import of information they possess, to learn to recognize its incriminating implications faster, and to demand more information from insiders and others in the course of their routine encounters and transactions.

Securities professionals—stockbrokers, investment advisers, attorneys, and accountants—the most sophisticated and astute group of outsiders, should be better trained to recognize the telltale signs of fradulent activities and to penetrate cover-up devices. Responsibility for providing seminars or educational materials to these professionals or to professionals-in-training might be delegated to the self-regulatory organizations such as stock exchanges, bar associations, the National Association of Securities Dealers, and the American Institute of Certified Public Accountants.

Responsibility for educating other members of the securities community (the telephone company, bankers, financial journalists and printers, landlords in the financial district, and others) falls to SEC enforcers. SEC regional offices might set up informal meetings with selected members of the securities community to improve their ability to recognize securities violations that they may observe or in which they may be unknowingly involved.

Many everyday con games and swindles as well as more complex white-collar crimes are actually securities frauds, because they are based on the investment of money in some scheme or enterprise in the expectation that it will appreciate in the future. But since these offenses rarely involve stockbrokers, stock exchanges, blue chip stocks, or publicly held corporations, their securities implications are less apparent, and information about them is more likely to diffuse to other social control agencies than to the SEC. Given their role of informational gatekeepers to potential SEC investigations, it is essential that these agencies be familiar with the vagaries of securities fraud. Personnel from federal agencies (such as the Federal Bureau of Investigation, the Internal Revenue Service, the U.S. attorneys' offices, the Commodity Futures Trading Commission, the Federal Trade Commission, and the Federal Election Commission—which the data indicate very rarely refer information to the SEC), state securities and other regulatory agencies, foreign agencies, local district attorneys and police departments, and self-regulatory agencies should be trained to recognize potential securities violations in the matters they encounter and to gather other intelligence that would be of value to SEC enforcers.

At present, the SEC invites officials from federal, state, and international agencies to its week-long Enforcement Training Conference. Designed primarily for new SEC staff, the conference introduces the securities laws, strategies of detecting, investigating, and prosecuting offenses,

techniques for interrogating witnesses or identifying "red flags" in accounting materials, and so on. Participation in the conference also creates networks that can later be exploited for intelligence purposes. Were other agencies encouraged to participate in greater numbers than they have so far (perhaps with some funding), the intelligence impact might be substantial.

A second strategy for facilitating referrals from other social control agencies is provided by multijurisdictional enforcement conferences, which have been held on occasion in some regions. It would be valuable to institutionalize these conferences at the regional level and to include more diverse enforcement roles—U.S. attorneys, local district attorneys, FBI and IRS personnel, state regulatory officials, self-regulatory and private social control agencies, as well as representatives from some of the newer white-collar crime enforcement programs.

The task of educating investors to better exploit the informational resources available to them is more difficult than that of educating other social control officials or members of the securities community. Investors are not always easily identifiable and therefore available for recruitment into an educational program; and many of them are considerably less sophisticated about securities matters and the signs of their own victimization. Still, the need for greater awareness is obvious—to protect investors from entering fraudulent transactions, to alert them to possible victimization early in their involvement, and to insure that their unique insights and experience in securities transactions can be exploited for intelligence purposes. In short, unwitting investors must be rendered witting and actual investor complaints transformed into solicited investor inquiries and referrals, disclosures that typically are made before offenses become stale and before many investors have been victimized.

How, then, can actual investors be transformed into solicited investors? One solution involves creating in the securities industry the kind of consumer movement found in other industries. Many middle-class consumers would not think of buying a major appliance without first checking *Consumer Reports* or some other source. Why should not investors, who may commit substantially more money to their stocks than they do to their refrigerators and vacuum cleaners, be intelligent consumers as well?[2]

Of course, the SEC could never become a public-sector equivalent of *Consumer Reports*. Proposals made prior to the formation of the SEC that a government agency be created to evaluate and rule on the merits of securities offerings were abandoned in favor of a "full disclosure model." The prevailing belief that government should serve as the conduit for the

2. I am not implying that all investors are not intelligent consumers. But from my perspective of acquaintanceship only with those victimized by securities fraud, it is clear that many are incredibly naive, gullible, trusting, and much too willing to part with their money.

disclosure of information that each prospective investor could then evaluate forms the cornerstone of the SEC mandate. The agency cannot advise potential investors on the wisdom of their investment decisions. But it could make its disclosure activities more accessible to individual investors.

SEC enforcers could mount a large-scale public relations campaign to encourage investors to check on potential investments before transactions are consummated. In this study I discovered, for example, that many of the most flagrant and insidious securities swindlers also failed to register their stock offerings with the SEC. Of course, some investment opportunities—intrastate or private placements, small amounts of capital to be raised—do not require full SEC registration. But revealing the registrant status of potential investments to prospective investors would save many of them from victimization and provide an early opportunity for SEC enforcers to gain intelligence about fraudulent schemes. This program, in which potential investors exchange often timely intelligence for information on SEC registration and the like, could be implemented with consumer hot-lines connected to SEC public reference rooms and regional offices. Much of this information has always been available, but less sophisticated investors had neither the awareness nor the incentive to avail themselves of the wealth of material disclosed to the SEC. Furthermore, because dissemination of information has traditionally been one-sided (investors simply consulted directories and reports) rather than interactive, SEC enforcers have been unable to exploit investors' informational needs for intelligence purposes.

Some Pittsburgh postal inspectors recently devised a victim "sting" operation. They created their own victimization opportunities, placing fraudulent advertisements (about weight loss and easy spare-time income) in thirty-seven newspapers. The more than four hundred consumers who responded to these ads were sent a letter from the postal inspectors warning them about opportunities that sound too good to be true. Thousands of others were alerted to the concept of mail fraud by the extensive media coverage given this innovative program (Haitch 1982, 49). Certainly SEC enforcers could initiate some of the promotional strategies adopted by securities swindlers (of which mass media advertising is one), snare the more gullible investors that typically fall victim to securities frauds, and then educate and "deputize" them as future sources of SEC intelligence.

How about the actual investors who have already committed money to the purchase of particular securities? Relatively limited current efforts by SEC staff to educate investors might be expanded. Perhaps all registered brokers could be required to offer free seminars to new clients to help sensitize them to the clues of securities fraud they may encounter. Or all

stock issuers might be required at the time of investment and with every proxy statement to provide informational packets developed by the SEC. The materials would alert investors to the telltale signs of various kinds of securities violations, to help reduce the likelihood that they will be victimized. Of course, these efforts would not help those who invest in corporations or with brokers not registered with the SEC, some of the most flagrant violators and swindlers.

Investors are increasingly more likely to represent organizational or institutional groups rather than single individuals. Institutional investors tend to be "repeat players" (Galanter 1974); their ongoing involvement in securities transactions affords them considerably more power and resources in their struggle against the wayward capitalists who victimize them. For institutional investors, the resources and incentives to be knowledgeable and to carefully scrutinize investments are much higher than for individuals. Furthermore, being a smaller and more easily identifiable group, institutional investors provide more efficient targets for SEC educational programs. Efforts to help educate and facilitate mutual cooperation among institutional investors may have significant intelligence value for SEC enforcers.

Disclosure incentives. The fact that the SEC has not heard from the insiders participating in and outsiders surrounding securities violations is not entirely because they are ignorant. Many of them have no incentives for disclosing their knowledge to agency enforcers or to anyone else. (The disincentives or lack of positive incentives for disclosures were described extensively in chapter 4.) Intelligence reform must also attempt to restructure the incentives that surround the disclosure process.

For those potential disclosure sources directly involved in illicit activities, the most powerful incentives are most likely negative ones—such as threatening an expanding pool of perpetrators or collaborators with culpability for their acts and promising leniency to the first to disclose information to the SEC. Efforts toward increasing definitions of culpability or responsibility for illegal acts are already underway by SEC enforcers, although their primary interest is in deterring marginal offenders from participating in offenses in the first place, rather than inducing them to disclose incriminating information. Attempts to expand the boundaries of culpability have been both vertical—charging corporate officers, directors, or managerial personnel for the illicit acts of their employees, regardless of the evidence of their direct responsibility or even knowledge of these acts—and horizontal—charging those in collaborative positions in outside organizations for their participation in the acts.

The latter strategy is reflected in the SEC "access points" theory. The theory argues for extending assumptions of culpability and legal action to

collaborators, coparticipants, or facilitators, directly or indirectly engaged in or aware of illegal activities. With the access points theory, the SEC has focused on expanding culpability to securities professionals, attorneys, and accountants who often provide the access necessary for illegalities to be executed. But there is no practical reason not to extend culpability to other collaborators as well—brokers, bankers, printers, "bird dogs," journalists, and others. There are some moral and legal issues (to be considered shortly) against extensions of this kind. But, clearly, expanding definitions of culpability and associating informed silence with complicity should result in increasing levels of disclosure (and possibly in retarding rates of collaboration).

Another alternative to induce insider disclosures involves redesigning disclosure incentives among culpable parties—to engineer rewards and punishments in such a way that an insider runs considerable risk by not disclosing information to the agency. The SEC's so-called voluntary program connected with its international bribery and questionable payments inquiries in the mid-1970s (U.S. Securities and Exchange Commission 1976; Kennedy and Simon 1978) provides one example. Here, the agency created a disclosure program in which corporations were requested to come forward voluntarily and disclose information about the illegal or questionable payments they made. Four hundred companies cooperated (Kennedy and Simon 1978). The disclosure incentives for these acts included promises that deviance confessed voluntarily would not be punished or would be punished with more lenience than that which the SEC might discover on its own without voluntary cooperation.

At least one positive incentive may be necessary for insider disclosure schemes to work. The use of plea bargaining and other contrivances of prosecutorial discretion may help to protect culpable insiders who disclose information. However, there are few protections for the nonculpable insiders who share information with the SEC, the "whistle-blowers." Whistle-blowers often endanger their jobs, future employment and promotion prospects, reputations, social relationships, mental health, and even their lives. In recent years, some legal protections for whistle-blowers have been enacted and others have been advocated. For example, Nader and his colleagues (1972) have proposed that individuals discharged from their positions as a result of their disclosures be allowed to sue for malicious discharge and for punitive damages. But so far, the positive incentives fail to offset the harsh reality of the social consequences of whistle-blowing. Sensitivity to the substantial social costs of disclosure is necessary if programs designed to increase insider reporting are to be successful.

For offense outsiders, for whom extensions of culpability are rarely appropriate, positive incentives may be more effective than negative ones. The payment of bounties, rewards, or other fees (like those available to

FBI informants) for information about securities violations might be entertained (Wilson 1978).[3] In the absence of empirical data, it is not clear how great an inducement this would be to many of the professionals now privy to considerable information or to those culpable or marginally involved in violations. But the monetary incentive might be sufficient to encourage nonculpable participants with access to illegal activities (for instance, secretaries), investors, or some members of the securities community to share information with the SEC.

Economic incentives should also appeal to investors. Research on traditional crimes suggests that victims are most likely to call the police when they assume that insurance or other forms of recompense necessitate such disclosure, and rates of reporting are generally highest for major property crimes such as auto theft (Reiss 1971a, 65—66). Securities investors must learn to associate the SEC with their economic interests. They must be convinced by education and example that the agency is protecting them, is responsive to their needs, is not co-opted by the industry, and that the outcomes of investigations they generate may be strong SEC enforcement cases that could result in restitution or rescission or become the basis for their own private lawsuits.

The disclosure incentives available for other social control agencies are more limited. Generally, they concern mutual cooperation, promises of reciprocity in intelligence, and the possibility that SEC involvement may reduce agency workload by providing investigatory or prosecutorial resources or assistance for the particular case referred or for other cases that the agency may encounter in the future.

Disclosure mechanisms. The least difficult approach to reforming the disclosure component of SEC intelligence pertains to improving the mechanisms by which disclosures are made, insuring that those who have relevant information and the proper incentives to disclose it will do so. Many of these disclosure mechanisms have been mentioned earlier. The requirement of self-scrutiny and deviance audits provides a formal mechanism for disclosing incriminating information to the SEC. Special programs such as the SEC voluntary program for disclosures about questionable corporate payments may routinize and minimize the disclosure process. Educational efforts, seminars, and conferences provided for members of the securities community and other social control agencies may create interpersonal networks and occasions for communication in which information can be shared.

Educational literature disseminated to investors might include com-

3. Wilson (1978) presents an interesting discussion of the trade-offs between these positive and negative incentives in the context of the enforcement work of the FBI and the Drug Enforcement Administration.

plaint forms through which they can easily communicate with the SEC. The adoption of tollfree hot-lines by other white-collar crime enforcement agencies has been highly successful (Hinds 1982, 20). Well-publicized SEC hot-lines might be established in major cities to facilitate disclosures by investors, insiders, or members of the securities community. In general, further steps should be taken to increase the visibility of the SEC and its regional offices to investors and to the public.

THE EXAMINATION OF ARTIFACTS

The examination of the artifacts of securities behaviors and transactions plays a part in SEC surveillance activities. The SEC market surveillance program is well-organized, complex, and sophisticated, probably the most refined of all SEC intelligence activities. Yet even it is criticized as being primitive ("A Computer Watchdog" 1980, 42). Until the recent advent of a policitical climate of deregulation and budgetary cutbacks, SEC officials campaigned hard for congressional appropriations to fund a more sophisticated and comprehensive computerized market surveillance oversight system (SEC Annual Report 1980, xii, 17–18). Under new leadership and increasing pressure from Wall Street and self-regulatory agencies, which believed that the system would be costly, intrusive, and duplicative of current stock exchange surveillance programs, the SEC has withdrawn proposals to improve its own market surveillance program ("SEC May Abandon Proposals" 1982, 37). But data from an experimental pilot program suggest that SEC and self-regulatory surveillance efforts are not duplicative: a quarter of the unusual trading activities—especially stock manipulation and insider trading—discovered by SEC surveillance was not detected by the exchanges (ibid.). It therefore appears that decisions to abandon updating SEC surveillance capacities are premature and inappropriate, given current SEC priorities for the control of marketplace violations particularly. The agency should further explore the ways in which improvements in its own surveillance technology would continue to expose offenses relatively immune from self-regulatory agency surveillance.

In contrast to the relative complexity and organization of market surveillance, SEC non-market surveillance activities are almost primitive, a system of accidental and fortuitous encounters that occasionally result in investigation. Given the quality of the intelligence so generated—involving major securities frauds of substantial scope and impact uncovered early in their development and forestalled—it seems sensible to better organize these practices. Perhaps each regional office could designate one or two surveillance officers and the Enforcement Division of the headquarters office could create a special non-market surveillance branch. Surveillance officers would be responsible for scouring the local press;

examining trade publications, records of civil, criminal, and bankruptcy litigation that pertain to securities issuers or their personnel; and routinely meeting with other regulators and law enforcement officials, bankers, members of the securities bar, members of the securities professions, and journalists to discuss potential problems in the industry. If the SEC decided to engage in sting operations or undercover work (described below), surveillance officers would be responsible for their implementation as well. If these efforts are to uncover matters different from the catch of market surveillance and other incursive detection strategies, it is essential that non-market surveillance pertain primarily to entities not registered with the SEC.

OBSERVATION

Another strategy for collecting data on human behavior utilizes observational methods. Of all the possible intelligence strategies available to SEC investigators, observational methods are the most underutilized. Indeed, the only observational work undertaken by SEC investigators is relatively incidental, occurring during the course of on-site broker-dealer or investment adviser inspections. During the period that SEC inspectors examine the books and records of these registered firms, they have some opportunities to observe office life—to overhear conversations, watch meetings and interactions at a distance, scrutinize the physical plant, assess the level of activity, note the kinds of business being conducted, and the like. That inspections do not provide useful observational intelligence, either because inspectors are not good observers or because their presence temporarily deters illicit activities, is confirmed by the fact that not a single investigation in the sample was so generated. All investigations resulting from inspections derived from the scrutiny of records and artifacts, not from observations of office life.

There are numerous obstacles to observation, both overt and covert, in the securities world. Illicit transactions are usually located in private places. They are relatively infrequent occurrences in a world where thousands of licit transactions are consummated each day. They are surrounded by "noise"; it is difficult to discriminate illicit from licit transactions. They are rarely "situationally specific" (Katz 1979b); no single interaction or transaction in itself betrays a fraudulent practice. Observations over a long period of time may be required to differentiate between licit and illicit practices. And their occurrence is not predictable. Stock fraud can emerge in any location, among any group of individuals, regardless of occupational position, on any social occasion. Although some frauds do occur on Wall Street, others may be found in rural

churches, beauty contests, steambaths, car dealerships, factories, board-rooms, seances, clubs, railroad yards, universities, and resorts.

But awareness of the qualities of securities offenses that protect them from observational penetration should not immediately foreclose the possibility of adopting observational intelligence at the SEC. Many other white-collar offenses enjoy similar immunities to detection. Yet, in recent years, innovative observational intelligence strategies have been devised and implemented by other white-collar crime enforcement agencies with great success. The FBI agents in the Abscam sting operation were able to observe private bribery transactions by joining these transactions as parti-cipants—setting themselves up as wealthy Arab sheiks and business rep-resentatives and offering bribes to congressmen while hidden videotape cameras rolled.

Two IRS agents, posing as wealthy art collectors, discovered tax fraud committed by a Los Angeles art dealer/tax shelter specialist from whom they purchased rare Egyptian art objects and by an art museum and university to which they donated the works. The dealer inflated the value of the art and the beneficiaries provided back-dated receipts so that the "couple" could claim excessive charitable deductions on the previous year's income tax return (Cummings 1982). Meanwhile, on the East coast, two undercover IRS agents posed as a business broker and a wealthy prospective restaurant buyer to uncover the skimming of cash in the Manhattan restaurant industry. Owners of three restaurants were caught after providing secret business records and disclosing their true income to the prospective buyer. In an oddly prophetic statement, one of the restau-rateurs observed to the (unsuspected) undercover agent, "I expect some-day the I.R.S. will come in like this and offer to buy the place and sit here and ask these questions." The restaurateur then "extended his arms in front of his body with his wrists together like a person about to be handcuffed and laughed" (Lubasch 1982).

There are any number of similar roles in the securities world that would bring SEC undercover investigators closer to the center of illicit activities for purposes of observational intelligence. They could become participat-ing members of suspected illicit organizations; they could join organiza-tions or adopt roles that facilitate securities violations; or they could adopt victim roles. Investigators could take positions in brokerage firms, under-writing firms, stock exchanges, investment banking firms, investment advisory firms, financial printing companies, public relations firms, per-haps even in stock issuing corporations. Investigators might pose as prospective investors or join the staffs of institutional investors and entice wayward capitalists promoting investment opportunities. Or SEC en-forcers might even create entirely bogus companies—brokerage firms or

potential stock issuers, for example—to examine the conduct of their business associates.[4]

Securing entree into these undercover roles in the world of wayward capitalism is not easy. Even if undercover agents can secure employment in offending organizations, it could take years before they are promoted to positions high enough in organizational hierarchies to provide access to behaviors worthy of observation. And access to even less central roles in securities offense scenarios is still considerably more difficult than in other undercover operations. It is much easier to authentically adopt the role of a John, a drug pusher or drunk, or even a wealthy Arab sheik, than it is to adopt the kinds of licit or illicit roles or organizations essential to secure access to the inner circles of securities fraud. Only the role of securities investor is readily and easily accessible to SEC undercover agents.

And even where entree is afforded and role authenticity is secured, there is still the problem of predictability—where to seek entree, which organizations to solicit as collaborators, which to attempt to "entrap," or where to deploy undercover potential victims. In the FBI and IRS examples cited earlier, agents received tips on which persons or organizations to pursue from con men, detected violators, business associates, and solicited victims. So, in a sense, undercover observation becomes an investigative strategy activated by disclosure-generated intelligence.

The use of undercover observation for initial detection is viable only where the number of potential violators can be narrowed considerably, where the loci of illicit behavior are more predictable. For example, if suspicions arise about several brokerage firms engaged in unorthodox promotions of speculative securities, SEC investigators could pose as principals of a new corporation seeking capital (still a rather major undercover commitment) or as interested investors and approach these particular firms. Or perhaps there are specific industries or geographic areas in which offending is likely enough to warrant an undercover operation, for example, securities fraud in the sale of interests in oil wells in the Southwest or silver mines in the Northwest. Here the likelihood of several attempts at securities fraud within a relatively circumscribed area with a fairly stable cohort of offenders might better insure successful observational opportunities.

In most cases, however, given the lack of predictability of the settings of

---

4. It is noteworthy that the FBI, with most experience in creating bogus enterprises like those used in Abscam, was allocated $7.7 million for undercover operations in 1981 alone (Maitland 1982, 22–23). Since creating securities firms and stock issuing corporations and other ancillary companies most likely requires more elaborate deception than setting up a few sheiks in a Georgetown townhouse, the costs of SEC sting operations could be even greater. And even these FBI figures are way out of the current SEC budgetary ballpark.

securities offenses, coupled with the difficulty of securing access to viable undercover roles and the tremendous commitment of time, resources, and manpower necessary to gather intelligence that might well be obtained in much easier ways, covert observation is not justified. The fact that SEC investigators rarely employ observational methods does not usually reflect lack of imagination or vigor, but good sociological judgment.

But a little real-world empirical exploration might be advisable. These strategies have well served other investigative agencies in the detection of particularly insidious offenses that are relatively immune from conventional intelligence practices. They might do the same for SEC investigators stymied by investor unwittingness, extremely subtle and complex violations, elaborate cover-up schemes, avoidance of public conveyances such as SEC registration, stock exchange listing, or mass-media advertising, extreme insider loyalty, and closely held conspiratorial networks. Agency enforcers might undertake a small experimental pilot program of undercover investigation—perhaps deploying agents into investor or broker roles—to explore the intelligence possibilities of covert strategies. After a short period of observation, the catch of the pilot program would be compared with that of conventional intelligence strategies and assessed for its redundancy, timeliness, accuracy, and the significance of the offenses snared.

SPIN-OFFS

According to the data, relatively few SEC investigations, particularly those of nonregistrants, result from previous investigative efforts. Either my assumptions that offenders recidivate and that birds of a feather flock together are wrong, or SEC officials are not sufficiently milking ongoing investigations for their intelligence insights—insights that are acquired easily compared to those secured by other intelligence methods. I suspect the latter to be true.

In order to capture more of this enormously valuable intelligence resource, every link in an investigated offense should be pursued with questions about whether principals have engaged in or are involved in any previous, simultaneous, or subsequent illegal activities; whether collaborators or facilitators, whatever their culpability, have engaged in or are involved in other offenses; whether witnesses have access to other unrelated information; whether victims have invested in any other questionable securities. Somewhat akin to the parole or probationary treatment of criminal offenders, securities violators should be routinely checked for possible recidivism. Since the spin-off is the only incursive strategy not limited by SEC registration, the spin-off potential of investigations of nonregistrants should be exploited relentlessly.

THE COST OF TECHNOLOGICAL UPGRADING

The implementation of these proposals obviously will increase the cost of SEC enforcement. Some proposals require substantial direct costs: the purchase of computer hardware, the hiring of new personnel, the rental of telephone hot-lines, the printing and distribution of instructional materials, and so on.[5] Others require significant indirect costs: lobbying for new statutory guidelines, prosecuting difficult cases to publicize the leading edge of enforcement policy and to deter would-be offenders, appealing unfavorable court decisions that undercut SEC charges of culpability. And others require little expenditure of SEC funds but impose substantial costs on SEC registrants or self-regulatory agencies. Like the intelligence technologies currently in place, the proposed intelligence programs are variably expensive. But officials have rarely if ever studied the cost of ongoing intelligence programs—of inspections, or market surveillance, or responses to investor complaints—let alone the price of new ones. Without these data, it is impossible to rationally evaluate the trade-offs between current or proposed intelligence programs.

These proposals for expanding intelligence technologies were made by imagining the theoretical possibilities implied in the research findings, not by weighing costs and benefits. I certainly do not advocate the wholesale adoption of the list of proposed reforms. I do recommend, though, that they provide the occasion for a wholesale evaluation of the SEC intelligence program. Estimates of the costs of intelligence strategies currently in place should be gathered and correlated with data presented here on the output of these strategies. And a series of small-scale pilot experiments with some of the reform proposals offered should be staggered over the next few years to gather data on their economic and organizational cost as well as on their output, with respect to kinds of violations, offenders, victims, offense seriousness and impact, and the accuracy and timeliness of intelligence. Armed with this information, policymakers can develop an intelligence program that best expends available resources and best meets enforcement priorities.

During a period of budgetary retrenchment, proposals to expand SEC enforcement programs may seem naive and academic. But when resources are scarce, the need to allocate them intelligently is all the more crucial. And the only way to properly expend scarce resources is to move from a passive intelligence program shaped by fortune, accident, and external pressure to one that is constructed by carefully analyzed policy

---

5. For example, SEC officials estimated that the market oversight and surveillance system would cost $12 million over five years ("A Computer Watchdog" 1980, 42).

preferences and empiricial data on cost and output. Furthermore, preoccupation with the current winds of political fortune is dangerously shortsighted. The SEC's course has been cyclical and oscillating. Although the present era represents a period of retrenchment, new cycles will inevitably follow. The scope of our imagination may be limited by the policies of the present, but its breadth may be essential to shaping the practices of the future.

LIMITS ON INTELLIGENCE: LEGAL AND MORAL ISSUES

Some of the technical, psychological, organizational, and economic obstacles to reengineering intelligence systems have been considered here. There are two other obstacles—of a different kind. Technological changes of the kind proposed may violate or be inconsistent with extant law, or they may be abhorrent to basic moral values, or both.

With respect to the legal impediments, there may simply be no legal support for some of the technological changes envisioned. Proposals for corporate self-audits for deviant conduct, for example, may be inconsistent with Constitutional guarantees against self-incrimination. An important inducement upon which many of the proposed strategies are based is one of extending culpability for illegal activities to more and more peripheral collaborators or facilitators. But there may be insufficient legal or evidentiary support to allege culpability of this sort. Several of the SEC access point cases, which extend culpability to collaborators such as attorneys and accountants, have been reversed in the courts (Hershey 1976). In a well-known civil case based on a similar premise, *Ernst and Ernst v. Hochfelder*, the court ruled that in order to collect damages in a suit against the accounting firm for failing to discover fraud, it was necessary to demonstrate that the offense was done "scienter," with evil intention to defraud, not simply negligence. If the court generally demands demonstrations of evil intention in charges against the facilitators of securities offenses, it may be difficult for the SEC to threaten these parties with culpability as a disclosure incentive where it is unlikely that willfulness could be adequately demonstrated. It may be necessary, then, to change elements of the securities laws if their potential negative sanctions are to be manipulated for intelligence purposes.

There may be moral obstacles to the implementation of intelligence reforms as well. The physical and social intelligence technology of Orwell's *1984* would undoubtedly assist SEC investigators in their intelligence efforts, but few would tolerate their use. The moral issues surrounding possible reforms of intelligence systems may seem obscure because the SEC has rarely been guilty of moral excess. But the example of the

scandals surrounding FBI, CIA, and even Royal Canadian Mounted Police intelligence highlights the many abuses and controversial questions that inhere in intelligence systems (Giniger 1981, 6). To how much privacy are persons and organizations, their activities, their transactions, or their records entitled? What amount of intrusiveness of government in peoples' lives is excessive? Should government be allowed to manipulate, intimidate, or deceive its citizens in order to gather intelligence? How just is the practice of discretionary prosecution, of letting a guilty person go free simply in exchange for information, or that of sending undercover agents to entrap would-be offenders? And so on. And there are more philosophical or ideological questions as well, concerning the extent to which citizens should be expected to pay for regulation and whether investors, shareholders, corporations, or professionals should bear the burden of enforcement costs. These questions cannot be resolved through the insights of social science, but only by serious introspection by all citizens.

INTELLIGENCE AND THE ENFORCEMENT PROCESS

The notion that the detection process provides a critical juncture for the operation of a system of social control, in that it defines the system's caseload, is an insight not unique to this analysis. For example, in their study of a police morals detail, Skolnick and Woodworth (1967) wrote:

> Awareness of infraction is the foundation of any social control system. Whatever the system of normative standards, whether these are folkways or mores, crimes or rules, a transgression must somehow be observed and reported before sanctions can be applied. The potential efficiency of a social control system, therefore, varies directly with its capacity to observe or receive reports of transgressions. . . . This idea may seem obvious, yet without exploring it, without analyzing the empirical relation between awareness and control, we shall be failing to examine some of the more serious problems and hidden consequences of control systems [99–100].

Leon Mayhew, in his study of antidiscrimination law enforcement, describes this phenomenon as that of jurisdiction or access to violation (1968, 16). Donald Black describes it as mobilization (1973).

The details of gathering an investigative caseload have implications for the likelihood that any one of a number of law enforcement purposes will be fulfilled. If policymakers seek to insure general deterrence, then it is essential that intelligence nets be cast widely and the full constellation of detection strategies be utilized, so that no category of offender is beyond

reach and therefore immune from the enforcement process.[6] If policy-makers seek to protect investors, then they need to allocate resources primarily to detection strategies that uncover offenses with the potential for substantial victimization but which catch them early. If they seek to control the behavior of SEC registrants, they must rely primarily on proactive detection strategies; if they seek to control that of nonregistrants, they must rely primarily on reactive ones. Other and sometimes inconsistent policy goals—the desire to maintain the integrity of the market system, to define the leading edge of securities law enforcement, to announce a new area of future law enforcement priority, to display the most flagrant abuses in hopes of securing new legislation—require different kinds of caseload and therefore different constellations of intelligence strategies.

The SEC recognizes the strategic role of caseload more than do many other social control agencies. Some of the data from sociological research on other administrative agencies—the Massachusetts Commission against Discrimination (Mayhew 1968), California's Industrial Accident Commission (Nonet 1969), and many others—suggest that, over time, these organizations become co-opted by the victims they are mandated to protect. The result is that they provide in essence a private-law system, a system in which law becomes trivialized, in which agencies ultimately become unable to institute strategic social change through their enforcement program. It is easy to understand how such a process could develop. With a constant and heavy input of victim complaints, the agency gets settled into a reactive posture of responding to the complaints rather than exerting the much greater effort of mounting a proactive intelligence program. And, in so doing, they have lost control over caseload and its strategic role in defining enforcement policy and outcome.

I cite this example because it appears that the SEC has reversed this trend. Over time, the agency has relied less and less on investor complaints to define its caseload. Especially in recent years, the agency has taken more intelligence initiative, developed better proactive strategies, pursued new categories of law violators. The result is that, while many

6. Most of the social science literature on deterrence has been preoccupied with sanctions, their severity, and their delivery. I find this focus misplaced. Given the impotence of most intelligence systems—the tiny percentage of infractions actually uncovered and the major categories of offenders that seemingly slip through intelligence nets entirely—concern for sanctions is irrelevant to most would-be offenders. Convinced of their relative immunity from detection, they are indifferent to the severity of punishment that is applied only to some of those detected. The primary task in deterrence, therefore, should be to decrease would-be offenders' assessments of their immunity from detection. Only after offenders are convinced that they may very well be caught does it make sense to manipulate sanctions in hopes of deterring infractions.

administrative agencies generate an increasingly trivialized caseload as they age, that of the SEC has become increasingly *less* trivial. This impression is clear not only from all the public rhetoric that surrounds the agency, but also from the twenty-five-year perspective on SEC history that I have acquired during this study.

In short, the attempt to realize any of the many and often conflicting goals of law enforcement policy is an active and not a passive process. Agencies do not have to become co-opted; they do not have to become captives of their reactive intelligence inputs. They always have the option of reengineering and rebalancing intelligence strategies, both reactive and proactive, in accordance with enforcement goals. I hope that this research has provided some insights about the varying consequences of particular detection methods that will be of value in the development of intelligence programs consistent with enforcement policy.

This book ends as it began: with the social institution of trust. The Securities and Exchange Commission was created when trust in America's securities markets was at its nadir. After the great stock market crash of 1929, investors discovered that fully half of their 25 billion dollars' investment in securities was worthless. They also learned that the abusive financing and trading practices that contributed to the great crash were pervasive. In the months that followed, the exchanges took little self-regulatory initiative. New issues of corporate securities were offered in only nominal amounts; trading on the exchanges was light. A former president of National City Bank of New York suggested that stock and bond quotations be renamed "Quotations of Risks and Hazards" (Vanderlip 1932, 3–4). Investor confidence disappeared.

But Americans have devised a brilliant solution to their crises of trust. In 1906, *The Jungle*, Upton Sinclair's novel about life in Chicago's stockyards, vividly revealed the unsanitary conditions in meat-packing plants—tubercular pork, moldy and white, being dosed with borax and glycerine and dumped into the hoppers along with the rats that infested the plants, poisoned bread meant to kill them, and the decomposed remains of unfortunate workers who slipped into the vats. The public uproar that inevitably followed was silenced by the passage of a federal meat inspection act, creating government certification of the purity of America's meat (Kolko 1963, 98–108). A quarter century later, when the great crash revealed the unhealthy condition of the nation's securities markets, an epidemic of public distrust was dosed with the passage of yet another federal act—this time for truth in securities—and the creation of a federal agency to insure its promises.

At last the role and function of the SEC becomes clear. It is the symbolic guarantor of trust in securities. The creation of the SEC was a clever

innovation. It allowed government to fabricate and guarantee the trust that the securities markets had lost. But the agency's initial promises of trust were only provisional; ultimately the SEC had to earn the trust of securities investors by deed rather than by word. So far the agency has performed well. Where other regulatory agencies have consistently earned the mockery and distrust of the American public, the reputation of the SEC has remained relatively untarnished and its role as symbolic guarantor of trust in the securities markets unquestioned (Cary 1964, 661; Ratner 1978, 2−3; Miller 1979b, D1; Subcommittee 1976, 11; Karmel 1982).

But shoring up the shaky foundation of trust is a fulltime job. With the slightest inattention or temporary lethargy, the capitalist structure might easily come crashing down. And this is where detection comes in. Obviously, the SEC cannot eliminate securities fraud. It is not necessary that it do so. But to maintain trust, the agency must reduce the opportunities for lawbreaking and insure complete enforcement coverage and the guarantee that no person, no corporation, no scheme is inherently immune from the enforcement process. Investors must believe that all wayward capitalists with whom they may inadvertently become involved have a real chance (and ideally a good one) of being caught by SEC enforcers and their illicit activities halted. Trust is therefore premised on universalistic application of the enforcement process.

Coverage or selective immunity or vulnerability to enforcement are byproducts of detection. The orchestration of detection strategies determines which wayward capitalists will be caught and which allowed to freely ply their trade, the likelihood that certain kinds of violators will be snared or spared, the likelihood that certain kinds of investors will be protected or victimized, and the likelihood that acts of wayward capitalism will be nipped in the bud or allowed to grow and flourish without disruption. SEC enforcers can easily maintain a respectable-size investigative caseload with little effort, imagination, or vigilance. And in this era of government contraction, budget cutting, and deregulation, the temptation certainly is to do just that. But the integrity of trust requires coverage as well as numbers. It requires that the full arsenal of investigative strategies be refined and deployed so that all forms of wayward capitalism are vulnerable to SEC enforcement. If word of selective enforcement leaked out, if securities fraud scandals became a common feature of the capitalist landscape, the shaky foundation of trust might crumble and the investment monies that feed the capitalist beast dry up.

I have proposed a number of programs to enhance the reach and timeliness of SEC intelligence strategies, some of them quite expensive. But the price tag of an intelligence program that would sustain the myth of the SEC's role as the symbolic guarantor of trust may be more afford-

able than it first appeared. In recent years, more than $1.5 trillion was invested in American corporations. The annual SEC appropriation represents less than .005 percent of this capitalist fund. Indeed, any million-dollar expense to expand the coverage of SEC intelligence technologies (not an insignificant sum by SEC budgetary standards) represents less than *seven-hundred-thousandths of one percent* (.00007 percent) of that investment in American corporations. Surely legitimate and even wayward capitalists can afford such a sum to insure the viability of the securities markets, in the former case, or the continued opportunity to victimize would-be investors, in the latter. From this perspective, it appears that the conduct of the SEC as a vigorous and terrifying David in a universe of Goliaths is truly astounding. And the remarkable power—yet delicate fragility—of trust is very real.

APPENDIX:

The Research: Design, Method, and Execution

ACCESS TO THE RESEARCH SETTING

The research upon which this book is based* emerged from my developing interest in the study of the control of white-collar crime at a time when, coincidentally, officials of the Securities and Exchange Commission (SEC) were visiting the Yale law school, where I was working. At that time, both the chairman of the SEC and the director of its Division of Enforcement participated in a special program on international bribery. Subsequently, the chairman was a visiting scholar at the law school and the director of the Division of Enforcement a guest lecturer and participant in an advisory conference on white-collar crime. From conversations with these officials, I learned that the SEC would provide a fascinating setting for research on the control of white-collar crime and that they would be receptive to such research.

These conversations began in early spring 1976. That summer, I was invited to visit the SEC headquarters office in Washington, D.C., to observe agency operations and learn more about the enforcement of the securities laws. To supplement my summer research experiences, I later requested formal access to nonpublic SEC enforcement records like those I had been shown during my summer in residence. It was not until late spring 1977 that full access and bureaucratic cooperation were extended and a second phase of research began. The long wait was not a function of bureaucratic delay and red tape. Rather, it reflected very serious consideration by SEC officials of whether the proposed research should be permitted and included more than one juncture where the possibility of any research at all seemed especially bleak.

My request for access to nonpublic enforcement records had no precedent. The SEC had considerable experience with requests by outsiders—the varied participants in securities transactions, the securities bar, and the media. The agency also had some experience with in-house economic research as well as with the commission of outside consultants. There were precedents as well for summer internships for law students, a status similar to that extended to me in the summer of 1976 (and undoubtedly the bureaucratic forerunner that made such an invitation possible). But apparently the SEC had never received such requests from academic researchers. SEC officials' unfamiliarity with academic research and the absence of precedent, on the one hand, and fear of the precedent that any positive response to the request might have, on the other hand, resulted in the activation of agency "big guns" in a matter of otherwise minor proportion.

*For a much fuller and more technical discussion of research method, see Shapiro (1980a, chapter 2).

The matters involved in negotiation were varied. SEC officials were primarily concerned about violations of privacy or confidentiality, the disclosure or collection of information that might identify SEC enforcement targets or reveal details of enforcement policy or strategy, and the implications of this grant of access for requests by others under the Freedom of Information Act or other vehicles. After I agreed to scrutinize only closed investigations, not to record either direct or indirect identifying information concerning parties under investigation, and to submit writings based on the research for prior clearance to the SEC general counsel (to guard against disclosure of nonpublic, confidential, or identifying information), SEC officials finally granted me access to their nonpublic enforcement records.

SOURCES OF DATA AND DATA COLLECTION STRATEGIES

The research was conducted in two phases, each with separate problems of access. The first phase, conducted for about six weeks during the summer of 1976, involved observation at the headquarters and one of the regional offices of the SEC. The second phase, conducted for about nine months, from the spring of 1977 until the following winter, involved the systematic examination and coding of SEC investigative records.

OBSERVATION STRATEGIES

During the observation period, I was affiliated with the Division of Enforcement in the SEC headquarters office in Washington, D.C. Like regular SEC employees, I was bound by sworn statements pertaining to disclosure of information, protection of privacy, conflict of interest, and the like. I was therefore permitted access to the meetings, conversations, documents, and miscellaneous information readily available to regular staff. I spent most of my time with a section of the division concerned primarily with management fraud—bribery, corruption, and self-dealing by or within publicly held corporations. However, as a matter of physical location, I floated through the division, occupying desks temporarily vacant when attorneys were out of the office or vacationing. This considerable mobility provided a broad perspective and the opportunity to learn by observation and conversation what might otherwise have required formal interviews. The sudden intimacy imposed by sharing a tiny office with someone for a day or two naturally generated small talk as well as opportunities for observation that provided colorful detail about the nature of his or her work.

My daily activities were varied. Most often, I engaged in interviews and conversations with SEC staff—commissioners and their law clerks, administrators, and especially enforcement attorneys. I became a voracious reader. Whenever there was a lull, I would read documents, reports, memos, press releases, or instructional materials provided by staff members with whom I had spoken. I scoured the SEC library for materials unavailable elsewhere.

I also sat in on the daily meetings of the SEC commissioners with their staff, most of which considered enforcement matters. These meetings, which usually lasted several hours, provided an excellent opportunity to learn about the enforcement problems of greatest concern to the agency at that time, about agency organization and decisionmaking, and about the development of enforcement policy. Although I was afforded the opportunity to attend these very private

commission hearings, opportunities to participate in smaller, less formal meetings were uncommon. I was included in few conferences between staff attorneys and was never invited to participate in those which included outsiders (subjects of investigation or their attorneys, witnesses, and so on). In some sense, I was given both binoculars and blinders.

Early in the period of observation, I attended an annual week-long Securities Enforcement Training Conference, conducted by the SEC, in which about a hundred persons attended formal sessions concerned with everything from recent amendments of the securities laws and current enforcement problems to techniques for obtaining testimony from witnesses to pointers on interpreting accounting work papers to strategies for discovering evidence. Later in the summer, I was also able to visit one of the regional offices of the SEC for a week of observation and interviews.

In the beginning, the most common reaction to my presence at the agency was one of distrust. I was the subject of gossip; a door was slammed in my face; people would awkwardly attempt to surreptitiously check up on my activities; certain staffers refused my requests for an appointment; and others were reticent in answering my questions. I also encountered occasional friendliness and cooperation. But as time passed, as I became a fixture in the office and easily recognizable as an insider, and as my interests and orientations became characterized as innocuous and nonthreatening, the distrust gave way to openness, candor, and, in some instances, almost comradeship.

The quality and quantity of data available from observational research strategies were affected only temporarily by problems of suspicion and distrust. However, after six weeks of expanding and perfecting observational methods, several other impediments to systematic research remained. They derive largely from the nature of SEC enforcement work and its amenability to observation. Many aspects of enforcement work are invisible, at least to the scrutiny of a single observer. They may be invisible for reasons suggested previously—because I was denied access to meetings or conversations in which investigation was conducted or strategy discussed. Invisibility may derive from related factors—telephone conversations I could not hear, written correspondence or documents I was not shown, out-of-town or out-of-the-office field investigations that I did not join.

But invisibility also derives from the fact that there is nothing to see. Typically, SEC investigations are protracted over a period of years. There may be weeks of intense investigation and then the matter may sit on a back burner for months. Where investigation is intense, there may be several simultaneous activities warranting observation; where it is not, there may be nothing to observe. Because of the complexity of cases requiring varied expertise and their extended course interrupted by personnel turnover, investigatory responsibility is typically diffused and delegated among many staff members. It may be difficult to reconstruct the process without observing or interviewing all these parties.

For the same reasons, specific enforcement activities become particularized. A two-hour commission meeting may involve consideration of the prosecution of only one participant in a massive securities fraud. Legal action against other participants may have been discussed previously. But without knowledge of these prior discussions, the particular observation is out of context and subject to considerable misinterpretation. Finally, because investigation and prosecution consume so much time, case turnover is relatively slow. Observational strategies, then, do not permit the accumulation of a very large base of data. Both the

quantity and, in many respects, the quality of data so obtained are limited.[1]

Observational strategies in this setting are suited to the development of an ethnography of the typical elements of enforcement experience, the day-to-day activities that are somehow aggregated and result in the enforcement of the securities laws. What observational strategies obscure, however, is a sense for the continuity of activity or for the formula of aggregation.

Because of the protracted period of investigation and the simultaneity of investigative activities, observational methods are almost necessarily cross-sectional. Observers are prohibited from contrasting developmental processes. They collect a series of "snapshots" taken at various points in different developmental sequences. These snapshots are clear and detailed, but a viewing of the films from which these stills were taken is also needed, to see how they began and how they ended, to see whether similar stills came from similar films, and to understand why dissimilar snapshots differ. The films lack the detail of the blown-up still shots, and, because they take longer to view, are accorded a greater superficiality of observation. But they serve as a useful corrective to the lack of continuity inherent in observational methods.

For this reason, I sought a data base that captured the diversity of enforcement activities but afforded the distance to appreciate their continuity, if only retrospectively. This was achieved by the archival phase of the research and the choice of the investigative record as the window through which enforcement activity would be viewed.

THE EXAMINATION OF ARCHIVAL MATERIALS

The second phase of research, on which most of this book is based, involved the examination of SEC investigatory records.[2] The choice of the formal investigation as the organizing device around which a dynamic perspective on enforcement activity would be constructed came easily, since it serves as the primary device by which SEC enforcers organize their own work. This archival research served as a corrective for some of the problems inherent in the observational research. Since materials are accumulated by case, it was possible to monitor all aspects of an investigation over time and the involvement of different staff in its conduct. Since all investigations were completed, it was possible to follow them from beginning to end. The reliance on records permitted access to events that might have occurred simultaneously or that might not have been otherwise observable. And, of course, the reliance on records maximized my own use of time—a larger quantity of activities could be monitored retrospectively than would have been possible if I had to wait for them to unfold.

These data, then, provided a sense for the continuity of events and permitted a larger sweep of "observation" than was possible through direct observation.

1. It is interesting that observational methods, the most accepted practice, indeed the state of the art in research on the social control of street crime (Skolnick 1967; Reiss 1971a; Rubinstein 1973; Manning 1977; Sanders 1977; Black 1980), fared so poorly in the SEC research. Observational methods are not equally successful because of the enormous differences between the social organization of street crime and securities or other white-collar crime enforcement practices. The differences are so pronounced that one recent definition of white-collar crime differentiates offenses on the basis of the problems they create for the enforcement process (Katz 1979b).

2. Since it was necessary to examine all investigatory records on SEC premises, I was able to continue observation and interviews throughout this second research phase, though less intensively and systematically.

Obviously they had associated costs: in superficiality of recorded information and in the rich details of investigative activity that are never recorded. Furthermore, the whole is not equal to the sum of its parts. Investigative cases cannot be aggregated to reconstruct a sense of the social organization of enforcement activity. Archival and observational methods complement each other nicely. They elaborate the whole and the parts, the static and the dynamic. Together they paint a comprehensible portrait. In this research, unfortunately, the observational and archival methods focused on different times and locations in agency experience. The composition is imperfect, but the insights are still of value.

The investigative file. At the time the research was begun, files gathering the materials generated by all SEC docketed investigations since the creation of the agency in 1934 had been saved and stored at the Federal Records Center in Maryland. Files ranged in size from several pages to dozens of boxes and thousands of pages. The average file in my sample had several hundred pages. The size of a file is usually correlated with the scope of investigation and the fact of and nature of formal prosecution. Some files, regardless of age, seemed more complete than others, but the majority shared a wealth of detail that is both gratifying and overwhelming to the researcher.[3]

Investigative files simply accumulated all the materials generated by an investigation. They were not prepared for any purpose other than storage, nor were they organized for presentation to some audience other than those attorneys conducting the investigation. Files contained scratch paper, notes, and rough drafts of memos arrayed among the more formal records or documents. Because these were working files, prepared for internal consumption, they were both detailed and candid. They lacked the public relations gloss or self-serving quality characteristic of records generated specifically for public audiences. The contents of investigative files were tremendously valuable for abstracting a full and realistic sense of investigative practice.

The quantity and quality of data available from the files varied considerably. Some files were incomplete, with missing records. In other instances, all necessary records were available, but it was clear in reconstructing the events that some details either were not recorded or records of them were missing from the files.

---

3. SEC investigatory files typically contain: (1) forms completed upon opening and closing the investigation, noting the circumstances of the investigation, the acts and statutes allegedly violated, dates, identities of investigators and of suspects investigated, the nature of the offense, the type and outcome of prosecution, if any, and justifications for prosecutorial choice; (2) quarterly reports noting the progress of investigation; (3) memoranda to the commission requesting formal orders of investigation or the institution of civil, administrative, and/or criminal proceedings, generally describing the offense and offenders in great detail and outlining relevant considerations and precedents for taking the action requested; (4) other memoranda between staff, summaries of meetings and telephone conversations; (5) copies of correspondence to and from the agency pertaining to offenders, victims, informants, and other enforcement agencies; (6) criminal reference reports transmitted to the U.S. Department of Justice requesting criminal prosecution (detailing the nature of the offense, the investigation, available evidence, prosecutorial rationale, and so on); (7) copies of civil complaints, indictments, administrative charges, and announcements of the outcome of proceedings; (8) press and other releases, newspaper articles, and clippings; (9) records of file searches for information on the prior record of subjects of investigation; (10) reports prepared for probation or presentence investigations; (11) transcripts of testimony, documents, records, copies of subpoenas, court exhibits, and papers.

For 19 percent of the cases in the sample, investigative files were missing entirely.[4] For all cases with missing or incomplete files, I examined a secondary record system, which summarized investigations and their enforcement history. In most cases, it provided enough information to reconstruct the basic contours of the offense and of the investigatory process. More frequently, materials in investigative files were redundant rather than incomplete, and I exploited these redundancies to check on the reliability of the records.

SAMPLING

The unit of analysis in the archival research is the formal docketed investigation conducted by the headquarters and regional offices of the SEC, for which a file was created and maintained.[5] Approximately 18,000 docketed investigations were opened from the inception of the SEC in 1934 until March 1977, when the research sample was drawn. A computer tape, developed by the SEC for in-house case management, documentation, and data retrieval, enumerated these 18,000 investigations and assorted characteristics. The sample was drawn from an extract of this tape, which listed all *closed* SEC cases.

It might have been desirable to weight the sample in order to focus on specific kinds of investigations or offenses—for example, criminal cases or only securities fraud—or to insure that they were adequately represented. However, documentation of these features of an investigation either was not included on the extract tape or was unreliable. Only the date of investigation was considered in the development of a sampling design.

As noted earlier, I was denied access to records of ongoing investigations for this research. SEC investigations typically continue for long periods of time, half of them for two years or more. The denial of access to open investigations resulted in a sharply reduced sample of cases reflecting contemporary investigative activity. Less than 43 percent of the SEC investigations instituted after July 1972 had been closed by March 1977, when the sample was drawn. If cases closed in random fashion, this fact would not be troubling, since it would be possible to correct for the problem through weighting. They do not, however. Cases involving larger corporations as violators, more complex, widespread, or long-term patterns of illegality, more serious violations, extended litigation, and multiple forms of legal action close more slowly. The inclusion of cases opened and closed during the mid-1970s, then, would bias and trivialize the sample by overrepresenting the quick investigation.

Choice of a precise cut-off date for the research sample considered biases of this sort as well as the possible effects of a major reorganization of the commission in August 1972 that resulted in the creation of a separate Division of Enforcement for the first time in commission history. All investigations opened after December 1972 were therefore excluded. Because the full arsenal of statutory provisions subject to SEC investigation was not complete until 1942—whereupon SEC enforcement activities were disrupted by the Second World War and a move of SEC

4. Files were missing for several reasons. Some had been lost, misfiled, or never returned to central storage by an SEC regional office or the Department of Justice; some were in use by other SEC personnel or by outsiders (under the Freedom of Information Act) at the time they were ordered for this research; others had been consolidated into another docketed case without proper notation.

5. For an extensive discussion of the implications for the generalizability of the research of defining docketed investigations as the unit of analysis, see Shapiro (1980a, 79–103).

central offices to Philadelphia—1948, the year of the agency's return to Washington, was selected as the starting date of the research.

The twenty-five-year period from 1948 to 1972 served as the time frame from which the sample was drawn and to which research findings generalize. Obviously, significant events intervened in the twenty-five-year-period—major amendments to the securities laws and drastic changes in the economy, in the state of the securities markets, in the conditions of the professional organizations that service them, in the vitality of the SEC itself, and in other political and social conditions.[6] Since I had no a priori reason to believe that a given era was more significant than another, my sampling rationale was to be as inclusive as possible. Certainly a narrow circumscription of years would present fewer problems, but also fewer findings of relevance to present or future SEC enforcement practices.

The listing of closed cases included 8,117 investigations opened between January 1948 and December 1972. Utilizing a sampling fraction of one-eighth, a simple random sample of 1,044 cases was drawn.[7] Selection was made without reference to any other case characteristics, and the probability of inclusion in the sample was equal for all cases opened during this time period. The desired target sample was 500 cases, but I drew a larger sample in case a substantial number of investigations were missing or data collection proceeded more quickly than expected. The 1,044 cases were randomly ordered through use of a random numbers table (Rand Corporation 1955), and they were coded in this order. This procedure also insured against bias in the sample introduced in the event that data collection was terminated prematurely.[8] However, it also insured that biases introduced by my

6. Given the long sweep of SEC history reflected in the archival research, one would have expected to find significant longitudinal trends in the data—in types of offenses or offenders investigated, characteristics of the enforcement process, and the like. There are surprisingly few, either because time periods large enough to yield statistically meaningful comparisons mask real change or because the content of what SEC enforcers do is relatively independent of the agency's status at large or the shifting economic fortunes of the nation. The twenty-five-year distribution of securities offenses is remarkably stable, especially for the most common violations, with small increases over time in technical violations, improper sales techniques, and investment schemes. The data suggest a modest trend toward greater prominence and scope in SEC enforcement targets (number of offenders, cost of victimization, size and age of organizational offenders, national and international victimizations) and shifts in the industries contributing to wayward capitalism (with fewer agricultural and mining firms and more numerous manufacturing and service firms). The data reflect some modest trends in SEC enforcement activity as well: the proportion of investigations generated by investor disclosures dropped from 35 percent in the late 1940s to 19 percent in the early 1970s. Since the late 1960s, rates of inspections and securities community referrals have increased and those of other social control agencies have decreased by much smaller proportions than that of investors. Over the years, the proportion of violations SEC enforcers chose not to prosecute decreased somewhat and the proportion of civil proceedings instituted by SEC enforcers increased, but proportions of criminal or administrative proceedings did not. Most of the other variables in this research—victimization patterns, offense duration, characteristics of wayward capitalists or of investigative technique—showed no major changes over the twenty-five-year period.

7. *A Statistical Package for the Social Sciences* subroutine was utilized to draw the sample (Nie et al. 1975, 128). I contrasted the population and sample on a number of variables included on the extract tape. Percentage differences between population and sample on any given category never exceeded 1 percent. Means, medians, modes, and standard deviations were remarkably similar.

8. Pursuant to a new act of Congress, many older SEC records had been scheduled for destruction about two months after data collection began. Fortunately, by the time that data collection was completed they had not yet been destroyed.

growing sophistication as a coder would be randomly distributed across the sample. Data on the first 526 cases in the randomly ordered sample were collected and coded. Thus, the actual sampling fraction was one-sixteenth.

A word about random sampling is in order. This aside is perhaps more relevant for the reader trained in law than in social science. The choice of random criteria in the selection of the research sample requires little justification for social science audiences. It would be the absence of random criteria that would require justification, because it would mean the impossibility or extreme difficulty of drawing inferences about the larger population on the basis of sample data. However, it would be strange indeed if a casebook in securities law was based on a random sample of all securities litigation or even if SEC annual reports commented on a random sample of the year's cases rather than its most significant groundbreaking ones.[9] That derives from the fact that the logic of legal reasoning and that of scientific reasoning are different. What is at first precedent in law is at first deviance in science.

One could do a fascinating scientific study of precedent-setting cases by drawing a random sample of a listing of all these cases. But it would be a different study. The one reported here is concerned with typical investigative work, not its unique examples. Once we have a sense for the contours of investigative work, for the common patterns, for what is not distinctive, for the endlessly repeated redundant activities that escape canonization in a casebook, we can begin to explore the distinctive ripples in the otherwise uneventful flow of events. We can ask when these ripples typically occur, what accounts for their occurrence, what is their substance, what are the patterns and processes according to which they become normalized and typical, and so on.

These observations are perhaps commonsensical. But their implications are radical. One gets an extremely different sense of reality from sampling the typical rather than the unusual, the frequent rather than the infrequent. If I had listed the names of the cases in the sample (which I could not because of assurances of confidentiality), even the finest scholar of securities law would recognize very few of them. And that is because they are not distinctive. These data, therefore, will look unfamiliar to the lawyer. But they will probably look unfamiliar to most SEC staff as well, especially those higher in the agency's hierarchy, whose vision is directed to the new, challenging, interesting, groundbreaking cases that are carefully built and often vigorously litigated and appealed.[10] Their blinders will exclude from their vision the typical violation quickly consented to by offenders because years of precedent and experience indicate that litigation would be pointless. It will exclude as well minor violations that never are formally prosecuted and therefore have little chance of inclusion in a casebook. To these observers, the work of the agency as reflected in these data will seem unfamiliar

9. Though perhaps bizarre, such an exercise would be fascinating and in some ways considerably more instructive than traditional presentations.

10. In his study of another federal regulatory agency, the Cost of Living Council, created to implement the nationwide wage-price freeze of 1971, Kagan makes a related observation. He notes that an examination of the top-level decisions, "generally the only ones reported and visible to those outside the agency," reveals a greater leniency, a tendency toward accommodation or change, than the more stringent decisions of "the part of the bureaucratic iceberg that operates beneath the surface of public visibility." This pattern derives from the fact that "mechanisms of upward referral of cases tend to send up those cases with the strongest arguments for changes or riskier interpretations of existing rules" (1978, 162).

and probably trivial. Indeed, one response to a preliminary report of my research findings was that they were "wrong." They are not wrong; they are different, and the difference derives from definitions of population and strategies of sampling.

THE CODING SCHEME AND CODING PROCEDURES

My examination of archival records of SEC investigations included in the sample generated two kinds of data. One recorded the detail and distinctive features of each case—concerning patterns of illegality, kinds of offenders and victims, and types of investigatory strategies—in pages of longhand notes. The other recorded standard information on each investigation amenable to quantitative analysis. This second data set required the development of a standard coding scheme, which defined relevant variables and specified objective categories along which cases could be classified.

Because of the difficulty of gaining access to these archival records, because of the possibility that many of the older records would soon be destroyed, because the files were so disorganized that it was necessary to skim through most of their contents and digest a mass of complex material even to abstract a small bit of information, and because my initial theoretical interests were general and unspecified, the coding scheme was developed to gather as much information as possible rather than to focus on a more limited set of variables. Specifically, it abstracted data on characteristics of the offense, offenders, and victims, details of investigative technique, including the circumstances under which the investigation was initiated, and details of case disposition. Two files of data were amassed, one that pertained to characteristics of the offense and investigation itself, the other to each of the 1,934 persons and organizations investigated in the sample. The file of offense-related data contained slightly more than 200 variables; that concerning offender-related characterisitcs, about 130 variables.[11]

SEC investigative files sometimes contained thousands of pages of material, and I skimmed through all their contents. The contents of files were often ordered randomly, without consideration for chronology, type of document, purpose of document, or any other criterion. Examination of the files often required skipping back and forth and reassembling materials to reconstruct the sequence of events. The examination and coding of a case took anywhere from about ten minutes to ten hours. However, the median amount of time spent coding each case was between one and one-and-a-half hours. Data collection continued for about seven months, from mid-May to late December 1977.

I was the only person to assemble, examine, or code any of the cases included in the pretest and sample. These data therefore reflect the biases, perspectives, and misunderstandings of a single individual but also offer the consistency so elusive with team research. Coding did not begin until an extensive pretest had been conducted, the scheme had been refined, and I had become very familiar with its categories and distinctions. Over the period of seven months, I undoubtedly became more sophisticated and developed a clearer sense for the distinctive features of particular kinds of cases and slightly different meanings for code categories. This process is unavoidable. However, the cases were coded in random order, so that any biases generated by this process should have been randomly

11. For most of these variables, rates of missing data were quite low, under 10 percent. Problems of missing or unreliable data were greatest for phenomena most remote from the investigative process, such as the age or prior record of offenders or the social background of victims.

distributed. After all data collection was completed, I reread the entire collection of codes, notes, and documents generated by this process to search for any patterns and inconsistencies that would reflect either error or changes in perspective or interpretation. Surprisingly few problems were discovered. Overall, the data reflect some of the fullest and most complete materials upon which a data set of this kind could be built.

References

Andersen, Raoul. 1980. "Hunt and Conceal: Information Management in Newfoundland Deep Sea Trawler Fishing." In Secrecy: A Cross-Cultural Perspective, edited by Stanton K. Teft, 205–28. New York: Human Sciences Press.

Barmash, Isadore, ed. 1972. Great Business Disasters: Swindlers, Burglars, and Frauds in American Industry. Chicago: Playboy Press.

Baruch, Hurd. 1971. Wall Street: Security Risk. Baltimore: Penguin.

Bernstein, Marver H. 1955. Regulating Business by Independent Commission. Princeton: Princeton University Press.

Biderman, Albert D., and Albert J. Reiss, Jr. 1967. "On Exploring the 'Dark Figure' of Crime." Annals of the American Academy of Political and Social Science 374:1–15.

Black, Donald J. 1973. "The Mobilization of Law." Journal of Legal Studies 2:125–49.

———. 1980. The Manners and Customs of the Police. New York: Academic Press.

Black, Hillel. 1962. The Watchdogs of Wall Street. New York: William Morrow.

Bloom, Murray Teigh. 1971. Rogues to Riches: The Trouble with Wall Street. New York: G. P. Putnam's Sons.

Blundell, William. 1974a. "Equity Funding Trustee Proposes to Give Common Holders Some Value on Shares." Wall Street Journal (October 24):5.

———. 1974b. "The Victims: Many People's Dreams Came Crashing Down with Equity Funding." Wall Street Journal (March 29):1, 19.

———. 1976. "Equity Funding: 'I Did It for the Jollies,'" in Swindled! Classic Business Frauds of the Seventies, edited by Donald Moffitt, 42–89. Princeton: Dow Jones Books.

Bok, Sissela. 1978. Lying: Moral Choice in Public and Private Life. New York: Pantheon.

———. 1982. Secrets: On the Ethics of Concealment and Revelation. New York: Pantheon.

Bowyer, J. Barton, pseud. 1982. Cheating. New York: St. Martin's Press.

Brandeis, Louis D. 1932. Other People's Money. New York: Stokes.

Brandt, Elizabeth. 1980. "On Secrecy and the Control of Knowledge: Taos Pueblo." In Secrecy: A Cross-Cultural Perspective, edited by Stanton K. Teft, 123–46. New York: Human Sciences Press.

Briloff, Abraham. 1976. More Debits than Credits: The Burnt Investor's Guide to Financial Statements. New York: Harper & Row.

Brooks, John. 1958. The Seven Fat Years. New York: Harper.

———. 1969. Once in Golconda: A True Drama of Wall Street, 1920–1938. New York: Harper & Row.

———. 1973. The Go-Go Years. New York: Weybright and Talley.

Bruck, Connie. 1980. "Waning Days for the Zealot at the SEC." The American Lawyer (November):16+.

Caplan, Gerald M., ed. 1983. ABSCAM Ethics: Moral Issues and Deception and Law Enforcement. Ballantine, for The Police Foundation.

Cary, William L. 1964. "Administrative Agencies and the Securities and Exchange Commission." Law and Contemporary Problems 29:653–62.

———. 1967. Politics and the Regulatory Agencies. New York: McGraw-Hill.

Cheek, James H., III. 1975. "Professional Responsibility and Self-Regulation of the Securities Lawyer." Washington and Lee Law Review 32:597–635.

Clinard, Marshall B., and Peter C. Yeager. 1980. Corporate Crime. New York: Free Press.

Cohen, Albert K. 1977. "The Concept of Criminal Organisation." British Journal of Criminology 17:97–111.

Cohen, Bernard. 1980. Deviant Street Networks: Prostitution in New York City. Lexington, Mass.: Lexington Books.

Comer, Michael J. 1977. Corporate Fraud. London: McGraw-Hill.

"A Computer Watchdog for Securities Trading." 1980. Business Week (May 5): 42.

Cormier, Frank. 1962. Wall Street's Shady Side. Washington, D.C.: Public Affairs Press.

Cressey, Donald R. 1953. Other People's Money: The Social Psychology of Embezzlement. New York: Free Press.

———. 1972. Criminal Organization: Its Elementary Forms. New York: Harper & Row.

Crock, Stan. 1981. "A Talk with the SEC's Enforcement Chief." Wall Street Journal (December 18):22.

Crowley, George D. 1975. "The Tax Fraud Investigation." Journal of Criminal Defense 1:155+.

Cummings, Judith. 1982. "I.R.S. Questions Gifts of Art in Coast Inquiry." New York Times (June 3):C17.

Currie, Elliott P. 1968. "Crime without Criminals: Witchcraft and Its Control in Renaissance Europe." Law and Society Review 3:7–32.

Daley, Robert. 1975. "Inside the Criminal-Informant Business." New York Magazine (March 24):31–35.

Dean, Arthur H. 1959. "Twenty-Five Years of Federal Securities Regulation by the Securities and Exchange Commission." Columbia Law Review 59:697–747.

DeBedts, Ralph F. 1964. The New Deal's SEC: The Formative Years. New York: Columbia University Press.

DeMott, D.A. 1977. "Reweaving the Corporate Veil: Management Structure and the Control of Corporate Information." Law and Contemporary Problems 41: 182–221.

Dirks, Raymond L., and Leonard Gross. 1974. The Great Wall Street Scandal. New York: McGraw-Hill.

Donnelly, Richard C. 1951. "Judicial Control of Informants, Spies, Stool Pigeons, and Agent Provocateurs." Yale Law Journal 60:1091–1131.

Douglas, Jack D. 1972. Research on Deviance. New York: Random House.

Dygert, James H. 1976. The Investigative Journalist: Folk Heroes of a New Era. Englewood Cliffs, N.J.: Prentice-Hall.

Edelhertz, Herbert. 1970. The Nature, Impact and Prosecution of White-Collar Crime. Washington, D.C.: U.S. Government Printing Office.

Edelhertz, Herbert; Ezra Stotland; Marilyn Walsh; and Milton Weinberg. 1977. The Investigation of White-Collar Crime: A Manual for Law Enforcement Agencies. Washington, D.C.: U.S. Government Printing Office.

Elias, Christopher. 1971. Fleecing the Lambs. Chicago: Henry Regnery.

Elsen, Sheldon H. 1969. "Securities Law Investigations." Review of Securities Regulation 2:873 78.

Farrand, James R. 1976. "Ancillary Remedies in SEC Civil Enforcement Suits." Harvard Law Review 89:1779 1814.

Ferrara, Ralph C. 1971. "SEC Division of Trading and Markets: Detection, Investigation and Enforcement of Selected Practices that Impair Investor Confidence in the Capital Markets." Howard Law Review 16:950 92.

Festinger, Leon; Henry W. Riecken, Jr.; and Stanley Schacter. 1956. When Prophesy Fails. Minneapolis: University of Minnesota Press.

Fidel, Kenneth. 1980. "The Dynamics of Military Conspiracy." In Secrecy: A Cross-Cultural Perspective, edited by Stanton K. Teft, 178 97. New York: Human Sciences Press.

Fisher, Jacob. 1948. The Art of Detection. New Brunswick: Rutgers University Press.

Flanagan, Timothy; David van Alstyne; and Michael Gottfredson, eds. 1982. Sourcebook of Criminal Justice Statistics—1981. Washington, D.C.: U.S. Department of Justice, Bureau of Justice Statistics.

Flowers, Theodore W. 1972. "SEC Investigations: A Current Appraisal." Pennsylvania Bar Association Quarterly 43:521 37.

Fried, Joseph P. 1982. "A Dentist's Plea of Guilt Voided in Sexual Abuse." New York Times (July 27):B1.

Friedman, Howard M. 1981. Securities and Commodities Enforcement. Lexington, Mass.: Lexington Books.

Gadsby, Edward N. 1959. "Historical Development of the S.E.C.—The Government View." George Washington Law Review 28:6 17.

Galanter, Marc. 1974. "Why the 'Haves' Come Out Ahead: Speculations on the Limits of Legal Change." Law and Society Review 9:95 160.

Galbraith, John Kenneth. 1955. The Great Crash, 1929. Boston: Houghton Mifflin.

Geis, Gilbert. 1967. "The Heavy Electrical Equipment Antitrust Cases of 1961." In Criminal Behavior Systems, edited by Marshall B. Clinard and Richard Quinney, 139 50. New York: Holt, Rinehart and Winston.

Geraghty, J. M. 1965. "One Face of the Informer—The Approver." University of Queensland Law Journal 5:66 73.

———. 1966. "Another Face of the Informer—The Police Spy." University of Queensland Law Journal 5:170 78.

Gerth, Jeff. 1981a. "New Enforcement Chief Backs S.E.C. Policy Shift." New York Times (June 30):D1, D18.

———. 1981b. "S.E.C.'s Chief Gives Blessing to Mergers." New York Times (July 14):D6.

Gesell, Gerhard Alden. 1940. Protecting Your Dollars: An Account of the Work of the Securities and Exchange Commission. Washington, D.C.: National Home Library Foundation.

Giniger, Henry. 1981. "Amid Criticism, the Mounties Lose Security Role." New York Times (August 26):6.

Godfrey, E. Drexel, Jr., and Don R. Harris. 1971. Basic Elements of Intelligence. Washington, D.C.: Law Enforcement Assistance Administration.

Goffman, Erving. 1952. "On Cooling the Mark Out." Psychiatry 15:473 502.

———. 1963a. Asylums. Garden City, N.Y.: Doubleday.

———. 1963b. Behavior in Public Places: Notes on the Social Organization of Gatherings. New York: Free Press.

———. 1969. Strategic Interaction. Philadelphia: University of Pennsylvania Press.

Greene, Robert W. 1981. The Sting Man: The Inside Story of Abscam. New York: E. P. Dutton.

Gregor, Thomas. 1980. "Exposure and Seclusion: A Study of Institutionalized Isolation among the Mehinaku Indians of Brazil." In Secrecy: A Cross-Cultural Perspective, edited by Stanton K. Teft, 81 99. New York: Human Sciences Press.

Guzzardi, Walter, Jr. 1974a. "The SEC's Crusade on Wall Street." Fortune 90 (November):139 204.

———. 1974b. "Those Zealous Cops on the Securities Beat." Fortune 90 (December):144 202.

Haitch, Richard. 1982. "Postal Trap." New York Times (May 16):49.

Harney, Malachi L., and John C. Cross. 1968. The Informer in Law Enforcement, 2nd ed. Springfield, Ill.: Charles C. Thomas.

Haswell, Jock. 1977. Spies and Spymasters: A Concise History of Intelligence. London: Butler & Tanner.

Hazard, John W., and Milton Christie. 1964. The Investment Business: A Condensation of the SEC Report. New York: Harper & Row.

Hazen, Thomas L. 1979. "Administrative Enforcement: An Evaluation of the Securities and Exchange Commission's Use of Injunctions and Other Enforcement Methods." Hastings Law Journal 31:427 72.

Hellerman, Michael. 1977. Wall Street Swindler. Garden City, N.Y.: Doubleday.

Hepworth, Mike. 1975. Blackmail: Publicity and Secrecy in Everyday Life. London: Routledge & Kegan Paul.

Hershey, Robert D., Jr. 1976. "Chipping Away at the S.E.C.: Supreme Court Cuts Back on its Mandate." New York Times (October 17):3:1, 9.

Hinds, Michael deCourcy. 1982. "New, Improved Fraud Hot Line." New York Times (October 5):20.

Jacobs, Harold. 1963. "Decoy Enforcement of Homosexual Laws." University of Pennsylvania Law Review 112:259 84.

Jaeger, Richard L., and Gregory C. Yadley. 1975. "Equitable Uncertainties in SEC Injunctive Actions." Emory Law Journal 24:639–68.

Jennings, Richard W. 1964. "Self-Regulation in the Securities Industry: The Role of the Securities and Exchange Commission." Law and Contemporary Problems 29:630–90.

Joffe, Edward M. 1975. "The Outside Director: Standards of Care under the Securities Laws." Emory Law Journal 24:669–96.

Jones, J. Edward. 1938. And So They Indicted Me! New York: J. E. Jones.

Kagan, Robert A. 1978. Regulatory Justice: Implementing a Wage-Price Freeze. New York: Russell Sage Foundation.

Karmel, Roberta S. 1982. Regulation by Prosecution: The Securities and Exchange Commission versus Corporate America. New York: Simon and Schuster.

Katz, Jack. 1977. "Cover-up and Collective Integrity: On the Natural Antago-
nisms of Authority Internal and External to Organizations." Social Problems
25:3–17.

———. 1979a. "Concerted Ignorance: The Social Construction of Cover-up."
Urban Life 8:295–316.

———. 1979b. "Legality and Equality: Plea Bargaining in the Prosecution of
White-Collar and Common Crimes." Law and Society Review 13:431–59.

Katzmann, Robert A. 1980. Regulatory Bureaucracy: The Federal Trade Commission and Antitrust Policy. Cambridge: MIT Press.

Kennedy, Tom, and Charles E. Simon. 1978. An Examination of Questionable
Payments and Practices. New York: Praeger.

Kinch, Sam, Jr., and Ben Procter. 1972. Texas under a Cloud. Austin: Jenkins.

Kohlmeier, Louis M., Jr. 1969. The Regulators. New York: Harper & Row.

———. 1976. "The Bribe Busters." New York Times Magazine (September
26):47+.

Kolko, Gabriel. 1963. The Triumph of Conservativism. New York: Free Press.

Kripke, Homer. 1979. The SEC and Corporate Disclosure: Regulation in Search
of a Purpose. New York: Law & Business.

Kwan, Quon Y.; Ponnusamy Rajeswaran; Brian P. Parker; and Menachem Amir.
1971. "The Role of Criminalistics in White-Collar Crime." Journal of Criminals
Law, Criminology and Police Science 62:437+.

Kwitny, Jonathan. 1973. The Fountain Pen Conspiracy. New York: Alfred A.
Knopf.

Laguerre, Michel S. 1980. "Bizango: A Voodoo Secret Society in Haiti." In
Secrecy: A Cross-Cultural Perspective, edited by Stanton K. Teft, 147–60.
New York: Human Sciences Press.

Lee, Nancy Howell. 1969. The Search for an Abortionist. Chicago: University of
Chicago Press.

Leff, Arthur A. 1976. Swindling and Selling: The Story of Legal and Illegal
Congames. New York: Free Press.

Levine, Theodore A., and Edward D. Herlihy. 1977. "SEC Enforcement Actions."
Review of Securities Regulation 10:951–55.

Lipman, Frederick D. 1974. "The SEC's Reluctant Police Force: A New Role For
Lawyers." New York University Law Review 49:437–77.

Loeffler, Robert M. 1974. Report of the Trustee of Equity Funding Corporation
of America. U.S. District Court for the Central District of California (October
31).

Long, Susan B. 1980. "The Internal Revenue Service: Measuring Tax Offenses
and Enforcement Response." Washington, D.C.: Bureau of Social Science
Research, Inc.

Loss, Louis. 1951. Securities Regulation. Boston: Little, Brown.

Lowenfels, Lewis D. 1974. "Expanding Public Responsibilities of Securities Lawyers: An Analysis of the New Trend in Standard of Care and Priorities of
Duties." Columbia Law Review 74:412–38.

Lubasch, Arnold H. 1982. "Restaurant Records Seized by I.R.S. in Broad Inquiry." New York Times (June 18):B3.

Lundy, Joseph R. 1969. "Police Undercover Agents: New Threat to First Amend-
ment Freedoms." George Washington Law Review 37:634–68.

MacKenzie, Norman I. 1967. Secret Societies. New York: Holt, Rinehart and
Winston.

Maitland, Leslie. 1982. "At the Heart of the Abscam Debate." New York Times Magazine (July 25):22+.

Manning, Peter K. 1977. Police Work: The Social Organization of Policing. Cambridge: MIT Press.

"Market Manipulation and the Securities Exchange Act." 1937. Yale Law Journal 46:624–47.

Marx, Gary T. 1974. "Thoughts on a Neglected Category of Social Movement Participant: The Agent Provocateur and the Informant." American Journal of Sociology 80:402–42.

———. 1980. "The New Police Undercover Work." Urban Life 8:399–446.

Masterman, John C. 1972. The Double-Cross System in the War of 1939 to 1945. New Haven: Yale University Press.

Mathews, Arthur F. 1971. "Criminal Prosecutions under the Federal Securities Laws and Related Statutes: The Nature and Development of SEC Criminal Cases." George Washington Law Review 39:901–20.

———. 1972. "The SEC's Tough Enforcement Record." New York Law Journal (December 11).

———. 1973. "The SEC's Enforcement Record." New York Law Journal (December 10).

———. 1974. "Enforcement: SEC's Won–Lost Mark in '74 Seen Good—on Balance." New York Law Journal (December 16).

———. 1975. "Effective Defense of SEC Investigations: Laying the Foundation for Successful Disposition of Subsequent Civil, Aministrative and Criminal Proceedings." Emory Law Journal 24:567–638.

Mathews, Arthur F., and Douglas G. Thompson, Jr. 1980. "The SEC's 1979 Enforcement Program: An Emerging Bit of Enforced Restraint." In SEC '80, vol. 8, edited by Herbert Schlagman, 13–47. New York: Law Journal Seminars-Press.

Maurer, David W. 1940. The Big Con: The Story of the Confidence Man and the Confidence Game. Indianapolis: Bobbs-Merrill.

Maxa, Rudy. 1977. Dare to Be Great. New York: Morrow.

Mayhew, Leon H. 1968. Law and Equal Opportunity: A Study of the Massachusetts Commission against Discrimination. Cambridge: Harvard University Press.

McCall, George J. 1978. Observing the Law: Field Methods in the Study of Crime and the Criminal Justice System. New York: Free Press.

McCall, George J., and J. L. Simmons, eds. 1969. Issues in Participant Observation. Reading, Mass.: Addison-Wesley.

McCauley, Daniel J., Jr. 1973. "The Securities Laws—After 40 Years: A Need for Rethinking." Notre Dame Lawyer 48:1092–1112.

McClintick, David. 1977. Stealing from the Rich. New York: M. Evans.

McCloy, John J. 1975. Report of the Special Review Committee of the Board of Directors of Gulf Oil Corporation (submitted to the U.S. District Court for the District of Columbia).

Miller, Judith. 1979a. "Enforcer Unit Loses Support in S.E.C." New York Times (October 23):D1, D13.

———. 1979b. "S.E.C.: Watchdog 1929 Lacked." New York Times (October 31):D1, D19.

Miller, Norman C. 1965. The Great Salad Oil Swindle. New York: Coward McCann.

Moffitt, Donald, ed. 1976. Swindled! Classic Business Frauds of the Seventies. Princeton: Dow Jones Books.

Morrison, Peter H. 1978. "SEC Criminal References." Review of Securities Regulation 11:991–96.

Nader, Ralph; Peter Petkas; and Kate Blackwell. 1972. Whistle Blowing. New York: Grossman.

Ney, Richard. 1970. The Wall Street Jungle. New York: Grove Press.

———. 1974. The Wall Street Gang. New York: Avon.

Nie, Norman H.; C. Hadlai Hull; Jean G. Jenkins; Karin Steinbrenner; and Dale H. Bent. 1975. SPSS: Statistical Package for the Social Sciences, 2nd ed. New York: McGraw-Hill.

Noble, Kenneth B. 1981. "Stalking Stock-Trading Abuses." New York Times (March 6):D1, D3.

Nonet, Philippe. 1969. Administrative Justice: Advocacy and Change in a Government Agency. New York: Russell Sage Foundation.

Office of Management and Budget. 1981. Budget of the United States Government, Fiscal Year 1982. Washington, D.C.: U.S. Government Printing Office.

O'Hara, Charles E., and James W. Osterburg. 1972. Criminalistics. Bloomington: Indiana University Press.

Orrick, Andrew Downey. 1959. "Organization, Procedures and Practices of the Securities and Exchange Commission." George Washington Law Review 28:51–85.

Orwell, George. 1949. Nineteen Eighty-Four, a Novel. New York: Harcourt, Brace.

Ottenberg, Miriam. 1962. The Federal Investigators. Englewood Cliffs, N.J.: Prentice-Hall.

Parrish, Michael E. 1970. Securities Regulation and the New Deal. New Haven: Yale University Press.

Patrick, Kenneth G. 1972. Perpetual Jeopardy: The Texas Gulf Sulphur Affair: A Chronicle of Achievement and Misadventure. New York: Macmillan.

Pecora, Ferdinand. 1939. Wall Street under Oath. New York: Simon and Schuster.

Pessin, Allan H., and Joseph A. Ross. 1983. Words of Wall Street: 2,000 Investment Terms Defined. Homewood, Ill.: Dow Jones-Irwin.

Peters, Charles, and Taylor Branch. 1972. Blowing the Whistle. New York: Praeger.

Phillips, Susan, and J. Richard Zecher. 1981. The SEC and the Public Interest. Cambridge: MIT Press.

Posner, Richard A. 1970. "A Statistical Study of Antitrust Enforcement." Journal of Law and Economics 13:365–419.

President's Commission on Law Enforcement and the Administration of Justice. 1967. "Police Operations—the Apprehension Process." Task Force Report: Science and Technology. Washington, D.C.: U.S. Government Printing Office.

Rabin, Robert L. 1971. "Agency Criminal Referrals in the Federal System." Stanford Law Review 24:1036–91.

Rand Corporation. 1955. A Million Random Digits with 100,000 Normal Deviates. New York: Free Press.

Ratner, David L. 1971. "The SEC: Portrait of the Agency as a Thirty-Seven-Year-Old." St. Johns Law Review 45:583–96.

———. 1978. Securities Regulation in a Nutshell. St. Paul: West.

Redlinger, Lawrence John. 1975. "Marketing and Distributing Heroin: Some Sociological Observations." Journal of Psychedelic Drugs 7:331–53.

Redlinger, Lawrence J., with Sonny Johnston. 1980. "Introduction: Secrecy, Informational Uncertainty, and Social Control." Urban Life 8:387–97.

Reisman, Michael. 1979. Folded Lies: Bribery, Crusades, and Reforms. New York: Free Press.

Reiss, Albert J., Jr. 1968. "Police Brutality, Answers to Key Questions." Society 5:10–19.

––––––. 1971a. The Police and the Public. New Haven: Yale University Press.

––––––. 1971b. "Systematic Observation of Natural Social Phenomena." In Sociological Methodology, 1971, edited by Herbert L. Costner, 3–33. San Francisco: Josey-Bass.

––––––. 1973. "Surveys of Self-Reported Delicts." Paper prepared for the Symposium on Studies of Public Experience, Knowledge and Opinion of Crime and Justice. Washington, D.C.

––––––. 1974a. "Discretionary Justice." In Handbook of Criminology, edited by Daniel Glaser, 679–99. Chicago: Rand McNally.

––––––. 1974b. "Citizen Access to Criminal Justice." British Journal of Law and Society 1:50–74.

Reiss, Albert J., Jr., and David J. Bordua. 1967. "Environment and Organization: A Perspective on the Police." In The Police: Six Sociological Essays, edited by David J. Bordua, 25–55. New York: John Wiley and Sons.

Rosen, Benson, and J. Stacy Adams. 1974. "Organizational Coverups: Factors Influencing the Discipline of Informational Gatekeepers." Journal of Applied Social Psychology 4:375–84.

Rubinstein, Jonathan. 1973. City Police. New York: Farrar, Straus and Giroux.

Ruder, David S. 1975. "Factors Determining the Degree of Culpability Necessary for Violation of the Federal Securities Laws in Information Transmission Cases." Washington and Lee Law Review 32:571–96.

Rule, James B. 1974. Private Lives and Public Surveillance: Social Control in the Computer Age. New York: Shocken.

Rushing, William A. 1966. "Organization Rules and Surveillance: Propositions in Comparative Organizational Analysis." Administrative Science Quarterly 10: 423–43.

Saferstein, Richard. 1977. Criminalistics: An Introduction to Forensic Science. Englewood Cliffs, N.J.: Prentice-Hall.

Sanders, William B. 1977. Detective Work: A Study of Criminal Investigations. New York: Free Press.

Schaefer, Richard T. 1980. "The Management of Secrecy: The Ku Klux Klan's Successful Secret." In Secrecy: A Cross-Cultural Perspective, edited by Stanton K. Teft, 161–77. New York: Human Sciences Press.

"SEC May Abandon Proposals to Improve Its Surveillance of Stock Market Activity." 1981. Wall Street Journal (October 5):37.

"The SEC's Top Cop." 1976. Time (July 12):54+.

Seidler, Lee J.; Frederick Andrews; and Marc J. Epstein. 1977. The Equity Funding Papers: The Anatomy of a Fraud. Santa Barbara: John Wiley & Sons.

Seligman, Joel. 1982. The Transformation of Wall Street: A History of the Securities and Exchange Commission and Modern Corporate Finance. Boston: Houghton Mifflin.

Selznick, Philip. 1960. The Organizational Weapon. New York: McGraw-Hill.

Seymour, J. Whitney North, Jr. 1972. Fighting White-Collar Crime. New York: Office of the U.S. Attorney for the Southern District of New York.

Shapiro, Susan P. 1978. "The Disposition of White-Collar Illegalities: Prosecutorial Alternatives in the Enforcement of the Securities Laws." Paper presented at the annual meeting of the American Sociological Association. San Francisco.

———. 1980a. "Detecting Illegalities: A Perspective on the Control of Securities Violations." Ph.D. diss., Yale University.

———. 1980b. "Thinking about White Collar Crime: Matters of Conceptualization and Research." Washington, D.C.: National Institute of Justice, U.S. Department of Justice.

Shaplen, Robert. 1978. "Annals of Crime: The Lockheed Incident." New Yorker (January 23):48+.

Sherman, Lawrence W. 1978. Scandal and Reform: Controlling Police Corruption. Berkeley: University of California Press.

Simmel, Georg. 1950. The Sociology of Georg Simmel. Translated, edited and with an introduction by Kurt H. Wolff. New York: Free Press.

Sinclair, Upton. 1906. The Jungle. New York: Doubleday, Page.

Skolnick, Jerome H. 1967. Justice without Trial. New York: John Wiley & Sons.

Skolnick, Jerome H., and J. Richard Woodworth. 1967. "Bureaucracy, Information, and Social Control: A Study of a Morals Detail." In The Police: Six Sociological Essays, edited by David J. Bordua, 99–136. New York: John Wiley & Sons.

Smith, Paul I. Slee. 1970. Industrial Intelligence and Espionage. London: Business Books.

Smith, Richard Austin. 1961. "The Incredible Electrical Conspiracy." Fortune 63:132+.

Smith, Richard B. 1971. "SEC—Past, Present, Future." Howard Law Journal 16:633–53.

Smith, Zay N., and Pamela Zekman. 1979. The Mirage. New York: Random House.

Sobel, Robert. 1965. The Big Board: A History of the New York Stock Market. New York: Free Press.

———. 1968. The Great Bull Market. New York: W. W. Norton.

———. 1972. AMEX: A History of the American Stock Exchange. New York: Weybright and Talley.

———. 1975. N.Y.S.E.: A History of the New York Stock Exchange, 1935–1975. New York: Weybright and Talley.

———. 1977. Inside Wall Street: Continuity and Change in the Financial District. New York: W. W. Norton.

Soble, Ronald L., and Robert E. Dallos. 1975. The Impossible Dream: The Equity Funding Story, the Fraud of the Century. New York: Putnam.

Sokol, David. 1970. Stock Market: Scams, Swindles, and Scoundrels. Los Angeles: Sherbourne Press.

Stinchcombe, Arthur L. 1963. "Institutions of Privacy in the Determination of Police Administrative Practice." American Journal of Sociology 69:150–60.

Stone, Christopher D. 1975. Where the Law Ends: The Social Control of Corporate Behavior. New York: Harper & Row.

Subcommittee on Administrative Procedure of the Senate Committee on the Judiciary, 86th Congress, 2nd Session. 1960. Report on Regulatory Agencies to the President Elect. Washington, D.C.: U.S. Government Printing Office.

Subcommittee on Oversight and Investigations of the Committee on Interstate and Foreign Commerce of the House of Representatives, 94th Congress, 2nd Session. 1976. Federal Regulation and Regulatory Reform. Washington, D.C.: U.S. Government Printing Office.

Sullivan, Colleen. 1977. "The Future of Futures Regulation." Washington Post (October 25−28).

Sutherland, Edwin H. 1949. White Collar Crime. New York: Holt, Rinehart and Winston.

Sykes, Gresham M. 1978. Criminology. New York: Harcourt Brace Jovanovich.

Teft, Stanton K. 1980. "Secrecy as a Social and Political Process." In Secrecy: A Cross-Cultural Perspective, edited by Stanton K. Teft, 319−46. New York: Human Sciences Press.

Thomforde, Fredrich H., Jr. 1975. "Patterns of Disparity in SEC Administrative Sanctioning Practice." Tennessee Law Review 42:465−525.

———. 1976. "Controlling Administrative Sanctions." Michigan Law Review 74: 709−58.

Tiffany, Lawrence P.; Donald M. McIntyre, Jr.; and Daniel L. Rotenberg. 1967. Detection of Crime. Boston: Little, Brown.

Tobias, Andrew. 1971. The Funny Money Game. Chicago: Playboy Press.

Treadway, James C., Jr. 1975. "SEC Enforcement Techniques: Expanding and Exotic Forms of Ancillary Relief." Washington and Lee Law Review 32: 637−79.

Trout, David. 1975. "The Inspectors." Journal of the Institute of Bankers 96: 302−06.

Twentieth Century Fund. 1980. Abuse on Wall Street: Conflicts of Interest in the Securities Markets. Westport, Conn.: Quorum Books.

Tyler, Poyntz. 1965. Securities, Exchanges and the SEC. New York: H. W. Wilson.

U.S. Department of the Treasury. 1979. Annual Report. Washington, D.C.: U.S. Government Printing Office.

U.S. General Services Administration. 1982. Code of Federal Regulations, Title 17. Washington, D.C.: U.S. Government Printing Office.

U.S. Securities and Exchange Commission. 1934−82. Annual Report. Volumes 1−48. Washington, D.C.: U.S. Government Printing Office.

———. 1941. The Work of the Securities and Exchange Commission. Washington, D.C.: U.S. Government Printing Office.

———. 1962. Staff Report on the American Stock Exchange. Washington, D.C.: U.S. Government Printing Office.

———. 1963. Report of the Special Study of the Securities Markets. Washington, D.C.: U.S. Government Printing Office.

———. 1971. Study of Unsafe and Unsound Practices of Broker-Dealers. Washington, D.C.: U.S. Government Printing Office.

———. 1976. Report on Questionable and Illegal Corporate Payments and Practices. Submitted to the Committee on Banking, Housing, and Urban Affairs, United States Senate, 94th Congress, 2nd Session (May 12).

———. 1978. The Work of the Securities and Exchange Commission. Washington, D.C.: U.S. Government Printing Office.

———. 1981. SEC Monthly Statistical Review 40, no. 8 (August).

———. 1982. SEC Monthly Statistical Review 41, no. 9 (September).

Vanderlip, Frank A. 1932. "What about the Banks?" Saturday Evening Post (November 5):3−4.

Vera Institute of Justice. 1977. Felony Arrests: Their Prosecution and Disposition in New York City's Courts. New York: Vera Institute of Justice.

"Violent Crime by Strangers." 1982. Bureau of Justice Statistics Bulletin (April).

Wagner, Walter. 1966. The Golden Fleecers. Garden City, N.Y.: Doubleday.

Washburn, Watson, and Edmond S. Delong. 1932. High and Low Financiers. Indianapolis: Bobbs-Merrill.

Weaver, Suzanne. 1977. Decision to Prosecute: Organization and Public Policy in the Antitrust Division. Cambridge: MIT Press.

Webb, Eugene J.; Donald T. Campbell; Richard D. Schwartz; and Lee Sechrest. 1966. Unobtrusive Measures: Nonreactive Research in the Social Sciences. Chicago: Rand McNally.

Wells, John A.; Manuel F. Cohen; and Ralph H. Demmler. 1972. "Report of the Advisory Committee on Enforcement Policies and Practices." Washington, D.C.: U.S. Securities and Exchange Commission.

Wheeler, Barbara, ed. 1983. New York Stock Exchange Fact Book 1981. New York: New York Stock Exchange.

Wheeler, Stanton, and Mitchell Rothman. 1982. "The Organization as Weapon in White-Collar Crime." Michigan Law Review 80: 1403−26.

Wheeler, Stanton; David Weisburd; and Nancy Bode. 1982. "Sentencing the White-Collar Offender: Rhetoric and Reality." American Sociological Review 47:641−59.

Wilensky, Harold L. 1967. Organizational Intelligence: Knowledge and Policy in Government and Industry. New York: Basic Books.

———. 1968. "Organizations: Organizational Intelligence." International Encyclopedia of the Social Sciences, vol. 11, 319−34. New York: MacMillan and Free Press.

Williams, Paul N. 1978. Investigative Reporting and Editing. Englewood Cliffs, N.J.: Prentice-Hall.

Willmer, M. A. P. 1970. Crime and Information Theory. Edinburgh: Edinburgh University Press.

Wilsnack, Richard W. 1980. "Information Control: A Conceptual Framework for Sociological Analysis." Urban Life 8:467−99.

Wilson, James Q. 1978. The Investigators: Managing FBI and Narcotics Agents. New York: Basic Books.

Wilson, Stephen V., and A. Howard Matz. 1977. "Obtaining Evidence for Federal Economic Crime Prosecutions: An Overview and Analysis of Investigative Methods." American Criminal Law Review 14:651+.

Winks, Robin W., ed. 1970. Historian as Detective: Essays on Evidence. New York: Harper & Row.

Index

Abscam: and observational intelligence, 76, 183; cost, 184*n*

Access, 188; and reactive detection, 47, 56; and insiders, 48; and disclosure, 51; and proactive detection, 57; and surveillance, 57, 60; and incursions, 61, 62; and spin-offs, 64, 66; and frequency of detection, 66; and detection, 94–95, 107, 112, 115; and misappropriation, 106; and accuracy of intelligence, 125–26, 128; and intelligence catch, 131*n*; and undercover operations, 184

Access points theory, 178–79; legal issues, 187

Accountants: as offenders, 3, 38; and misrepresentation, 13–14; and detection, 44, 48–49, 65; disclosures by, 52, 53; and cover-up, 92; SEC investigators, 142; and administrative proceedings, 153, 157; diffusion of information to, 175; and access points theory, 179; culpability, 187. *See also* Professionals; Securities community

Administrative proceedings, 152, 153–54, 157–59; SEC authority, 5; consent, 153; appeal, 153, 157; parties subject to, 153, 157; ancillary remedies, 153–54, 158–59; sanctions, 153, 158–59; frequency, 154–56; outcome, 157–58; litigation, 157, 158; and offense characteristics, 162–63; choice of, 162–63; and offender characteristics, 162, 164; trends, 199*n*

Advisers. *See* Investment advisers

American Stock Exchange: scandal, 140

Ancillary relief: civil proceedings, 153, 156–57; administrative proceedings,

153–54, 158–59; versus sanctions, 158–59

Anti-trust violations: disclosure of, 86

Appeals: administrative, 153, 157; civil, 156; criminal, 161

Artifactual methods, 71–72, 73, 89–92; and SEC intelligence, 89, 90; accuracy, 89, 90, 91*n*; and market surveillance, 90; inferential, 90; reactivity, 90; and cover-up, 90, 91–92; vulnerabilities, 91–92; and records, 92; and intelligence reform, 181–82

Attorneys: and misappropriation, 18; relationship to victims, 35; as offenders, 38; and detection, 44, 49, 51; disclosures by, 52, 53; SEC investigators, 141, 142, 151; evidence from, 144; and administrative proceedings, 153, 157; diffusion of information to, 175; and access points theory, 179; and non-market surveillance, 182; culpability of, 187. *See also* Professionals; Securities community

Auditors. *See* Accountants

Audits: and cover-up, 174

—deviance, 174; legal issues, 187

—special, 174; and informal remedies, 147; as disclosure mechanism, 180

Bankruptcy: among offenders, 4, 40, 41; SEC jurisdiction over, 5; and self-dealing, 20; and detection, 54, 111; and choice of legal action, 164; receivership proceedings, 165

—receivers: disclosures by, 53; and SEC investigation, 144*n*